Learning Hiragana and Katakana

(Japanese Made Simple)

A Beginner's Guide and Integrated Workbook

Learn how to read, write and speak Japanese, with the Kana alphabets

Dan Akiyama

JAPANESE FOR BEGINNERS | SYSTEMATIC LEARNING APPROACH

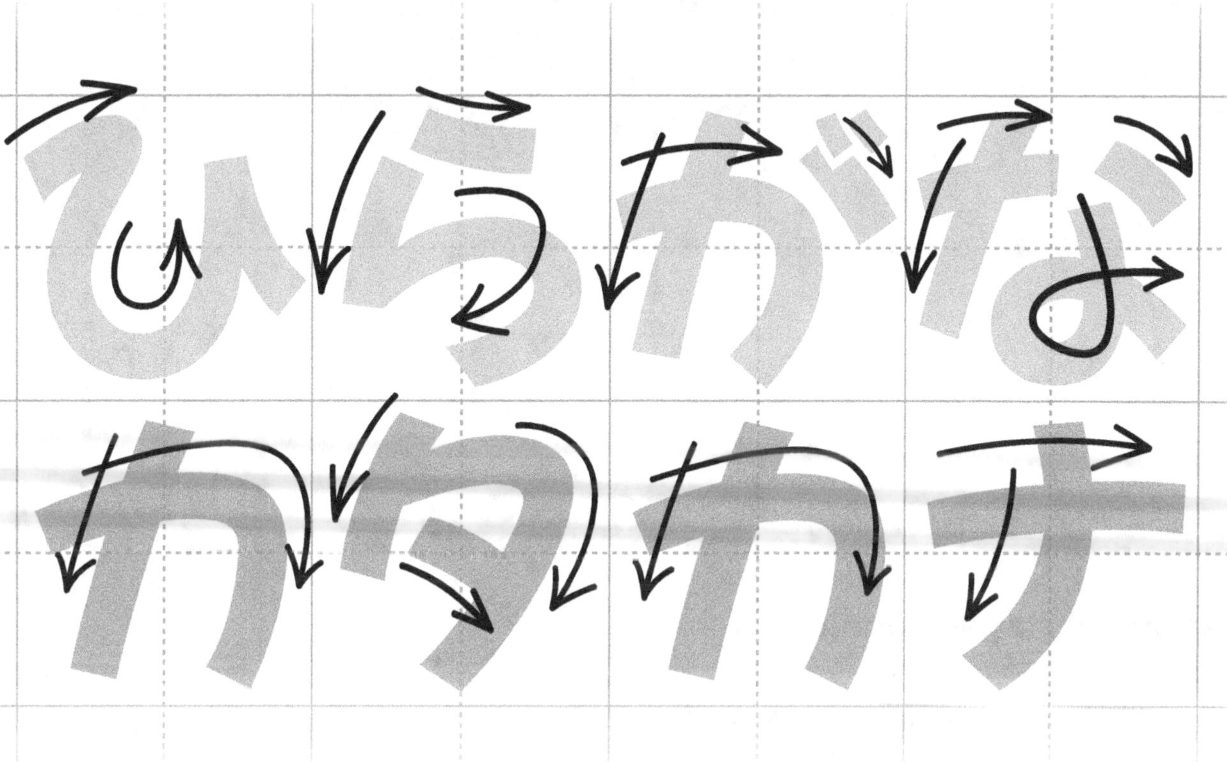

HIRAGANA + KATAKANA MADE SIMPLE

LEARN HOW TO READ, WRITE AND SPEAK JAPANESE WITH KANA!

ひらがな
カタカナ
漢字

- Memorize **Hiragana** and **Katakana** *fast* and *intuitively*
- Practice **reading and writing**, and develop *powerful* **mnemonics**
- Learn how to pronounce the sounds **for *all* Japanese** Language
- Includes *extra* **tools and templates** to help you study

BEGINNER'S GUIDE + INTEGRATED WORKBOOK

DAN AKIYAMA

Learning Hiragana and Katakana
Japanese Made Simple
Beginner's Guide and Integrated Workbook

---

by Dan Akiyama

ISBN: Print 978-1-7392387-5-9 (Paperback)
First Edition

Contents

//////////////////////////////////// **PART 1**

Introduction

日本語

Welcome to my combined **Hiragana and Katakana workbook**, part of the *Japanese Made Simple* series. Each book in this series is designed specifically for beginners, with all the tools you need to start reading, writing, and speaking Japanese.

Consisting of three *'alphabets'* and thousands of unique and complex written characters, many people refer to Japanese as one of the most challenging foreign languages to learn. When approached correctly, however, it can be made simple! I aim to make Japanese faster and more straightforward by presenting essential information in the most intuitive, step-by-step way.

In this book, you will learn about the *elementary* Hiragana and Katakana scripts, known collectively as the ***Kana***, representing the sounds needed to pronounce everything in Japanese. They each have different functions relating to grammar and 'spelling' in the broader writing system, so they are also pre-requisite for studying Japanese kanji. They take little time to memorize and make everything else a little easier, so it makes sense to do this before attempting to learn vocabulary.

Starting with the basics, the guided self-study materials in this workbook will help you reach your goals quickly. By the end, you will have learned how to read, write and pronounce two of the three 'alphabets' and be well-equipped to study the third - ***Kanji!***

About this Book

This book emphasizes writing practice to learn and remember characters. Most would probably concede that manual handwriting is not required much in any language since most communication has moved into digital and online spaces. Writing skills are not a high priority when learning other foreign languages, such as French or Spanish, but they play a different role when studying one with an entirely new set of characters or letters.

Writing and spaced repetition remain one of the most effective tools for memorization, so this workbook provides space to practice your penmanship. This technique helps to build muscle memory and make information stick, helping you recognize and recall characters' shapes later. Neat written Japanese is an essential skill that you will achieve naturally.

It will help to practice pronouncing each character out loud as you learn to write them in the correct stroke order. The process of repeatedly writing out characters and pronouncing the terminology will help attach sounds to shapes. Mnemonics are valuable tools for learning kanji, so use the space provided on the kana pages to practice - any connection you can make with a sound, shape, or meaning will make characters much easier to remember.

It is always good to begin immersing yourself in the language as soon as possible. Find ways to read, watch, or listen to Japanese language materials, even though you may not understand them. Hearing the sounds will make saying things aloud in Japanese feel less awkward and help improve pronunciation to become more natural-sounding.

How hard is it?

When you learn the right way, *Japanese is not that difficult*. Many of the common problems and frustrations that learners face are caused by simply starting with the wrong strategy. They often choose a difficult study route without knowing that there are other, better ways. *By buying this book, you have already taken a step in the right direction.*

Anybody beginning with a path that involves learning random words or spoken phrases at the start will find themselves confused sooner or later. Without understanding how all the pieces go together, they are likely to waste a lot of time or become discouraged when the difficulty ramps up - *and it will.*

Every aspect of the language works relatively logically, so it makes sense to also take a systematic approach to your studies. This book will help you understand how the whole language works making your study more efficient and saving you lots of time and effort at every stage.

Learning Japanese

Learning Japanese will seem incredibly difficult to do right now, which is why this workbook will start with the basics, introducing more information only when it will be helpful. This chapter will begin with a quick assessment of what lies ahead.

At an elementary level, there are three stages to learning Japanese. Each subsequent level will be more demanding than the previous, relying on the knowledge you gain in the last stage - there is no practical way to skip ahead. That said, there are more and less effective ways to learn about some topics:

1. Learning Kana

What: The kana *'alphabets'* enable you to read and pronounce all Japanese as they effectively spell everything out in a way that's easy to understand.

How: Memorizing the shapes and pronunciations through repetition. There are two sets of 46 basic symbols, plus a few extras to learn afterward. It could take just a day or two but should not be rushed. Practice them frequently, as they are the foundation on which you will build everything else.

2. Acquiring Kanji

What: More complex symbols representing whole words, making up a large part of Japanese - are often pronounced multiple ways and have multiple meanings. *A command of the kana scripts is a pre-requisite for kanji study.*

How: Due to the sheer number of unique characters, they inevitably take longer than learning kana. There are a variety of routes and methods, and, with the right strategy, they do not have to be as tricky as they seem.

3. Adding Grammar

What: Equipped with kanji knowledge *(or a dictionary)*, you can understand lots of Japanese when you learn about sentence structure, how to make other word forms, can recognize particles, and appreciate respectful speech.

How: We will examine different types of words and how to use them; learn about verb conjugations, and explore some of the most useful grammatical patterns that you can start using in everyday Japanese language.

All of my workbooks are divided into sections to help structure your learning in the most effective way. This *combined Hiragana and Katakana workbook* consists of five parts, and should be approached in chronological order:

Section 1

An overview of the Japanese writing systems that will begin by explaining what each of the different *'alphabets'* or scripts are, and how they come together to form the language. You will also learn about the way that we read, write, and pronounce individual characters and fuller texts.

Section 2

The second chapter will teach you all about the ***Hiragana,*** the first of Japan's two phonetic *'alphabets,'* or syllabaries. The 46 basic characters are divided into groups of 'letters' with similar sounds, to make everything a little quicker. Here, you will learn how to write each symbol with the correct stroke order, and how they should sound when spoken. Each group ends with exercises that will help you to memorize the shapes and pronunciations you will have learned.

Section 3

You will jump straight into the ***Katakana*** and learn in the same way as the previous chapter. It should be easier and quicker, as the syllable sounds are all the same!

Section 4

Once you have mastered the basic characters, you will learn about the way that additional sounds are shown with extra written markings. The shapes you will have learned about up to this point will be re-used to write some extra, but fairly similar, pronunciation sounds. On completion of this section, there are no more Hiragana characters to learn.

Section 5

This section of the book consists of some useful study tools, including extra, blank grids for further writing practice. Generally, I would reccomend purchasing a separate notepad for practicing your Japanese, but these sheets may be handy for repetition of characters that you might have found particularly tricky.

Towards the rear of this chapter, and the book overall, I have included some double-sided pages of cut-out study tiles or *'flashcards'* which you can use to create a deck of helpful prompts for testing your memory. *Feel free to make copies if you prefer not to remove pages.* They might not be as large or durable as real 'cards', but they are nice to have without an extra cost, and work well as part of writing exercises. You could use them to check whether you remember the stroke order for hiragana in a randomized sequence.

The 'Alphabets'

You will use ***four different types of characters*** while learning the language, although *one isn't strictly Japanese*. We will refer to each set as an *'alphabet'* for ease since that is a more familiar concept that will simplify your initial studies. The *main* alphabets are ***Hiragana, Katakana, and Kanji,*** and they are frequently used together:

Katakana Kanji Hiragana

クリスは日本語を勉強しています

Kurisu wa nihongo o benkyō shite imasu ← Romaji

Translates as: *"Chris is studying Japanese."*

Romaji

Romaji is the ***English lettering*** used to transcribe Japanese symbols into a format that beginners can read and understand. It illustrates the sounds that make up the language when first starting, but it's not truly compatible with Japanese sounds, so often inaccurate. You will find that romaji transcriptions may also vary from one learning resource to another and inconsistencies like that inevitably lead to confusion later.

With very few practical uses beyond learning pronunciations, you should aim to reduce your reliance on romaji and eliminate it from your studies as soon as you can memorize the kana scripts. *After all, you aim to learn Japanese!*

Hiragana & Katakana

The subsequent two alphabets are known collectively as the ***Kana scripts***, and they are distinctly *Japanese-looking* by comparison. Each consists of 46 basic characters (or *'letters'*) and they are used frequently throughout the language, often together.

Kana characters are very different from other alphabets. Technically, ***Hiragana and Katakana*** are ***'phonetic syllabaries,'*** meaning individual symbols represent a sound instead of a letter. It also means that each character is pronounced as a separate, distinct *'syllable'* when speaking Japanese. They are essential for kanji study *(the fourth character system)*.

Japanese writing typically contains characters from each of the hiragana, katakana, and kanji scripts, although we never mix hiragana and katakana within a single word. You will soon recognize which is which, but they are easy to tell apart when you look at the general shapes:

Hiragana tend to have more rounded shapes and are drawn or written with curved, sometimes sweeping, lines *(a little like cursive handwriting)*. Katakana generally have more angular or pointy shapes, by comparison:

ひらがな
hi ra ga na
Hiragana Characters

カタカナ
ka ta ka na
Katakana Characters

The two sets of kana represent the same sounds, but each script has different uses within the language. Very briefly, hiragana is used to show how to pronounce kanji *(effectively spelling them out)* and also to show grammatical information. On the other hand, Katakana is used to spell words from outside Japan - *foreign vocabulary, such as names, objects, brands, etc., from overseas* - and for spelling your name. Later in the book, you will learn more about the different ways in which you can use both of the kana scripts.

Kanji

Japanese Kanji characters are *extremely numerous* compared to the kana, and there are tens of thousands in existence, with more created over time. To be considered literate in Japan, one must memorize over two thousand, but you can start reading lots of everyday Japanese with a knowledge of *just a few hundred*.

The kanji writing system is very different from the kana scripts, as the characters represent large blocks of meaning and vocabulary - for the most part, verbs and nouns. Essentially, they are the types of words that make up most of any language. Some of the characters are simple in appearance, even resembling the kana in some instances, but lots of kanji are far more complex-looking. Kanji are also combined to make additional words with new, often related meanings.

Initially adopted from the Chinese language, Japanese kanji often have more than one meaning, and most will usually have several different pronunciations. It's easy to see why Japanese is considered one of the most challenging languages to learn. The writing system works relatively logically, making it easier to study than you may think.

漢字 'Kanji' *in Japanese*

Pronounced: **かんじ** *"kan-ji"*
Meaning: *Chinese characters*

From: **漢** *(China)* + **字** *(letters)*

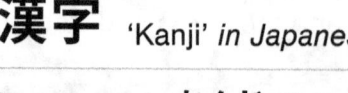

Writing in Japanese

In addition to helping with memorization, the careful writing of characters or texts is a part of learning Japanese. Both the way and order in which we draw lines can affect the shape and legibility of your writing. Before you begin learning about hiragana, the following pages provide some practical information about Japanese text and writing.

Text Direction

When Japan first imported the kanji writing system from China, it adopted the vertical writing configuration, show to the right *(A)*. Vertical text is written and read in columns, starting in the upper right, from top to bottom, and from right to left. The spine of all books, magazines, and newspapers with vertical text is positioned on the right side. *They are, effectively, read back to front compared to books written in English.*

Modern Japanese uses the more familiar horizontal writing direction *(B)*. Text is read and written in rows, from *left to right*, and top to bottom, as in European languages that use the Roman lettering system.

The text direction tends to be apparent from the line spacing, creating a gap for certain types of notation. *You can read more about this in a later chapter on kanji.*

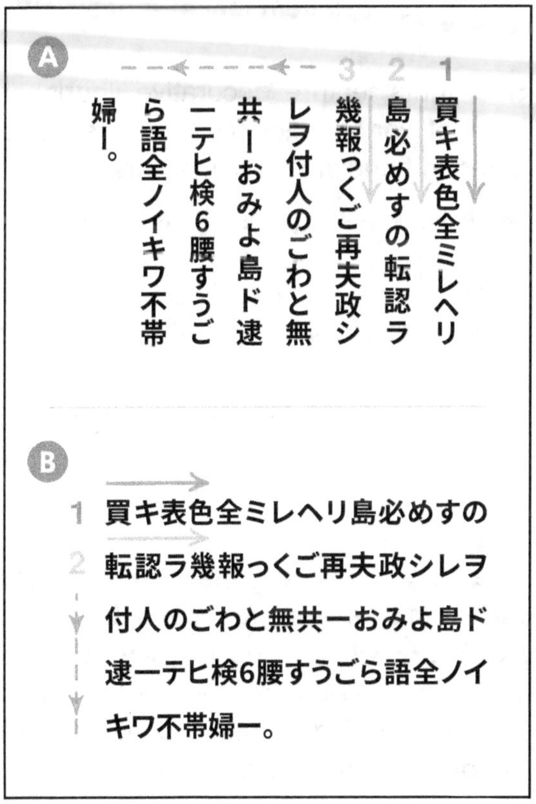

Above: the same dummy text in (A) vertical and (B) horizontal writing directions.

Stroke Order

The lines that make up Japanese characters are all drawn in a set order. You will learn the correct way to write individual kana and develop muscle memory through practice.

In most cases, two rules apply: we start in the upper left of a symbol, and make strokes from left to right, top to bottom until reaching the lower right.

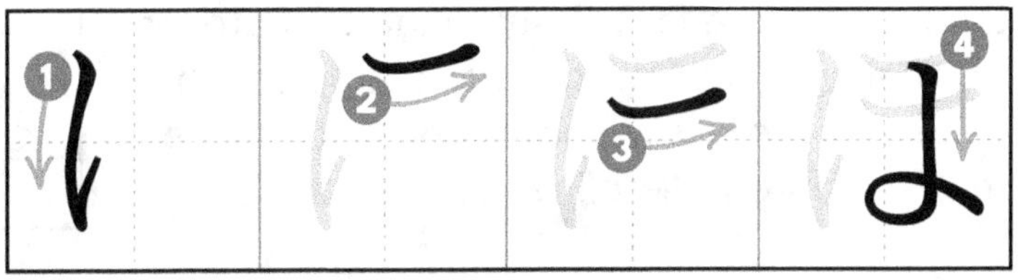

Some slightly extended rules apply to kanji, but the same general steps still apply.

Text Styles

Japanese characters can be presented in a wide variety of styles, from ornate, brushed calligraphy, to the contemporary, bold typefaces featured on packaging designs. While words and characters may have a completely different appearance from one place to another, they always mean the same thing.

Just as there is a wide range of fonts or typefaces available for *Roman* lettering, the style of Japanese symbols can be altered to suit different styles, tones, and designs. There are two types of system font at a basic level with slight but notable differences:

Serif fonts feature decorative flourishes and lines of varied thickness, replicating details found in handwritten characters:

- Similar style to: [**Times New Roman**]

Sans-serif or *Gothic* fonts are more uniform or *'plain,'* with consistent line thicknesses and no added decoration:

- Similar style to [**Century Gothic**]

Above: kanji **日本語** *means "Japanese (language)"*

Like any language, Japanese handwriting comes in all shapes and sizes, both tidy and... *less so*. As with any calligraphy, you can often see *how* characters have been written, and the more writing practice you do, the easier it becomes to recognize characters written by other people:

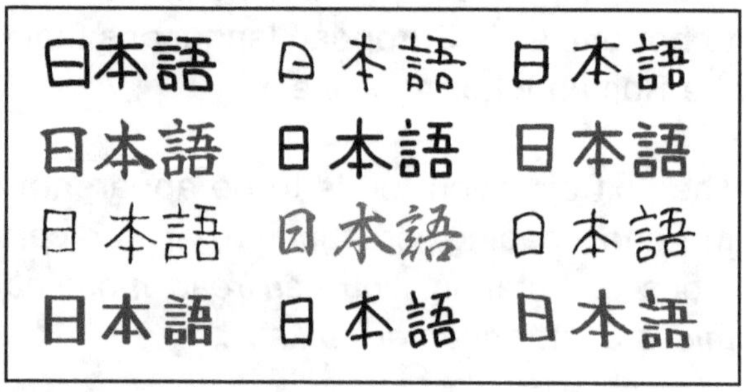

Bold and modern fonts provide lots of options for contemporary designs. Some can be pretty abstract, but most make for effective display typography. Decorative flourishes tend to be more for the style than they are for replicating handwriting. The characters that you know are easily understood, with shapes that are more well-defined:

Kana and kanji can look significantly different without losing their meaning, as long as their overall *proportion and shapes remain the same* relative to the other characters.

Stroke Types

There are three distinctly different types of mark that you can make with your pen. It may be tricky to emulate these shapes unless using a a brush-tipped pen and, in some ways, this style of writing is comparable with cursive handwriting, so not *essential*.

Referred to as a *'tome'* or *'stop stroke'*, from **止める (とめる)**, or *Tomeru*, which means *"to stop"*, these lines have clearly defined start and end points. Your pen or pencil is brought to a hard stop before lifting from the page:

The second type of mark, known as a *'sweep'* or *'harai'*, comes from the Japanese **払う (はらう)**, or *Harau*, meaning *"to sweep"*. It also features a well-defined start point but as you approach the end of the stroke, you would flick your pen from the paper. The line should continue in the same direction, slowly trailing off before lifting completely from the page:

Typically referred to as a *'hane'*, from the Japanese **跳ねる (はねる)**, or *Haneru*, which means "to jump". These strokes are confident lines where your pen or pencil is flicked from the paper, usually in the opposite direction:

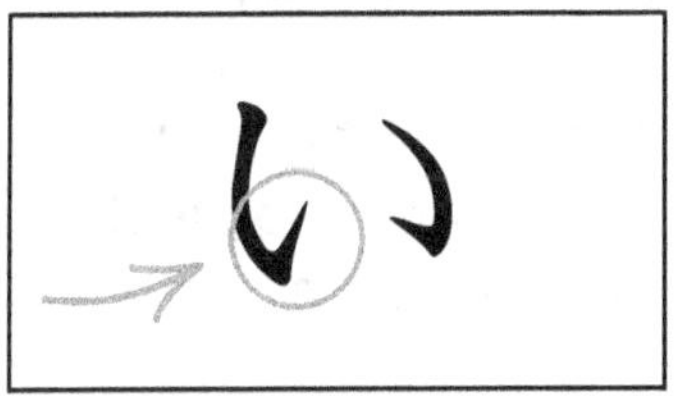

Most people use a ballpoint pen or pencil to write, making it difficult to achieve this level of accuracy. Unless you intend to practice more traditional styles of calligraphy, concentrate on the shape of your kana characters before addressing these details.

Writing in this Book

This workbook is for writing in, and while the paper is relatively good quality, you should try to avoid using any markers or pens with especially wet ink that is prone to bleeding. The pages are better suited to ballpoint pens, pencils, or even gel-based stationery, which should not transfer to the pages beneath. *You can test your writing tools in the spaces below, checking how they affect the following pages:*

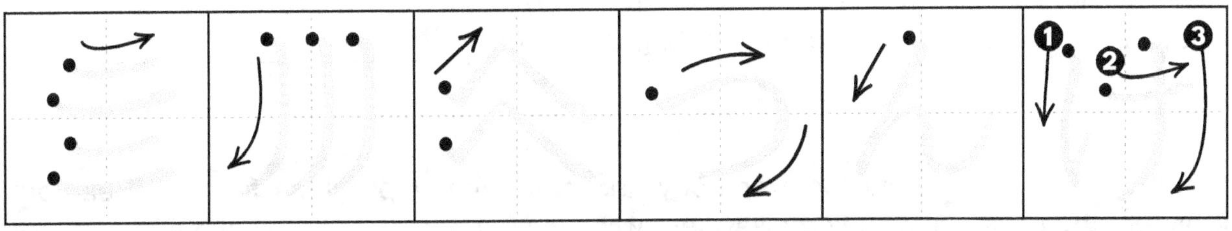

Once you have learned and practiced the kana, it could be worth investing in a notebook with a high-quality paper for advanced studies. A traditional brush-style pen can make your Japanese writing more natural-looking but require more specialist types of paper.

About Mnemonics

Mnemonics are simply tools that can aid with memorization. They are particularly effective for those learning Japanese, and we use them to remember what each of the characters represents.

Essentially, we can either associate new information with something we already know or develop a mechanism to prompt our brain to recall what we are learning. The kana scripts are visual representations of sounds, so we create mnemonics based on their shapes. An example may help to illustrate the point:

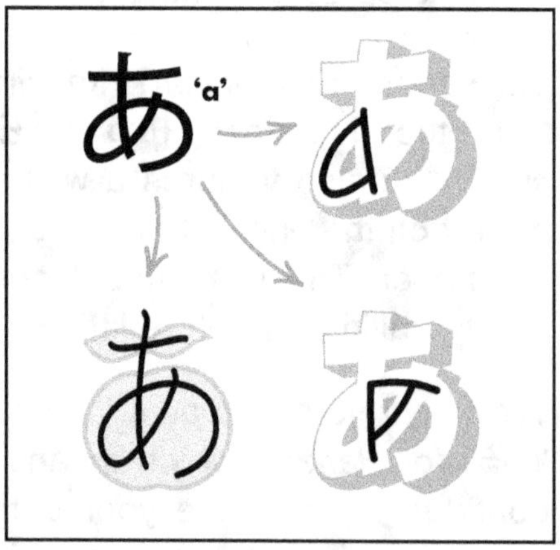

The hiragana **あ** represents an *'a-'* or *'ah'* sound. We transcribe it as equivalent to the letter 'a' in romaji, pronounced as a short *'ah,'* similar to the *'a'* in car, father, or apple.

It may be easier to remember if you visualize **あ** as having the shape of an apple *(also starting with the letter 'a')*. The shapes of the letters *'A'* and *'a'* also hide within the character **あ**. It doesn't matter how vague or obvious the connection, so long as it will remind you that **あ** = *a / or an 'a- sound.'*

Examine the shape of each new symbol and the sound it represents. Look for any sort of immediate connections that can be made between the romaji version, the pronunciation, and its general appearance. You may need to think outside the box for some shapes, but even the most abstract ideas, once visualized a certain way, are not forgotten as quickly, and *that's the whole idea!*

Another example *(right)* shows a mnemonic created for the hiragana **け** *(or 'ke')*, pronounced in a similar way to the *"ke-"* in the word ***"keg."*** The character has a shape that looks a little like a barrel or *keg of beer*:

One of the more *obvious* mnemonics now, this time for the hiragana character **の** *(or 'no')*, which sounds and looks similar to the *"no-"* in the word ***"nose."*** This shape could be compared to a *'**no** smoking'* sign too:

Mnemonics may not work for everybody and can hamper progress for some learners. Some of the examples you find elsewhere will seem inaccurate or silly, putting people off their use. Try to come up with personal visualizations before dismissing them altogether. Even if you only recall a character from an especially bad mnemonic, it will have served its purpose and helped you to remember.

About 'Syllables'

Japanese is one of the few languages where pronunciation is based on timing and rhythm. We structure sounds around a system of ***'mora,'*** which are simply timing units in the context of language and speech. For ease, you can think of ***'morae'*** *(the plural of 'mora')* as *beats.* A *'moraic system'* organizes sound units differently to languages based on syllables, such as English.

Each kana character represents one syllable sound, and they all take one *mora*, or one *beat*, to pronounce. Words written with two kana take twice as much time to pronounce as one kana*, and those with three or four kana are three or four beats long. The actual amount of time is unimportant and will vary from one person to another, depending on how fast they talk.

"banana" [バナナ]

バ	ナ	ナ	*Katakana*
ba	na	na	*Romaji*
•	•	•	*Mora*

Above: 3 Syllable Word, 3 Mora.

If you're wondering the difference between a syllable and a mora, ***syllables*** are broad chunks of sound that can be of different lengths. Each syllable has a vowel in the middle, with consonants on one or both sides. ***Morae*** are smaller, timed units of sound that set an underlying rhythm by which we pronounce all Japanese sounds.

In the example (*right*), the kana have separate sounds that we say over two distinct beats in the Japanese pronunciation. The English pronunciation has just one syllable because the 'n,' without a vowel, attaches to the *'ka-'* sound. Syllables in Japanese can contain multiple morae, but mora can have only one syllable sound:

かん		かん
ka •	n •	kan •
2 Mora (Japanese)		*1 Syllable (English)*

To further illustrate the difference: the Japanese word for *'teacher'* is 先生*, or 'Sensei.'* This is a word that's also used in the English language to describe martial arts teachers. There are two units of sound *(two syllables)* in the English pronunciation, *"sen-say."* We spell the kanji *'reading' (pronunciation)* using four hiragana, so it's four morae long and said in 4 equal beats. *Morae are the way that we differentiate between long and short syllables:*

"teacher" [先生]

sen •	sei •	*Syllables (English)*

せ	ん	せ	い	*Hiragana*
se	n	se	i	*Romaji*
•	•	•	•	*Mora*

We still speak Japanese in syllables, but morae dictate the timing with which each sound is made. We pronounce individual sounds at a fixed rate (at regular intervals), all roughly equal length. Hopefully, that should make some sense, but it may take some time and practice with the language to fully understand how mora work.

* Two characters are not *always* pronounced as two morae, but you will learn more about special *'combination kana'* and their sounds in a later chapter.

PART 2

Hiragana

ひらがな

In some ways, hiragana is the most crucial alphabet to learn. Firstly, hiragana represent every sound that you need to speak Japanese. It's also an essential tool for further study, as we use it to read all of the kanji, effectively *'spelling'* kanji words out with sounds.

Eventually, you will use hiragana across the whole writing system as they are suffixed to kanji (Japanese words), like verbs and adjectives, to provide extra information. Later still, you will use hiragana as particles to add structure to sentences and implement grammar. Before looking at any of those topics, the most important thing you can do is learn the alphabet.

As you work your way through this chapter, pay particular attention to how characters are pronounced. The *'alphabet'* in the following chapter represents the same sounds. Doing a thorough job here could save lots of time later.

The chart to the right shows all of the ***46 basic hiragana symbols*** you are about to learn. You should see that romaji vowels are written to one side, with consonant letters above, and most symbols follow a consistent pattern where two sounds are combined - we take a consonant (top row) and add a vowel sound afterward (right column), with just one exception.

This pattern will become your key to mastering the pronunciation of most hiragana. The basic vowel sounds in the right column are carried across the chart, with subsequent consonant sounds added in front to pronounce the others characters. All characters in the 'A-row' will sound similar, *e.g. ka, sa, ta, etc.*

Traditional Japanese texts are written and read from top to bottom, and from right to left, column by column. This chart should be read the same way but, in reality, you will find everyday modern Japanese texts are written from left to right - just like in English and other European languages.

Over the following pages, you will learn the alphabet in groups, roughly column by column. Learning the letters in chunks will make it more manageable. Each block of letters ends with a revision section to test your memory and determine where you might need more practice.

Notes:

* ん iis the only character in this table that we pronounce as a syllable without adding any of the vowel sounds.

** を is a *"particle"* and is used for grammar. We write it as *"wo"*, but it is transcribed in romaji as either *"o"* or *"wo"*.

Hiragana

w	r	y	m	h	n	t	s	k		
わ wa	ら ra	や ya	ま ma	は ha	な na	た ta	さ sa	か ka	あ a	a
	り ri		み mi	ひ hi	に ni	ち chi	し shi	き ki	い i	i
ん * n	る ru	ゆ yu	む mu	ふ fu	ぬ nu	つ tsu	す su	く ku	う u	u
	れ re		め me	へ he	ね ne	て te	せ se	け ke	え e	e
を ** wo	ろ ro	よ yo	も mo	ほ ho	の no	と to	そ so	こ ko	お o	o
p. 087	p. 081	p. 075	p. 069	p. 061	p. 055	p. 046	p. 038	p. 030	p. 022	

H1. The Vowel Column

The first column of the basic hiragana chart is arguably the most important. Learning how to pronounce all five characters in this group properly is going to make the rest much easier. They set you up with sounds that are used across the whole alphabet so it is worth spending time to practice these well.

Symbols in this learning block.

あ	い	う	え	お
a	i	u	e	o

Pronunciation

Each of the vowel characters have a short, sharp pronunciation and these sounds should not drawn out or elongated. For example, the first symbol あ is pronounced as a short *'ah'* sound (like the *'a'* in *'apple'*) and not as *'ahh'*.

The second symbol い is shown in romaji as *'i'* but never pronounced like *'I' (or, eye)*. It always has a shortened 'ee' sound, similar to the *'i'* in *'igloo'*.

When you pronounce the 'oo' sound for the third character, 'u' or う, your lips make a round shape and move forwards - try saying the word 'pool' once or twice. This is less pronounced with the Japanese *'u'* sound, and the *'oo'* sound is shorter.

The sound for the character え or *'e'* is similar to normal pronunciation in the middle of a word. It is a short *'eh'* sound, *like the 'e' in bed, tell, send, and so on.*

Lastly, お is the Japanese vowel sound for *'o'* and it is pronounced as *'oh', like the 'o' in 'no' or 'original'.*

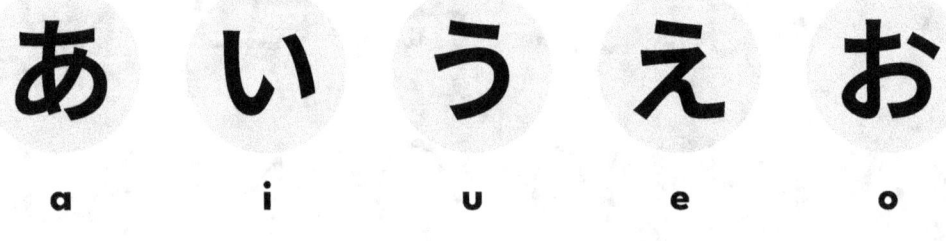

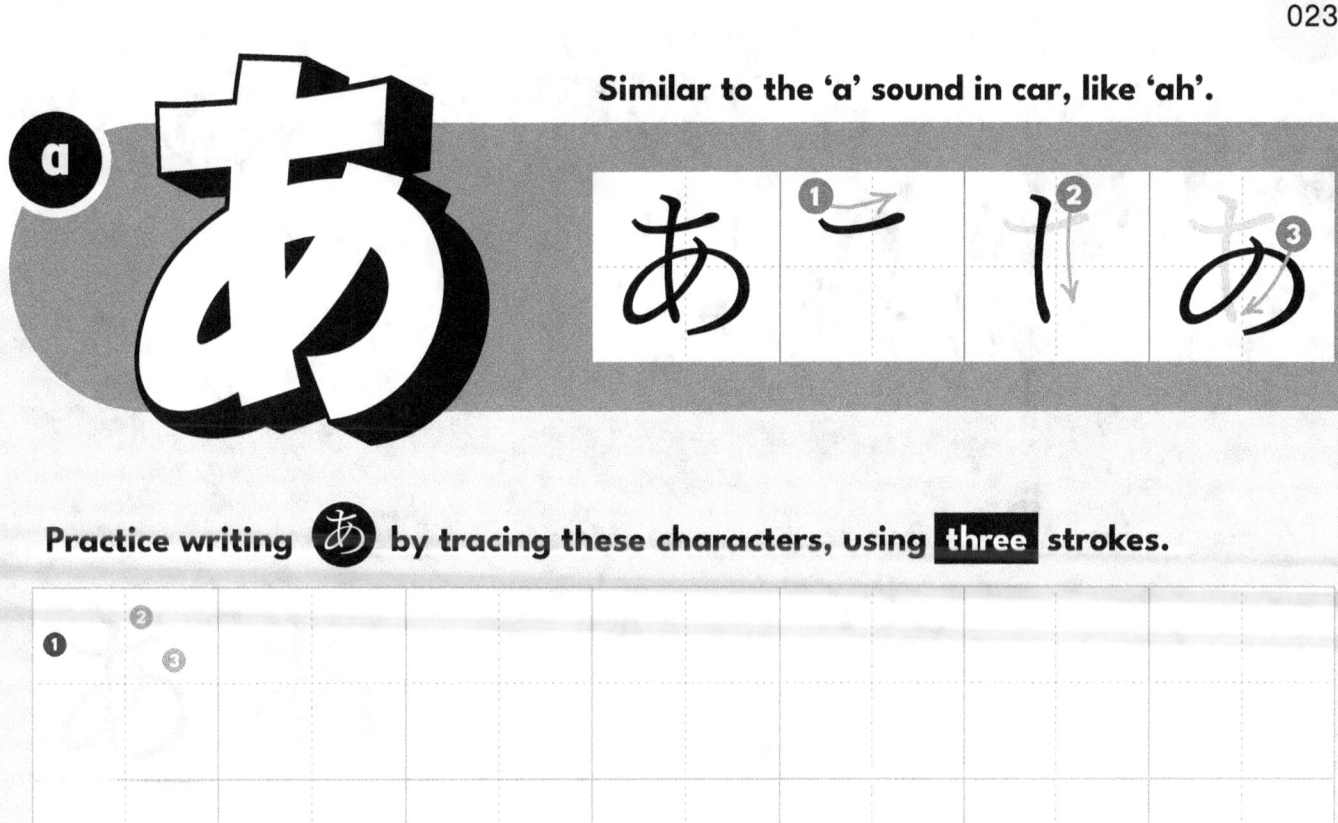

a あ

Similar to the 'a' sound in car, like 'ah'.

Practice writing あ by tracing these characters, using three strokes.

Try to maintain accurate shapes while writing あ on a smaller scale.

Mnemonic.

Examples.

- Shape of an apple
- Contains letter 'a'

i い

Sounds like 'i' in king, or 'ee' in cheek.

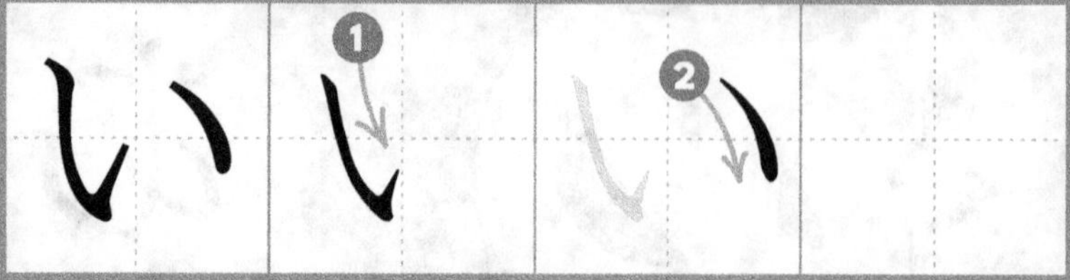

Practice writing い by tracing these characters, using **two** strokes.

Try to maintain accurate shapes while writing い on a smaller scale.

Mnemonic.

Examples.

- Letter 'i' x 2
- Picture two feet
- Pair of eels

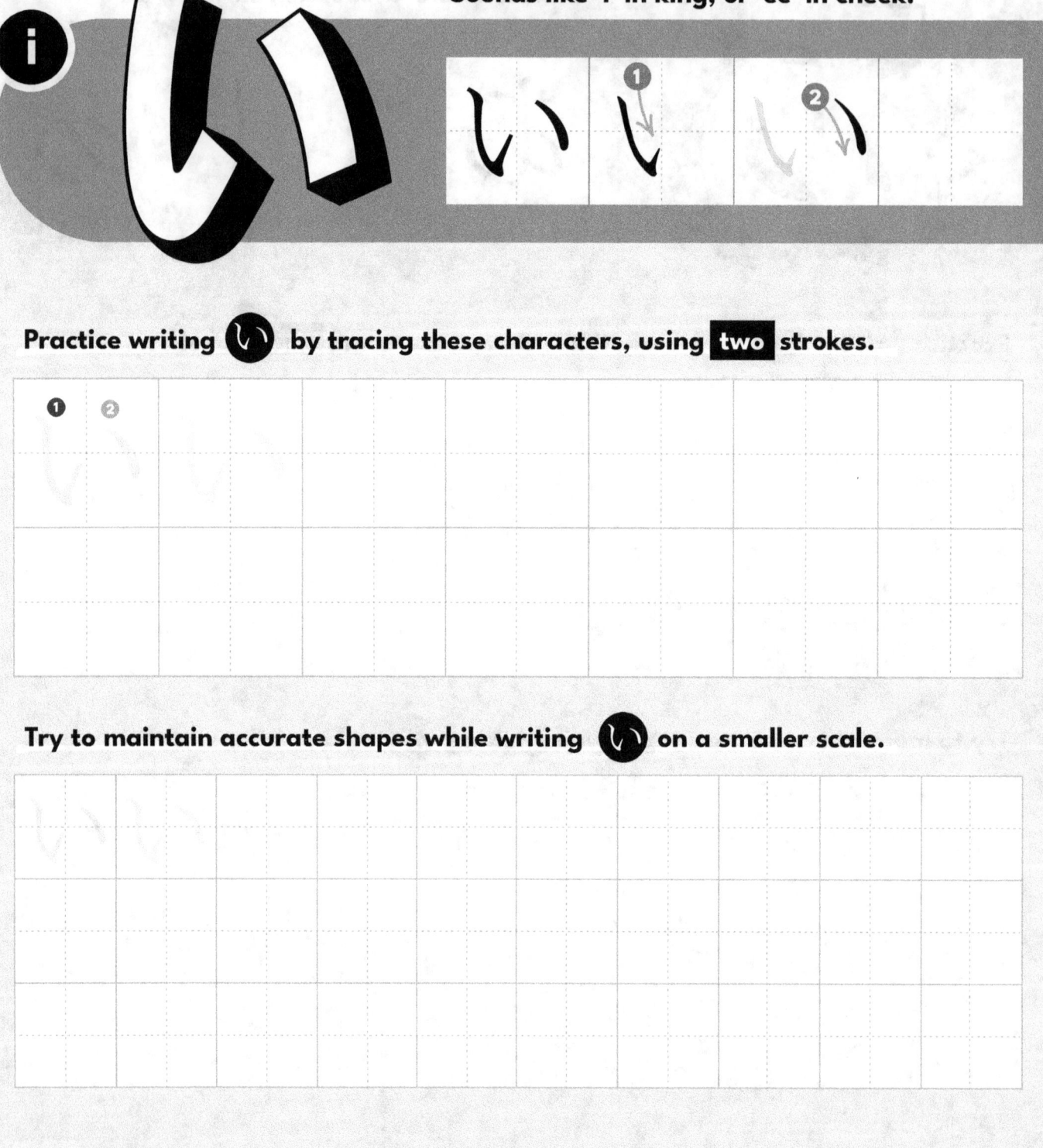

u う

Similar to 'oo' but like the 'ue' in true.

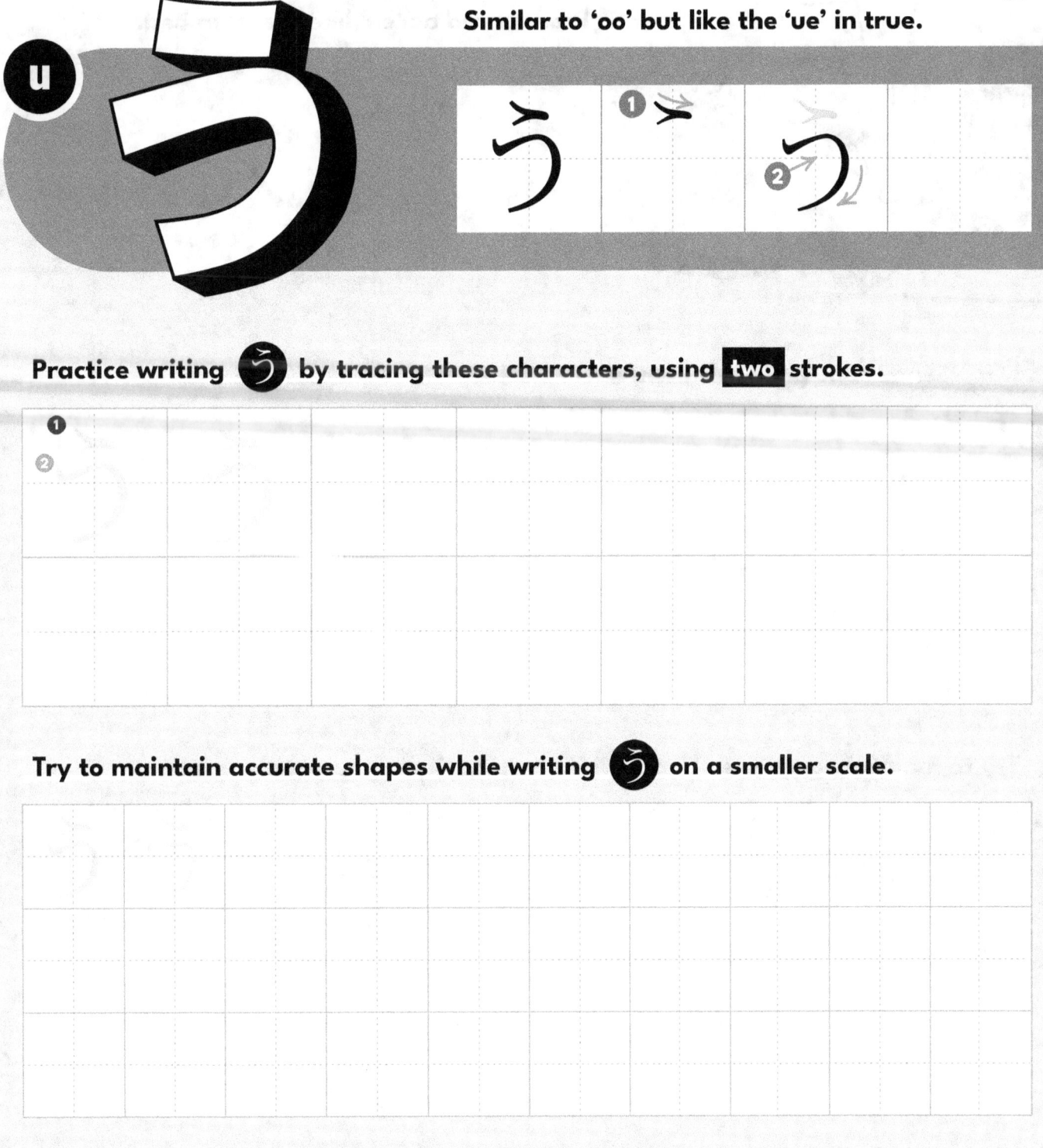

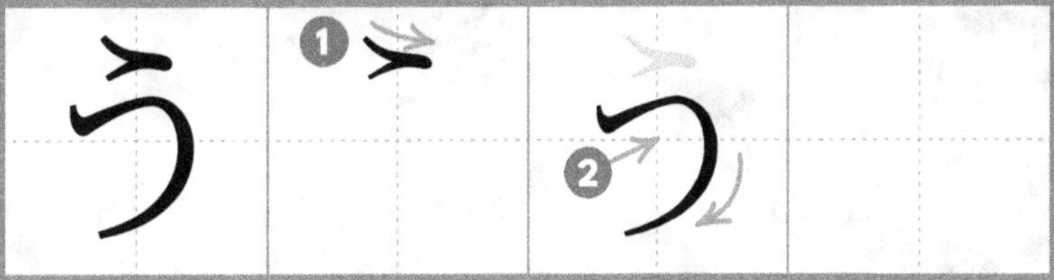

Practice writing う by tracing these characters, using two strokes.

Try to maintain accurate shapes while writing う on a smaller scale.

Mnemonic.

Examples.

- Sideways letter 'u'
- Imagine an open mouth eating f<u>oo</u>d

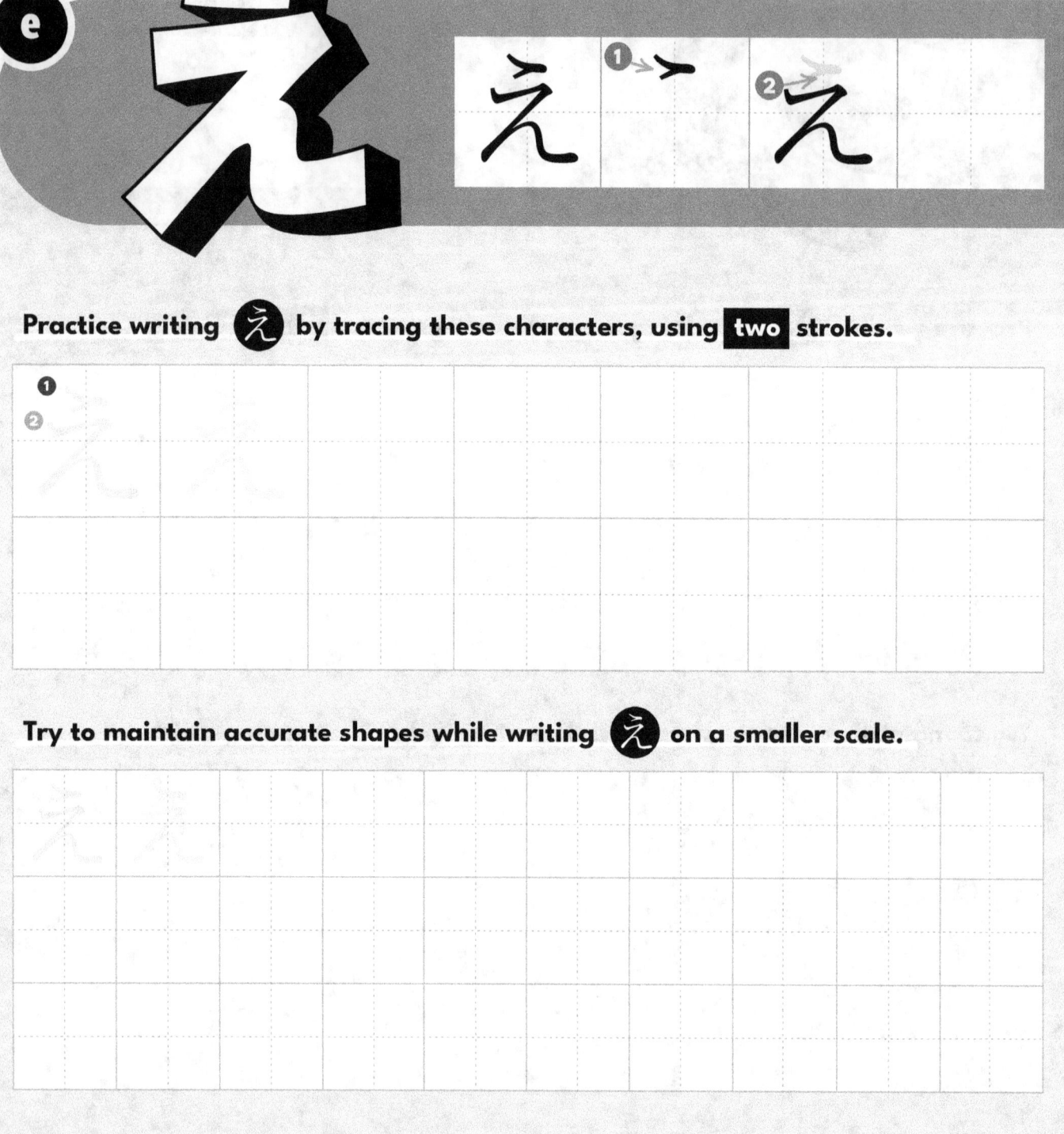

e え

Pronounced as 'eh' like the 'e' in bed.

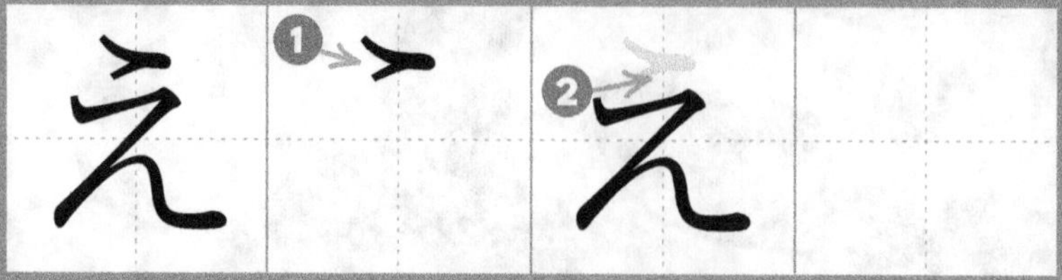

Practice writing え by tracing these characters, using **two** strokes.

Try to maintain accurate shapes while writing え on a smaller scale.

Mnemonic.

Examples & ideas.

- Looks energetic, like a running man
- Shape of exotic bird

お

o

Sounds like the 'o' in box.

Practice writing お by tracing these characters, using **three** strokes.

Try to maintain accurate shapes while writing お on a smaller scale.

Mnemonic.

Examples.

- Picture an Olive on a stick
- Contains letter 'o'

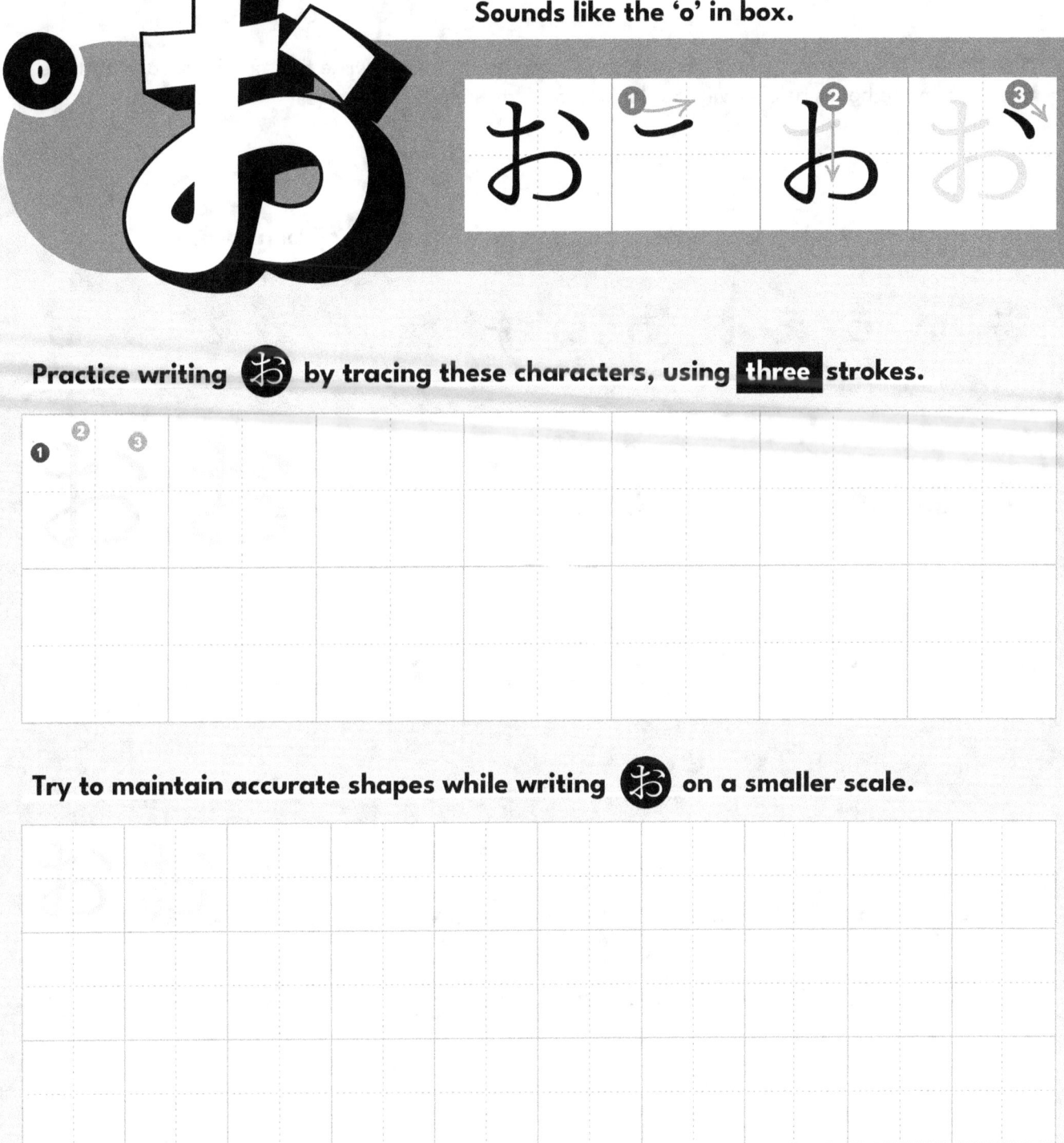

How good is your memory? This exercise should be easy but try to write the romaji for each of these hiragana in the boxes below - without looking back at the previous pages.

Practice pronouncing each symbol as you write the romaji beneath.

あ	い	う	え	お	あ	い	お	う	あ	え	あ	う	あ
え	お	あ	い	う	え	お	い	あ	え	お	い	う	え
い	う	あ	え	お	え	う	あ	お	あ	う	い	お	あ

Take a break for 5 minutes, and then do the same for these symbols too.

う	い	う	あ	え	い	え	い	お	い	あ	お	え	う
い	え	う	あ	お	う	お	え	い	お	え	う	あ	い
あ	い	え	あ	い	え	あ	う	い	あ	え	あ	い	お

Reading Practice

With the ability to recognize the sounds that each character represents, you can start to read Japanese words. Reading is a great way to practice the language and simultaneously collect new vocabulary. You should try to practice your pronunciation at the same time by reading aloud.

When we read Japanese words, each *'syllable sound'* should take the same length of time to say. When we write characters together to form words, we pronounce each character one after the other - the sounds are not usually* merged. For example, the term **あい** *(meaning love)* is pronounced as *'a-i'* so that both sounds can be heard *("ah-ee")*.

The pronunciation of vowels like *'a'* and *'i'* often changes when they are joined together in English words. Compare how you pronounce the word *"man"* to the word *"main"* or how the vowels sound when you say *"bit," "bat,"* and *"bait."* Some describe Japanese as more straightforward to learn as a foreign language than English because what you see is often what you say.

We can write several words using just those five hiragana you have learned so far. Some examples are shown below, with space to write the romaji for each:

あう			to meet	**あい**			love/ indigo
いえ			house	**あお**			blue
おい			nephew	**ああ**			ah! / oh!
うえ			up/above	**いい**			good
いう			to say	**おう**			chase/King

** Certain letter combinations can be written and pronounced differently. You will learn more about these later in this book.*

H2. The K Column

The second column of the chart has similar pronunciation to the vowel column. All that is needed to pronounce these characters is a *'k-'* sound in front of the vowel sounds. In other words, the *'eh'* sound of え becomes a *'keh'* sound, and so on.

Symbols in this learning block.

か	き	く	け	こ
ka	**ki**	**ku**	**ke**	**ko**

Pronunciation

The *'k-'* sound that you add to each of the vowel sounds is made in much the same way as in English. Your tongue is pressed up into the upper part of the mouth, towards the back of your mouth.

This is a *'voiceless'* consonant sound, meaning that your vocal chords are not used when you say it out loud. The sound is made as you push air through them and out of your mouth. These types of sounds have relatively high levels of aspiration when pronounced by an English speaker.

Aspiration is just the name for the force that is applied to air being pushed out of your mouth. You can feel the level of aspiration your normal *'k-'* sound has by holding your hand in front of your mouth and saying words like *'key'* or *'kelp'*. The real Japanese *'k-'* sound is not as strong, so try to hold back some of that force as you pronounce the sounds.

ka か

Pronounce like the ‘kha’ in khakis.

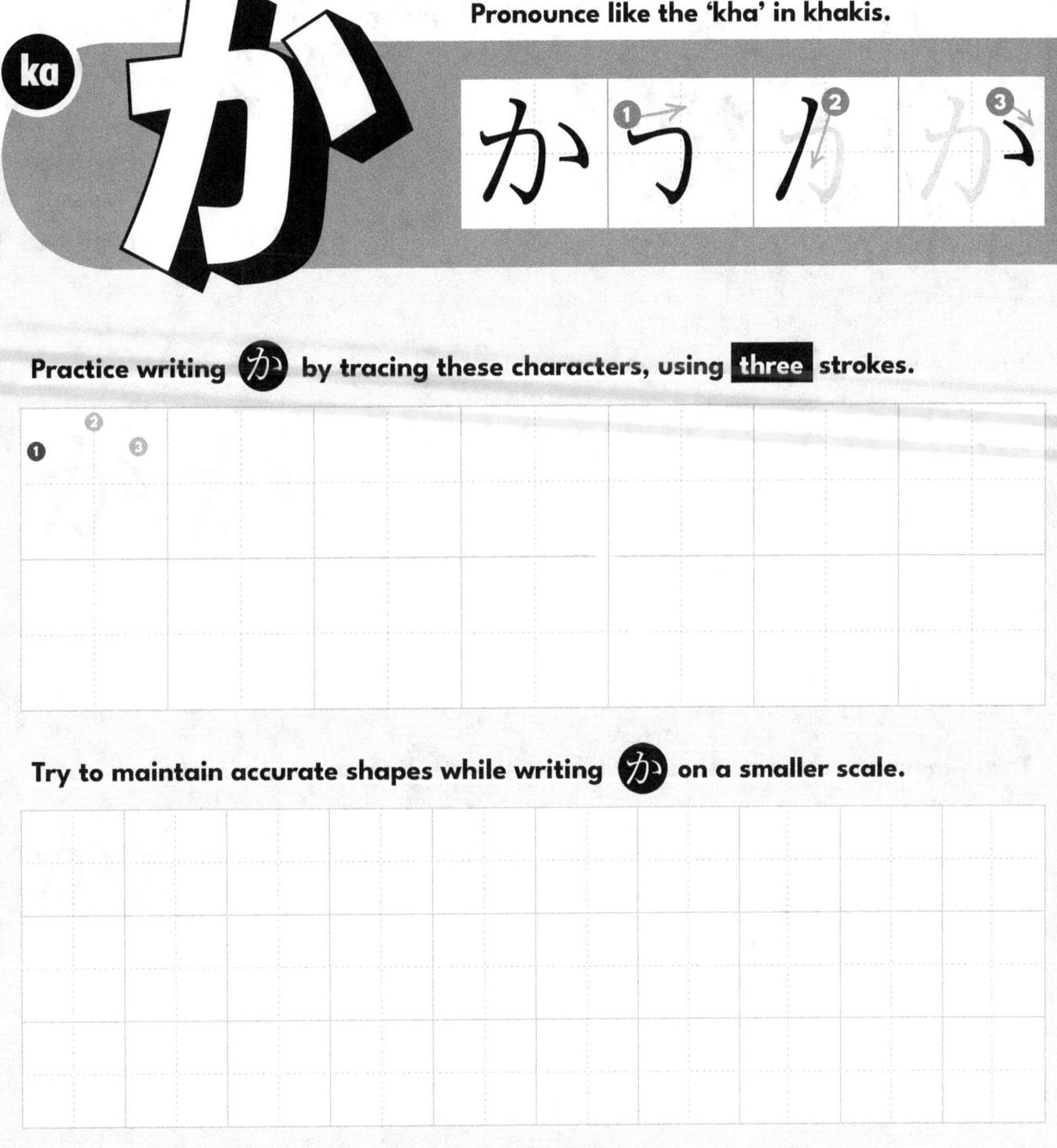

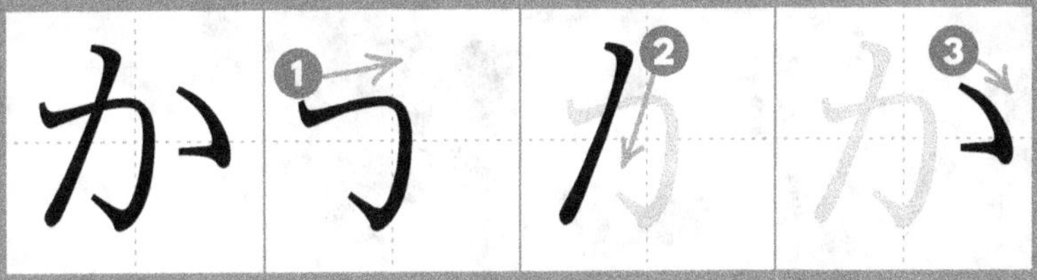

Practice writing か by tracing these characters, using **three** strokes.

Try to maintain accurate shapes while writing か on a smaller scale.

Mnemonic.

Examples.

- Letter ‘k’ shape with piece broken off
- Picture kicking a can up in the air.

ki き

This kana looks and sounds like a 'key'.

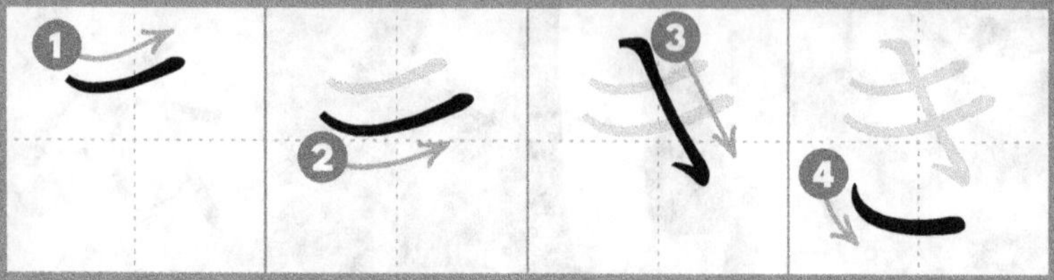

Practice writing き the correct way, with **four*** strokes (not three).

Try to maintain accurate shapes while writing き on a smaller scale.

Mnemonic.

Examples.

- Looks like a key, for the 'ki' sound

ku く

Pronounced like the 'coo' in cool.

Practice writing く by tracing these characters with just one stroke.

Try to maintain accurate shapes while writing く on a smaller scale.

Mnemonic.

Examples.

- Picture the beak of a cuckoo bird.
- Or any coo-ing bird

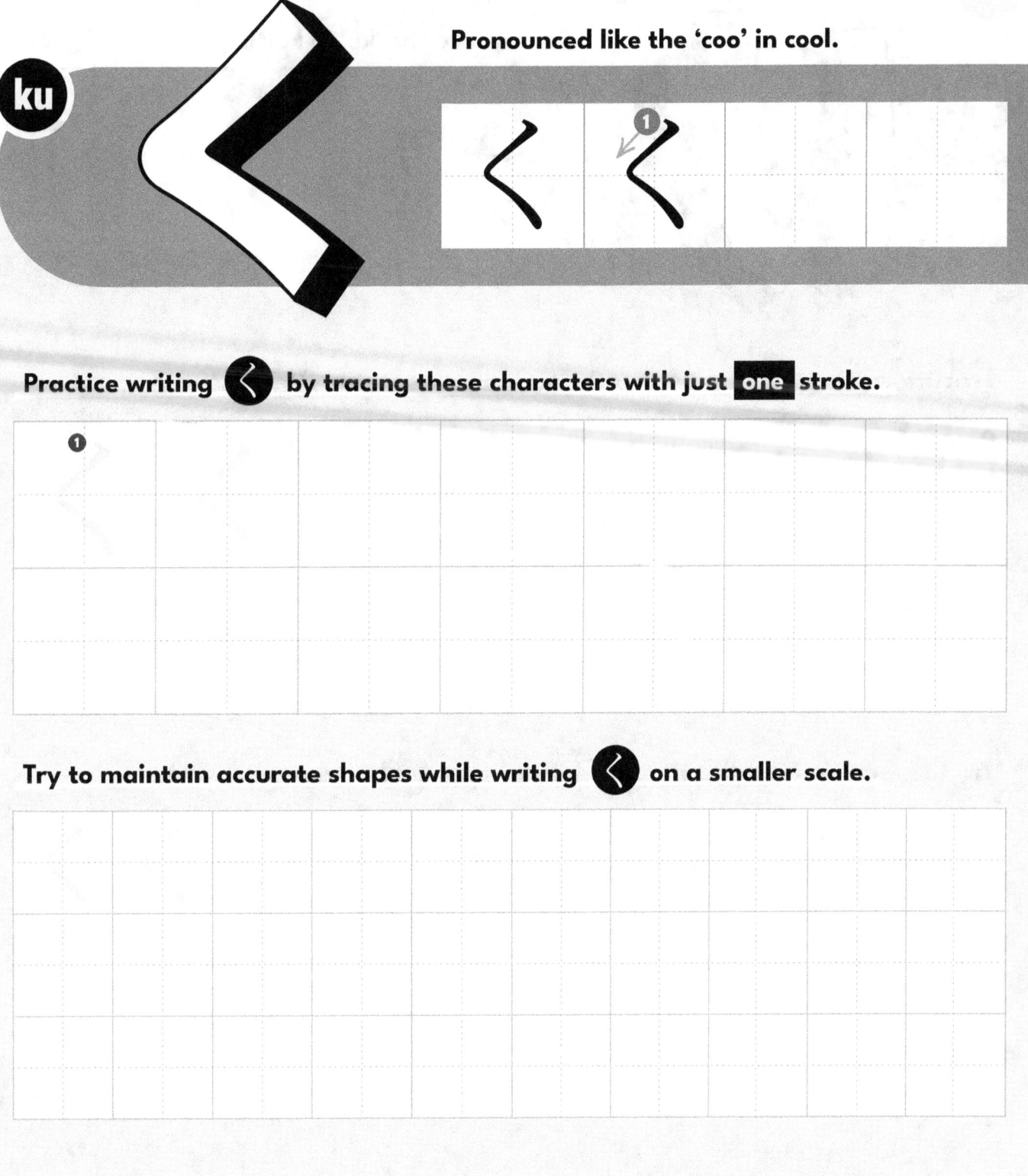

ke け

Sounds like the 'ke' in kettle.

け ① ② ③

Practice writing け by tracing these characters, using **three** strokes.

Try to maintain accurate shapes while writing け on a smaller scale.

Mnemonic.

Examples.

- Picture as a barrel shape, or keg
- Could be a broken kettle

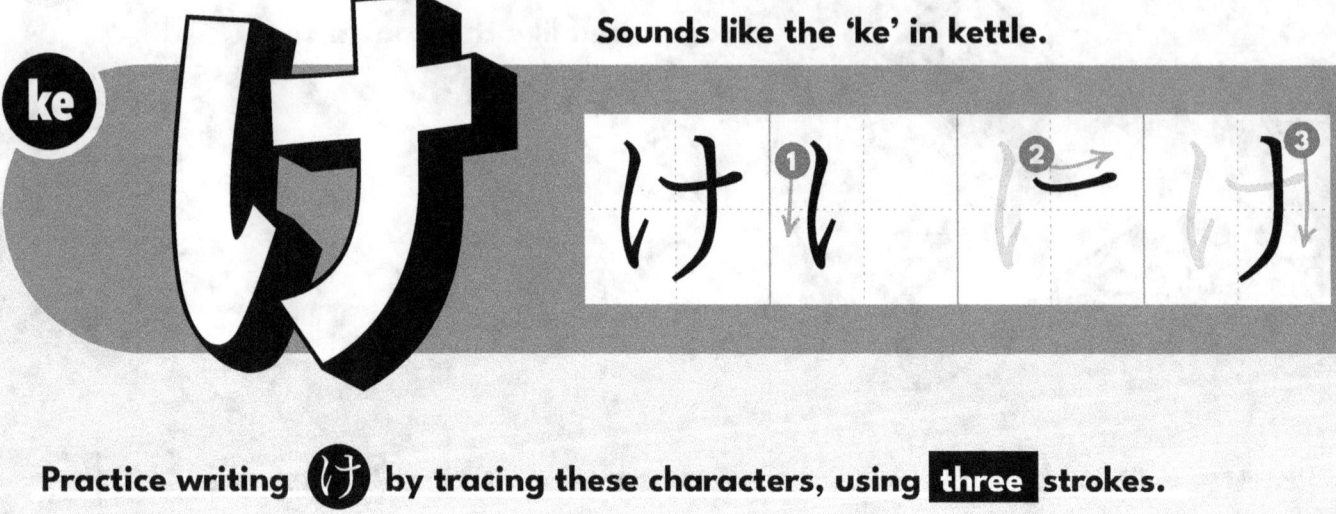

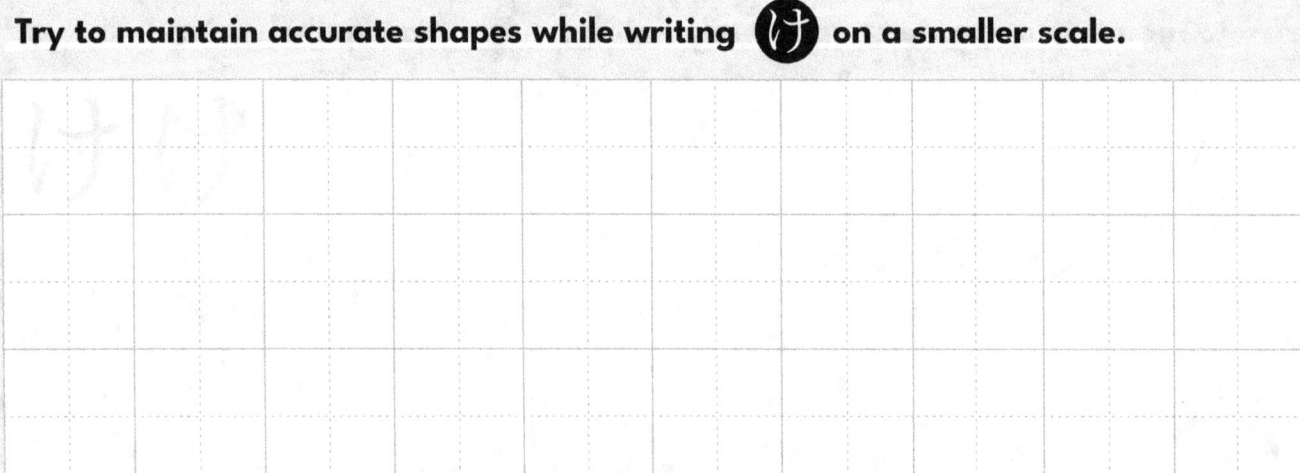

ko こ

Sounds like the 'co' in comb.

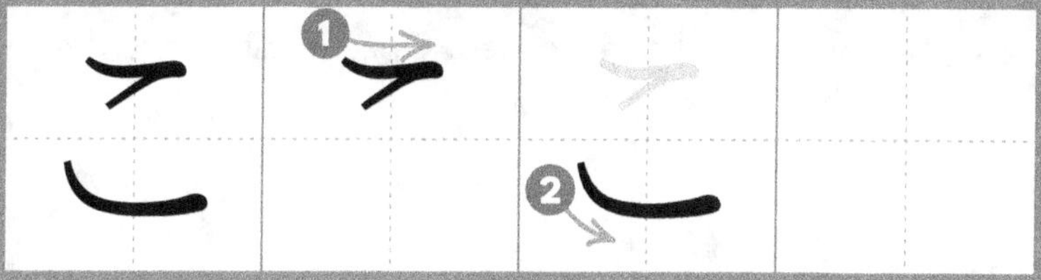

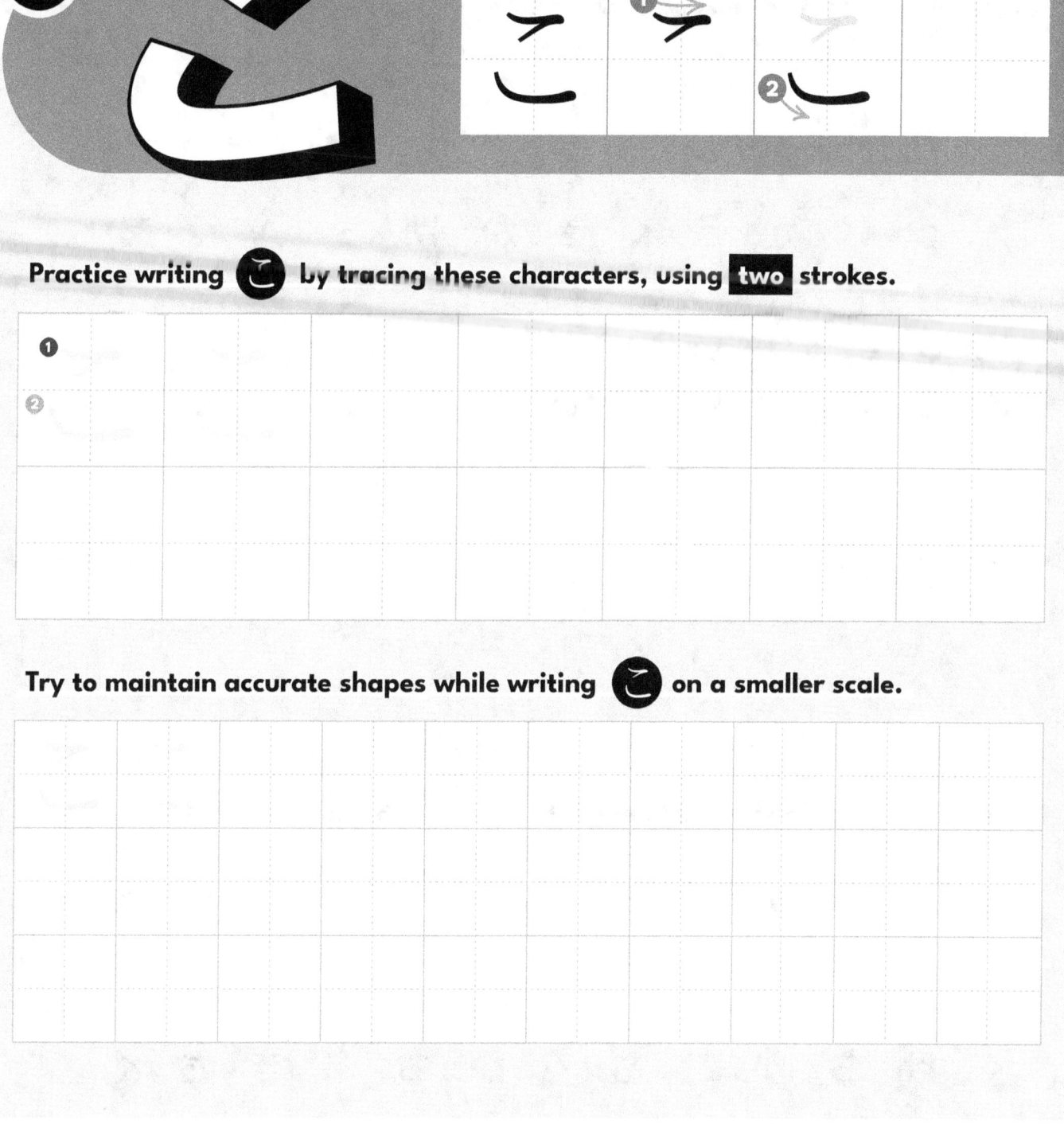

Practice writing こ by tracing these characters, using **two** strokes.

Try to maintain accurate shapes while writing こ on a smaller scale.

Mnemonic.

Examples.

- Could resemble a round coin shape
- Maybe a corner?
- Rolling can of cola?

This set of exercises should be more challenging than the previous set, as it includes all ten of the hiragana you have learned. Once again, write the romaji for the characters below.

Practice pronouncing each symbol as you write the romaji beneath.

え	う	け	か	う	く	き	か	け	お	い	く	あ	こ

え	こ	か	お	け	こ	お	え	く	か	け	あ	こ	お

く	き	い	お	か	く	こ	あ	き	い	け	き	け	き

Take a 5-minute break, and then do the same for this set of symbols too.

き	か	け	お	え	こ	け	い	か	く	き	い	え	く

く	け	お	か	こ	お	く	か	お	あ	き	お	く	う

い	こ	う	こ	け	お	え	き	く	か	き	あ	こ	け

Practice reading and writing words with characters from all group so far.

あい love		あう meet	
うえ above / top		こえ voice	
お hill		かく write	
きく hear / ask		おけ wooden bucket	
こけ moss		かお face / honor	
いけ pond		あき autumn	
かう buy		いう say	
えき station		あかい red	
いく go		あおい blue	
ここ here		きおく memory	

H3. The S Column

The ***[consonant*** + ***vowel]*** pattern applies to most groups of symbols, but not all. This third group contains the first of a few exceptions you will meet along the way. Fortunately, they are not any more difficult to pronounce.

Symbols in this learning block.

さ	し	す	せ	そ
sa	**shi**	**su**	**se**	**so**

Pronunciation

With the exception of the second character, the symbols in this column follow the usual pattern. Simply add a normal *'s-'* sound to the vowels you have learned.

The exception here is し or *'shi'* which is pronounced slightly differently. Instead of saying *'si' (like 'see')* this character is *'shi'* and sounds like the English word *'she'.*

Accurate pronunciation of a Japanese 'sh-' is not far from the English 'sh' and it is unlikely to cause problems. If you want to achieve a more accurate sound, the tongue would need to make a slightly different shape. You may be able to feel the difference by saying the words *'he'* and *'she'* alternately a few times. The tongue tends to be pushed upwards with a bend in the middle when you say 'he'. Introduce more of this tongue shape into your pronunciation of *'shi'.*

sa さ

Sounds like the 'sa-' in sarcasm.

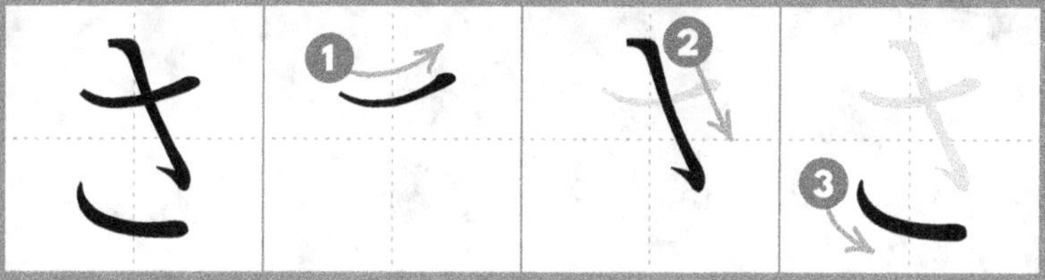

Practice writing さ the proper way, with three* strokes (not two).

Try to maintain accurate shapes while writing さ on a smaller scale.

Mnemonic.

Examples.

- Imagine the shapes as a sad face?
- Similar to KI, but not the same

shi

し

Sounds exactly like the 'shi' in sashimi.

し し

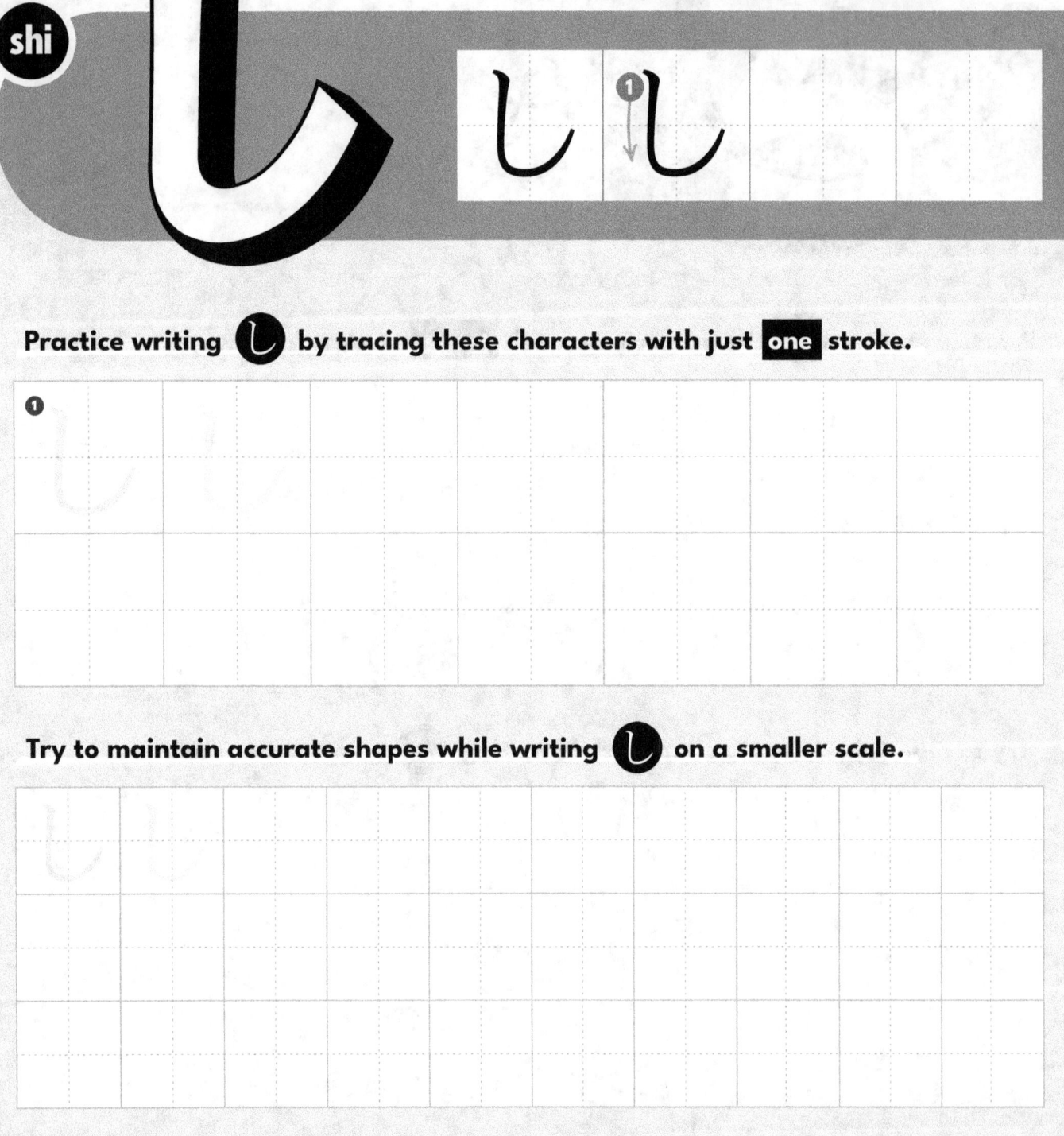

Practice writing し by tracing these characters with just **one** stroke.

Try to maintain accurate shapes while writing し on a smaller scale.

Mnemonic.

Examples.

- A fishing hook
- She has long hair

su す

Sounds similar to the 'sou' in soup.

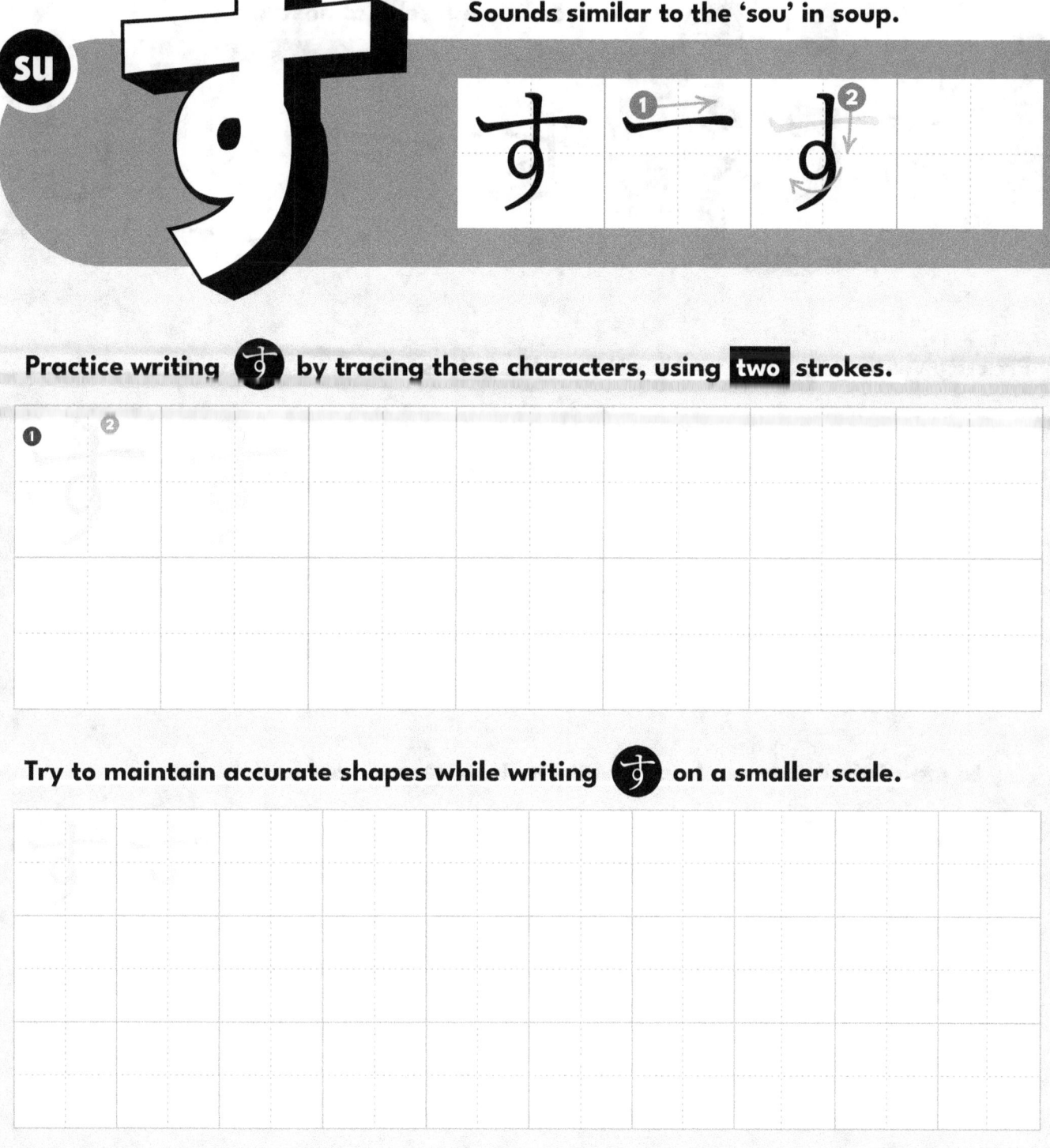

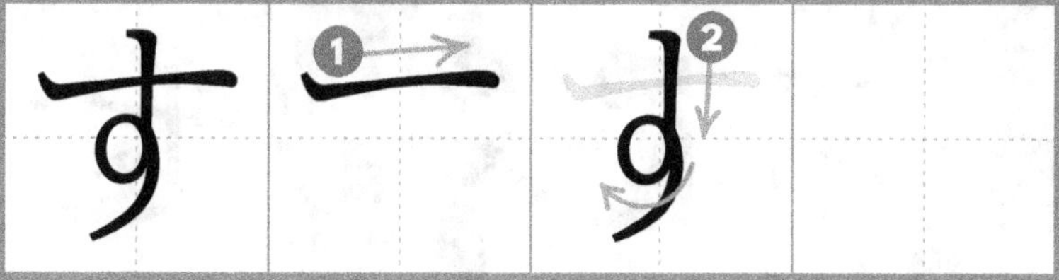

Practice writing す by tracing these characters, using **two** strokes.

Try to maintain accurate shapes while writing す on a smaller scale.

Mnemonic.

Examples.

- Picture a pig with a curly tail, called <u>Sue</u>
- Somebody wearing a hat, oh it's <u>Sue</u>

se せ

Pronounced 'seh' (almost like say).

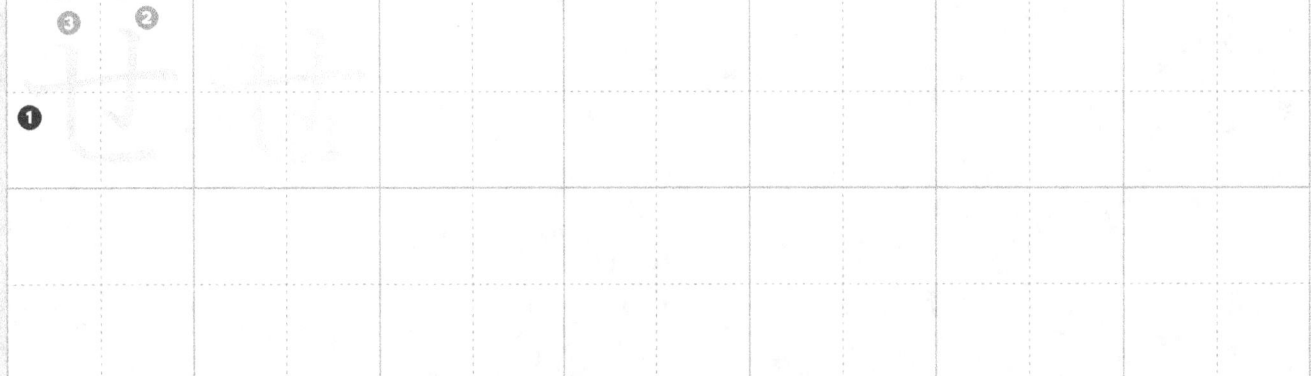

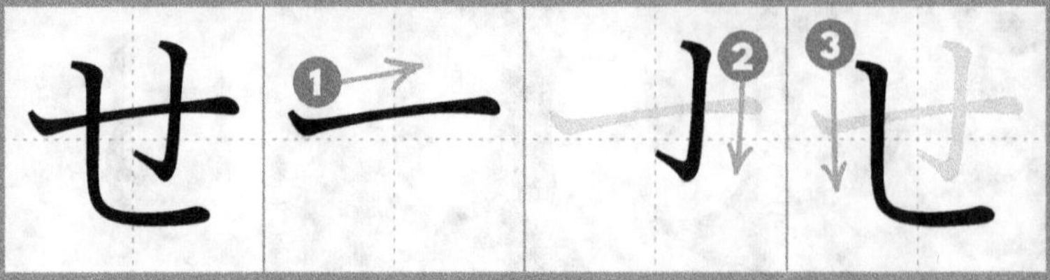

Practice writing せ by tracing these characters, using **three** strokes.

Try to maintain accurate shapes while writing せ on a smaller scale.

Mnemonic.

Examples.

- imagine its a mouth seh-ing something
- Upside down sevens

SO そ

Sounds like the 'so-' in soccer or sorry.

そ ①そ

Practice writing そ by tracing these characters with just one stroke.

①

Try to maintain accurate shapes while writing そ on a smaller scale.

Mnemonic.

Examples.

- It's so abstract
- Picture a sewing needle and thread

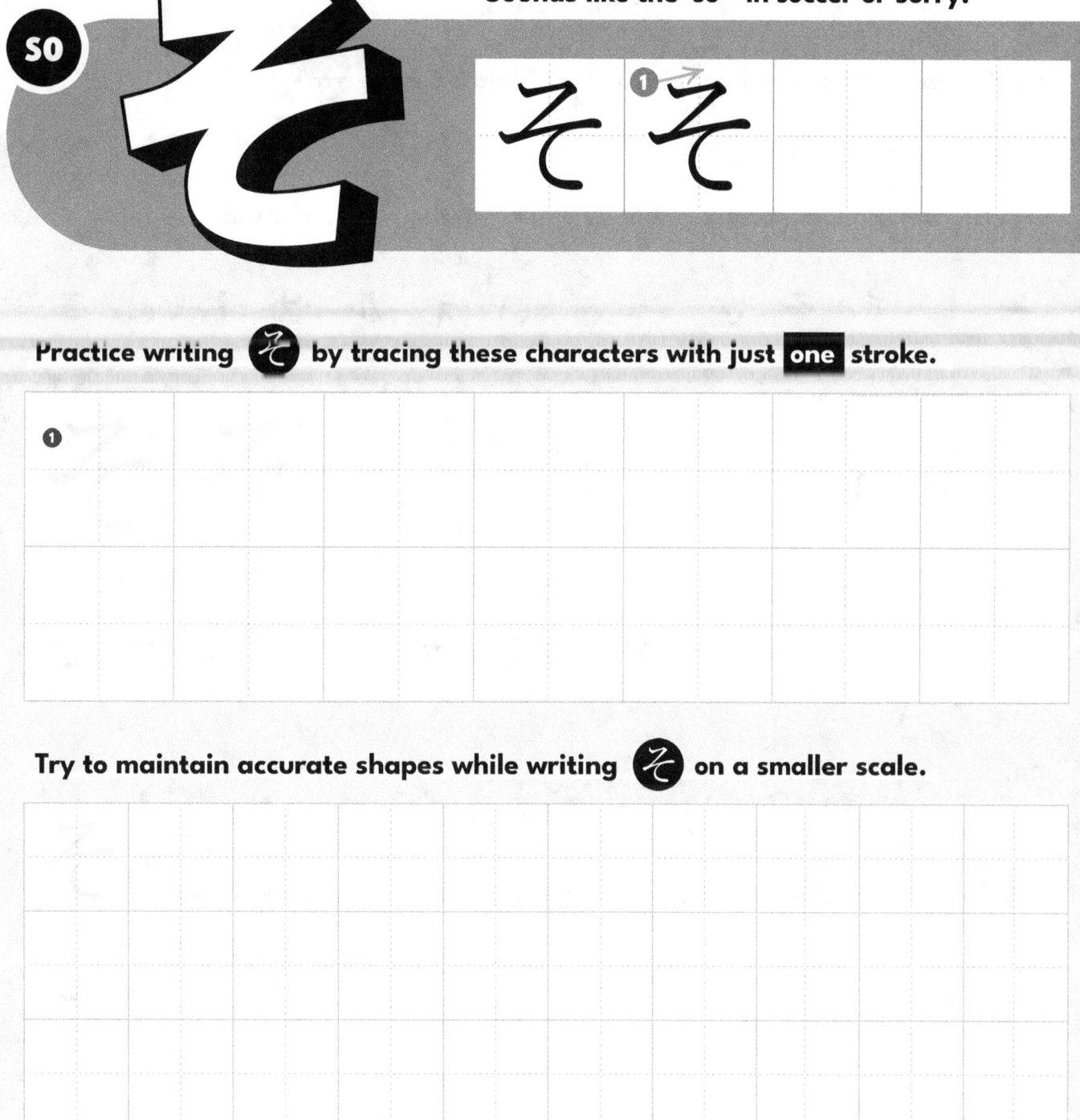

Now that the five new hiragana have been added to the others, repeat this memorization exercise. Take a break between each set, as this will help to improve recall.

Practice pronouncing each symbol as you write the romaji beneath.

そ	し	す	そ	さ	そ	こ	い	え	か	せ	お	し	そ

せ	さ	せ	き	す	う	し	く	さ	す	か	う	す	き

こ	あ	か	け	き	け	そ	い	せ	こ	し	す	さ	せ

Take a 5-minute break, and then do the same for these symbols too.

か	き	い	す	そ	せ	さ	く	き	け	そ	さ	お	せ

さ	か	こ	し	あ	せ	こ	し	う	す	さ	そ	せ	し

か	け	す	き	う	せ	し	す	す	そ	せ	え	い	こ

This time, take a 10-minute break and come back to complete these.

き す く し す さ か そ せ か う せ そ さ

す し か せ こ そ さ お き き す せ え い

あ さ け い う こ こ け し そ そ せ し す

After a much longer break, add the romaji for each symbol below.

せ そ あ す お く き そ さ し か こ け う

き う す せ け そ さ え す こ そ こ か お

く し そ す か い き せ さ す せ い し そ

H4. The T-Column

The fourth column contains two characters that fall outside the usual pattern but, once again, they are not difficult to say and simply need to be remembered. They only really seem like exceptions because of the romaji beneath and, before long, you will simply recognize the character as the sound that it represents.

Symbols in this learning block.

た	ち	つ	て	と
ta	**chi**	**tsu**	**te**	**to**

Pronunciation

Characters with the pure *'t-'* sound are simple enough to pronounce. The tip of your tongue touches the top of your mouth, just behind your upper teeth, and air is released with some aspiration. Try to reduce the amount of force and air that is released.

The second character in the T column is simply pronounced as *'chi'* or a short *'chee-'*. While not exactly the same as the *'ch-'* in English pronunciation, this will be close enough. To achieve a more accurate pronunciation, the tip of your tongue would make contact with the roof of your mouth still, but further back from the position for a pure *'t-'* sound. It would be located on the area that feels slightly ribbed, at the end of the ridge that runs across the roof of your mouth, from front to back.

Finally, the character つ represents a *'tsu'* sound. The *'u'* part of the sound is the same as the basic vowel character う but the *'t-'* sound is now a *'ts-'*. Try not to view this as a silent *'t'*, as it should certainly be heard. Instead, try to isolate the sound of *'-ts'* from words like *'boats'* or *'knots'* and add the short *'oo'* sound to that. This almost sounds like the word *'zoo'* but shorter and with the *'t'*. Remember that this syllable is no longer than the others and is pronounced in the same length of time.

ta た

Sounds like the '-ta' in Santa.

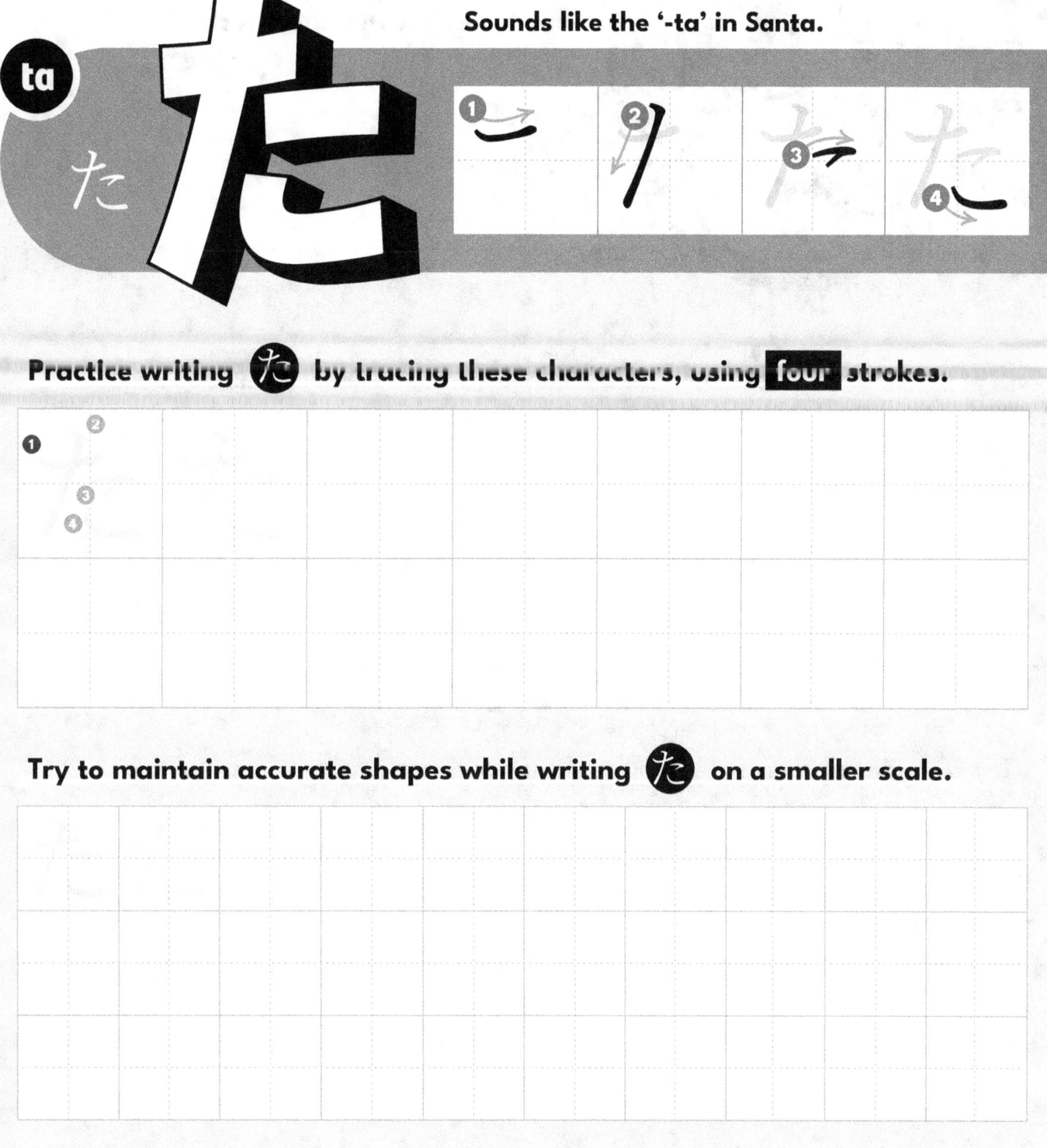

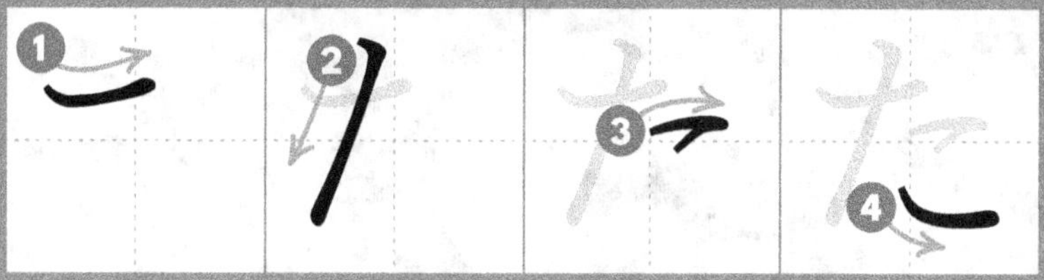

Practice writing た by tracing these characters, using **four** strokes.

Try to maintain accurate shapes while writing た on a smaller scale.

Mnemonic.

Examples.

- Looks like letters 'ta'
- Tackling a ball

chi ち

Sounds just like the 'chee' in cheeks.

ち ① ② ち

Practice writing ち by tracing these characters, using **two** strokes.

Try to maintain accurate shapes while writing ち on a smaller scale.

Mnemonic.

Examples.

- A face, from the side with no chin
- It sneezes, Aachioo!
- A cheap number 5?

tsu つ

Sounds just like the name 'Sue'.

つ つ

1

Practice writing つ by tracing these characters, with just one stroke.

1

Try to maintain accurate shapes while writing つ on a smaller scale.

Mnemonic.

Examples.

- A tsunami wave

te て

Sounds like the 'te-' in teddy bear.

て て

Practice writing て by tracing these characters with just **one** stroke.

1

Try to maintain accurate shapes while writing て on a smaller scale.

Mnemonic.

Examples.

- Letter T for ten.
- Terrible number 7

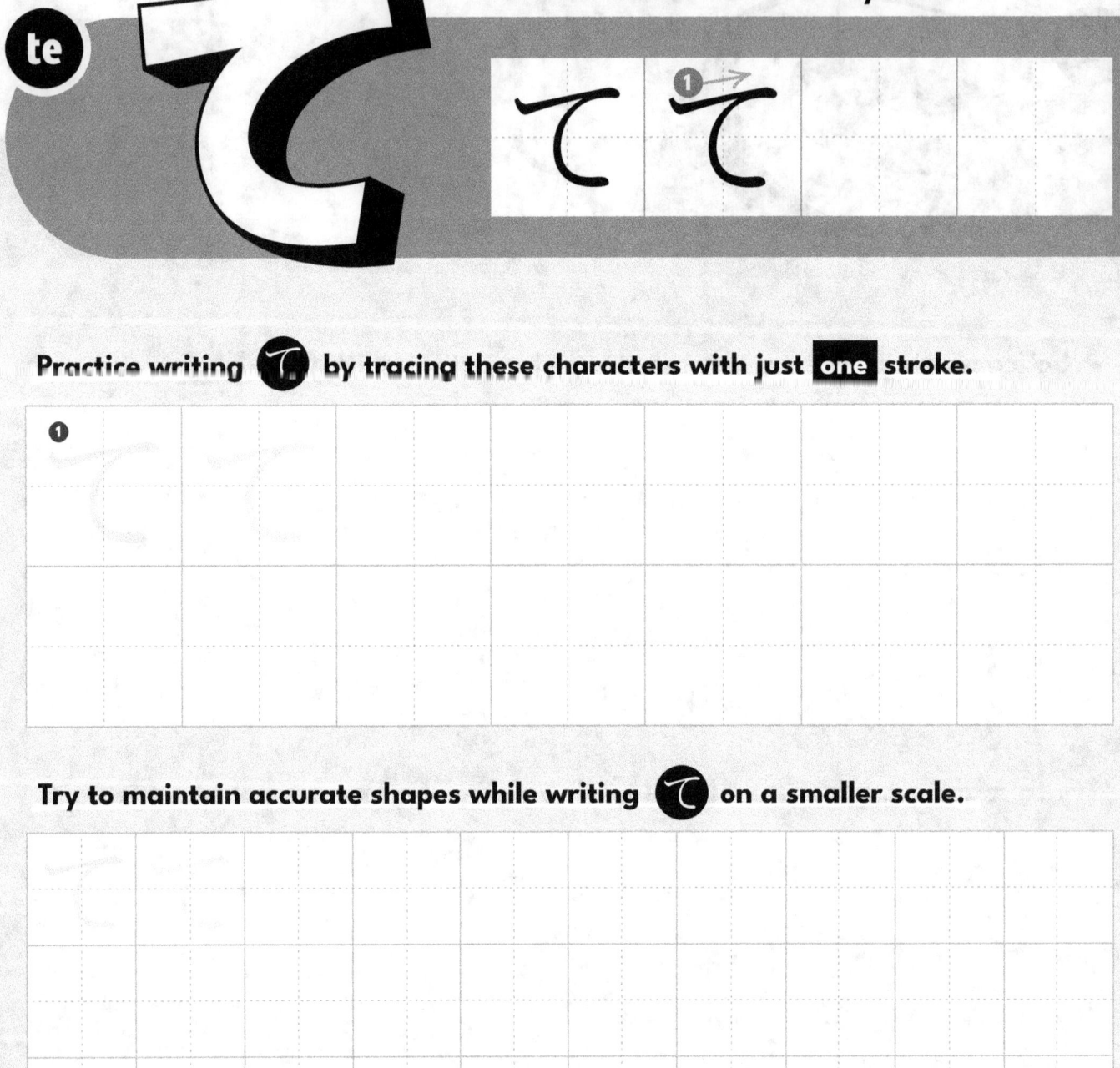

to と

Sounds like the 'to-' in tonic.

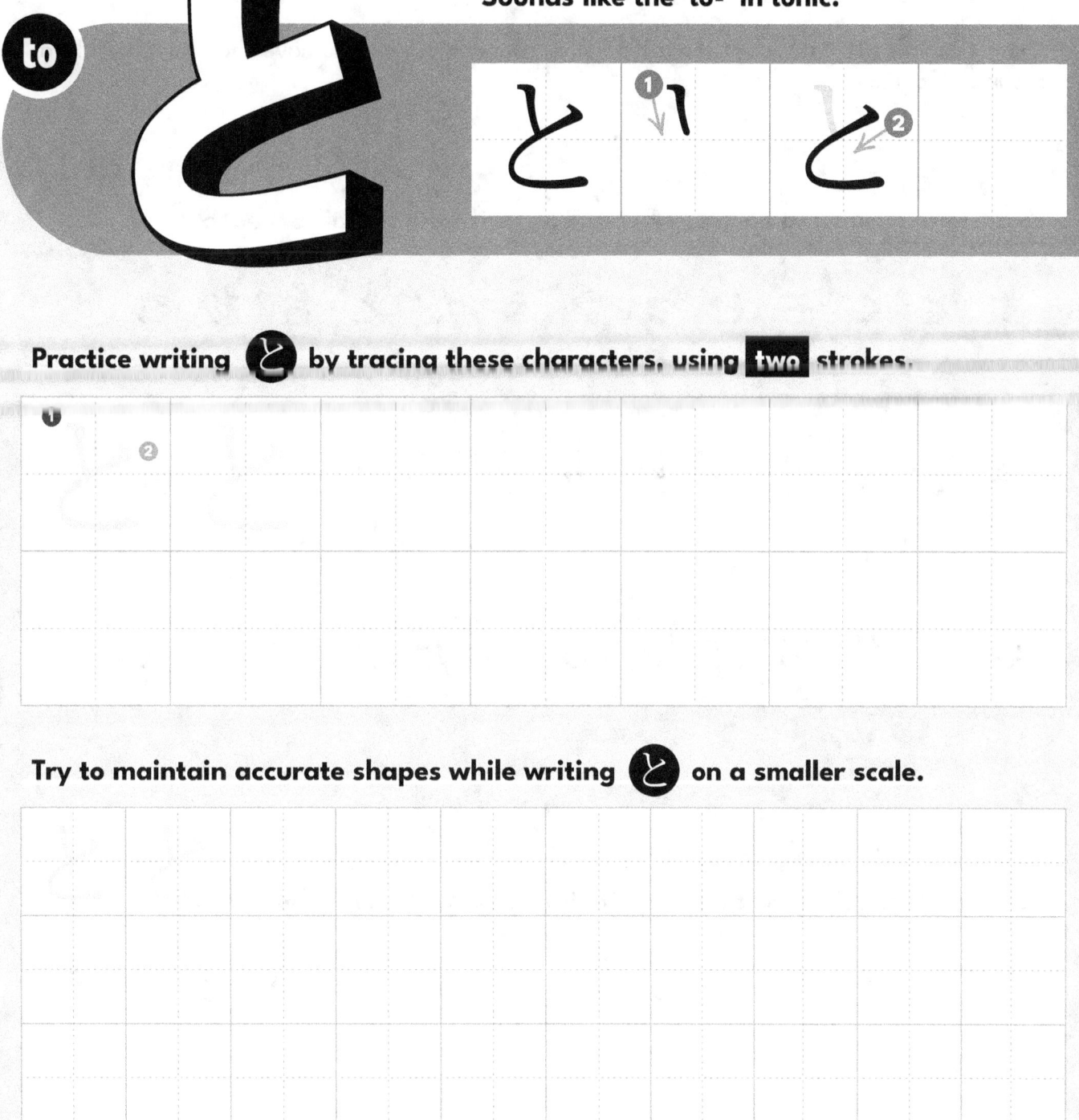

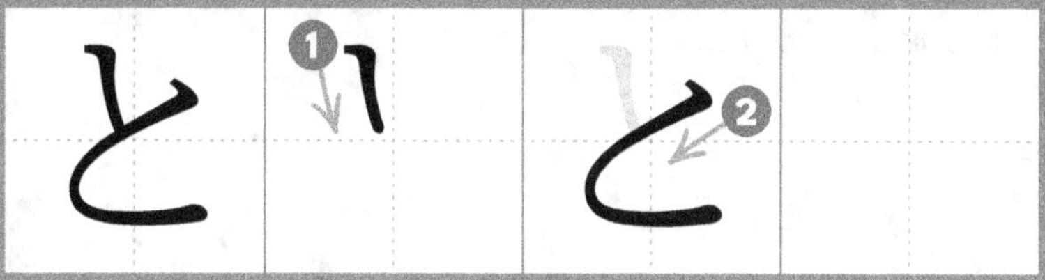

Practice writing と by tracing these characters, using **two** strokes.

Try to maintain accurate shapes while writing と on a smaller scale.

Mnemonic.

Examples.

- Picture a big toe with a splinter
- Imagine a thorn in your tongue

These exercises will test your memorization of all twenty hiragana you have encountered. Take a break and continue.

Practice pronouncing each symbol as you write the romaji beneath.

す	と	く	そ	と	つ	さ	う	た	と	ち	あ	つ	ち
そ	せ	え	て	た	き	け	こ	と	ち	つ	こ	か	て
し	た	せ	お	ち	さ	あ	す	た	せ	い	て	し	つ

Take a 5-minute break, and then do the same for these symbols too.

う	た	そ	せ	さ	い	き	そ	お	ち	か	け	す	う
ち	か	て	そ	あ	て	え	た	け	し	こ	と	す	お
せ	さ	う	き	つ	え	こ	す	と	あ	つ	せ	と	し

Your brain should be saving earlier symbols to your longer-term memory, making them easier to recognize and recall.

This time, take a 10-minute break and come back to complete these.

し	ち	た	つ	あ	て	す	か	さ	ち	け	い	う	え
け	え	さ	て	そ	せ	こ	お	す	き	と	う	そ	し
お	す	き	そ	せ	ち	あ	し	つ	と	か	せ	た	こ

After a much longer break, add the romaji for each symbol below.

お	き	こ	す	せ	こ	あ	う	け	ち	そ	て	ち	す
と	つ	た	せ	け	さ	そ	さ	と	お	し	か	え	し
せ	ち	と	つ	か	う	あ	た	い	そ	す	き	え	た

Practice reading and writing words with characters from all group so far.

すし
sushi

つち
soil

そと
outside

さけ
sake

こと
thing

くつ
shoes

かこ
past

てつ
iron/steel

せき
cough

たつ
to stand/leave

とち
land

うた
song

かた
shoulder

しち
seven

さす
to point

あした
tomorrow

とおい
far

きせつ
season

さとい
clever

ちかてつ
subway

H5. The N & H Columns

This group is a little larger than the previous few and, largely, follows the *[consonant + vowel]* pattern. One symbol will immediately stand out as different. Instead of having a *'h-'* sound added, like the others in this column, it is shown with *'f-'* and it is pronounced with a sort of mixture of sounds - generally, this should almost sound like *'hfu-'* when you pronounce it.

Symbols in this learning block.

な	に	ぬ	ね	の
na	**ni**	**nu**	**ne**	**no**

は	ひ	ふ	へ	ほ
ha	**hi**	**fu**	**he**	**ho**

Pronunciation

Most of this group will sound exactly how it reads. Add a regular *'n-'* and *'h-'* sound like those used when saying words like *'north'* and *'house'* to the basic vowel sounds. Both are voiced consonants, and the *'n-'* sounds are nasal sounding.

The pronunciation of ふ is a little odd and may be sound like *'fu'* and *'hu'* depending on use. Generally, this has a *'hfu'* sound that is made by trying to say *'foo'* without your teeth making contact with your lip. You still need to bring your lips closer together but the huff of air is expelled through open lips, instead of the puff of air generated by touching your lip against the upper teeth.

na な

Sounds just like the '-na's in banana

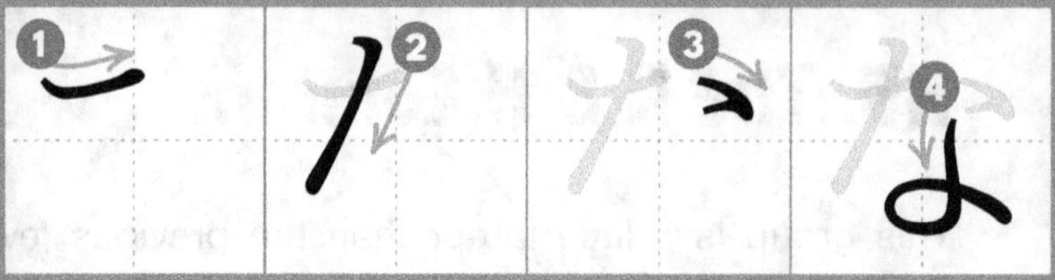

Practice writing な by tracing these characters, using four strokes.

Try to maintain accurate shapes while writing な on a smaller scale.

Mnemonic.

Examples.

- A naughty person, praying at a cross.

ni に

Sounds similar to the word 'knee'.

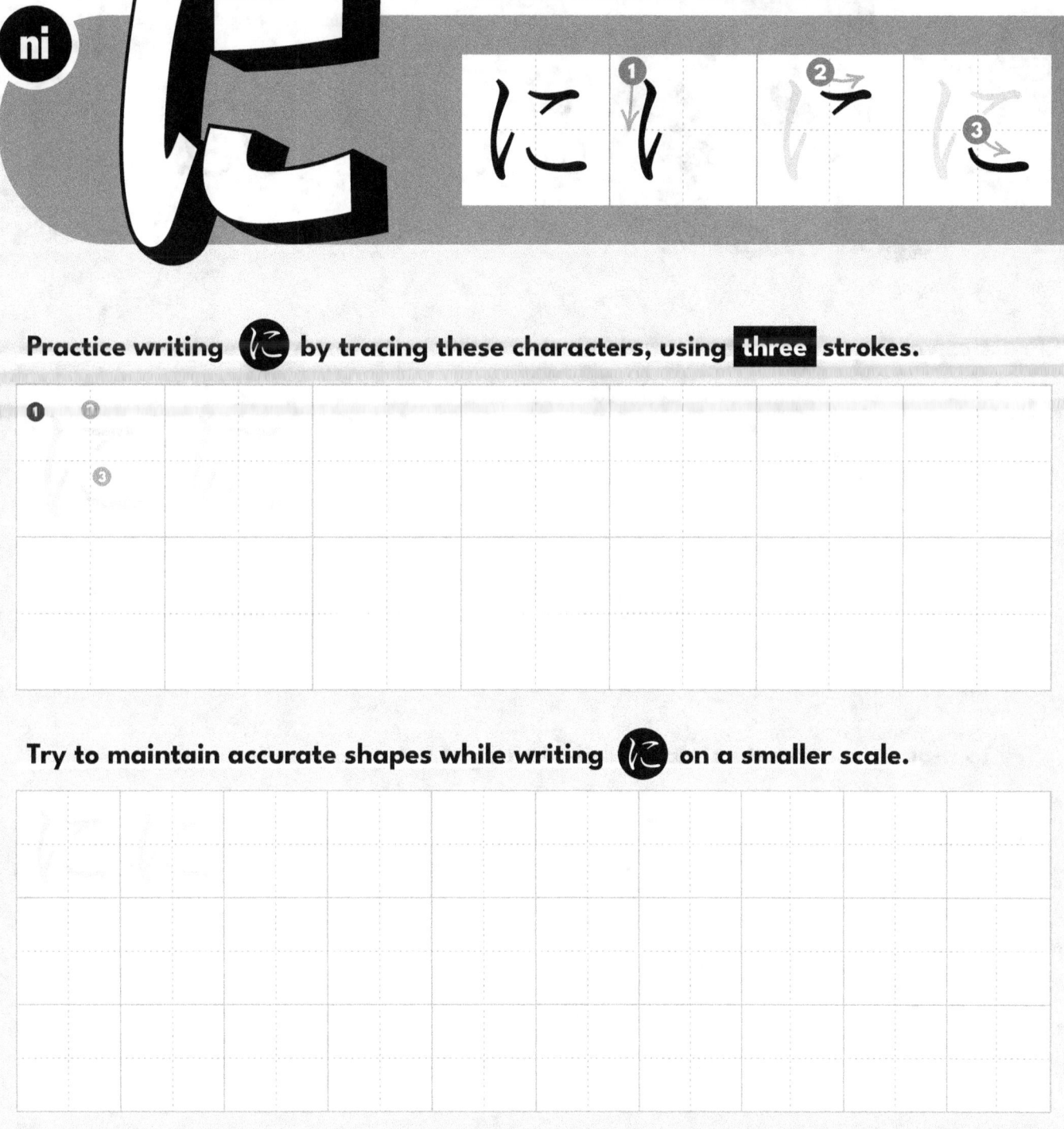

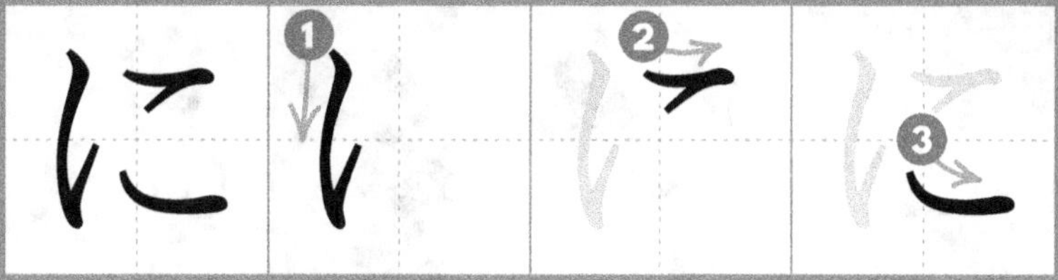

Practice writing に by tracing these characters, using **three** strokes.

Try to maintain accurate shapes while writing に on a smaller scale.

Mnemonic.

Examples.

- Picture as a knee
- Nearly a square?

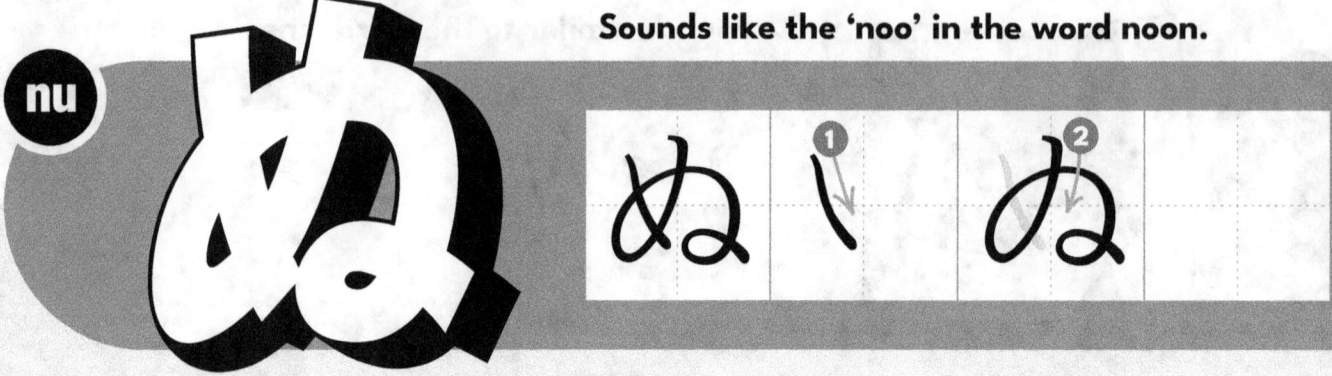

nu ぬ

Sounds like the 'noo' in the word noon.

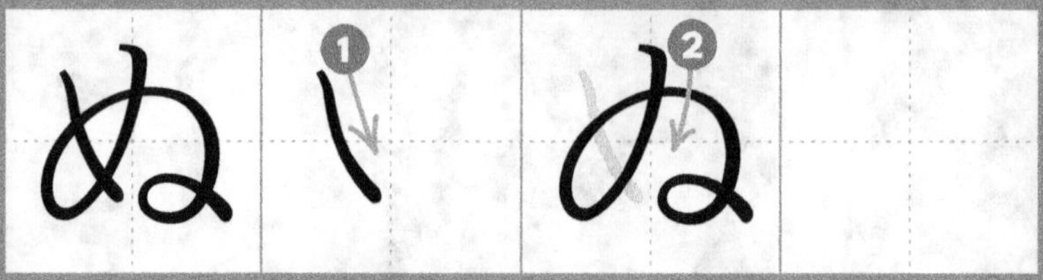

Practice writing ぬ by tracing these characters with just two strokes.

Try to maintain accurate shapes while writing ぬ on a smaller scale.

Mnemonic.

Examples.

- A bowl of noodles with chopsticks
- A clockface, and it's almost noon

ne ね

Sounds similar to 'nay' or 'neigh'.

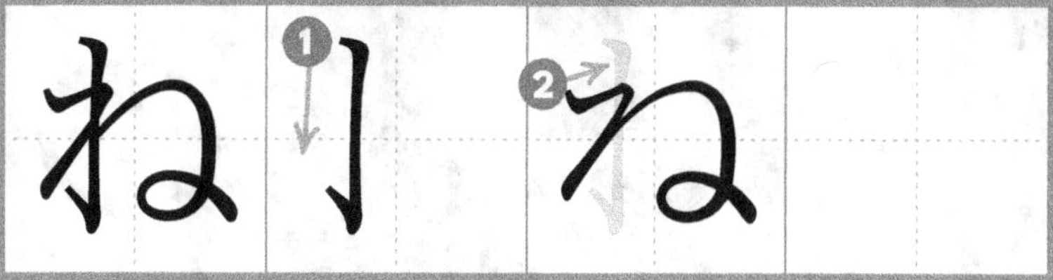

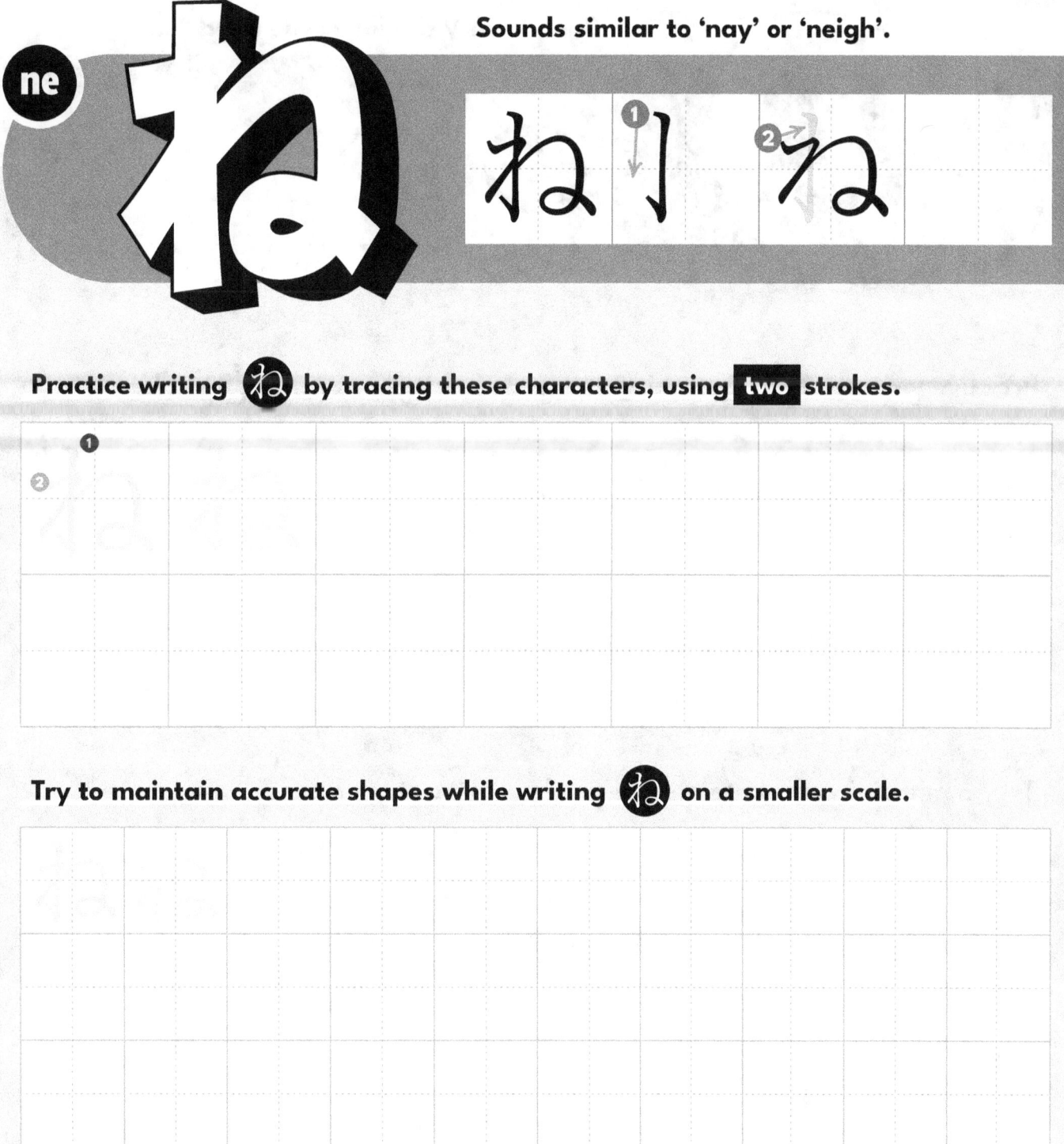

Practice writing ね by tracing these characters, using two strokes.

Try to maintain accurate shapes while writing ね on a smaller scale.

Mnemonic.

Examples.

- Nelly the elephant, with a curly trunk
- A cat, curled up, or 'neko' in Japanese

Sounds very similar to the word 'No'.

no の

のの

Practice writing の by tracing these characters, using **one** stroke.

Try to maintain accurate shapes while writing の on a smaller scale.

Mnemonic.

Examples.

- A pigs nose
- A sign that says NO Smoking

ha は

Pronounce as 'ha' like in hand.

は ① ② ③

Practice writing は by tracing these characters, using **three** strokes.

Try to maintain accurate shapes while writing は on a smaller scale.

Mnemonic.

Examples.

- Looks like letters 'h' and 'a', for 'ha'

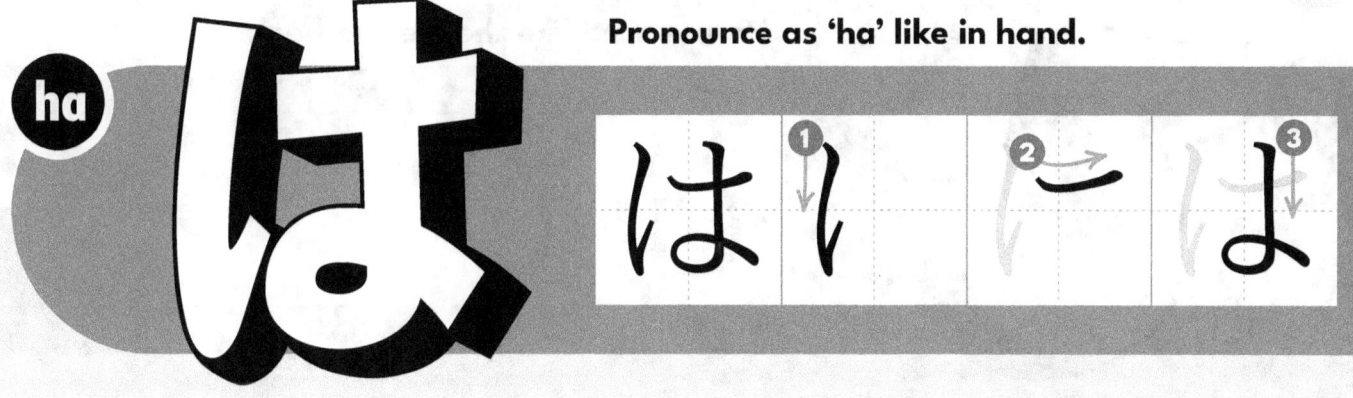

hi ひ

Pronounced like the 'hee' in heel.

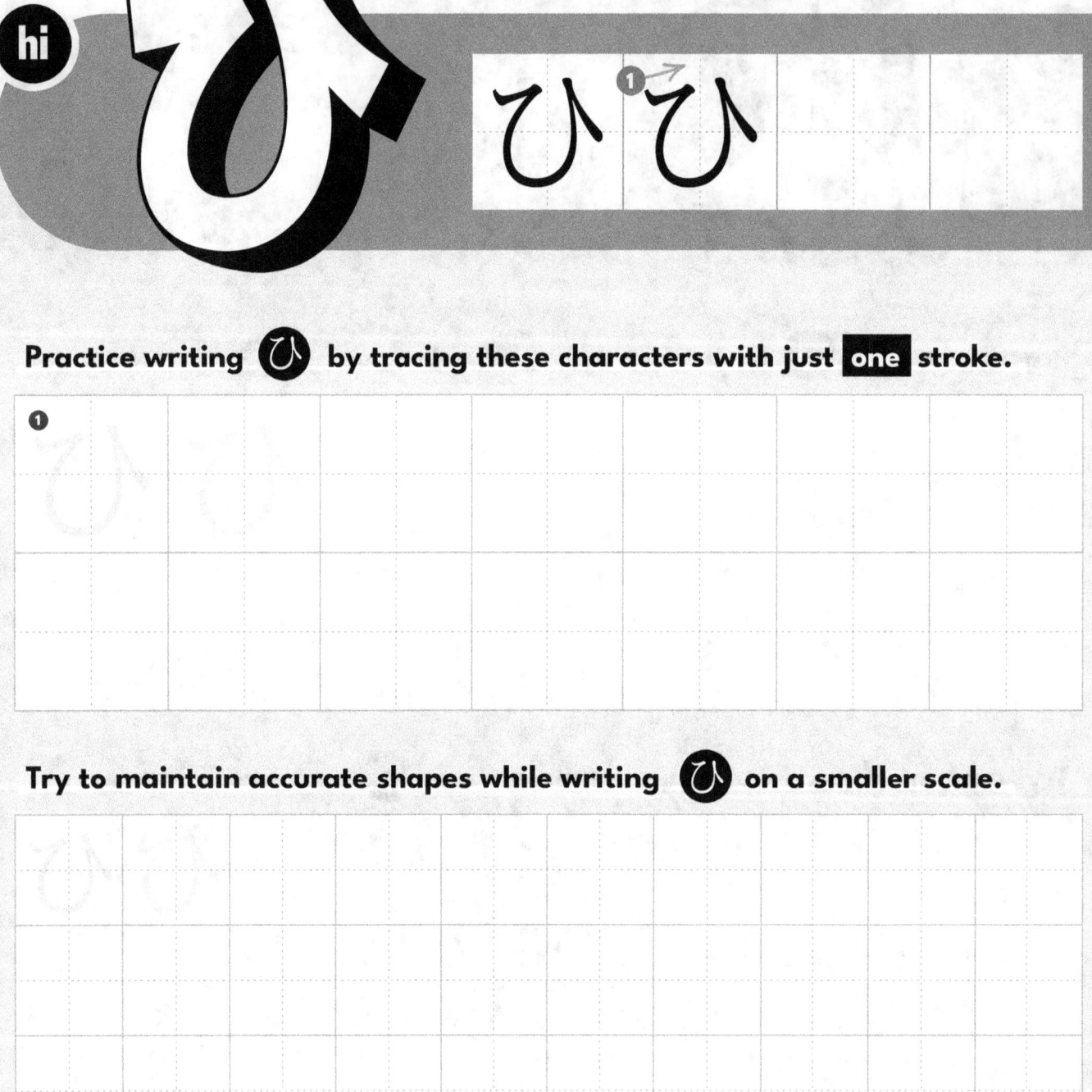

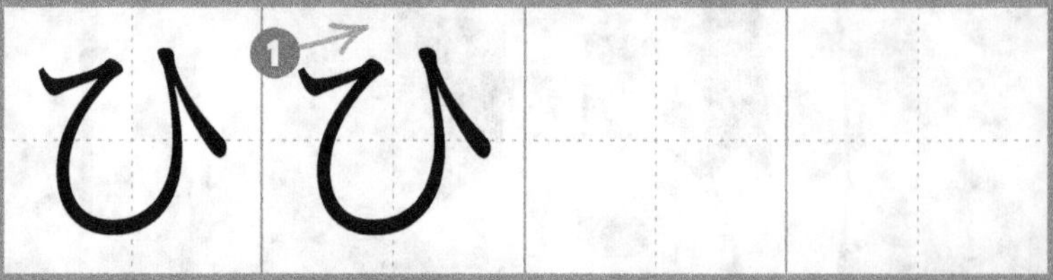

Practice writing ひ by tracing these characters with just one stroke.

Try to maintain accurate shapes while writing ひ on a smaller scale.

Mnemonic.

Examples.

- Big smile, laughing mouth, "hee hee!"
- Like a mans nose, He has a big nose

Sounds like both 'fu' and 'hu' - or 'hfu'.

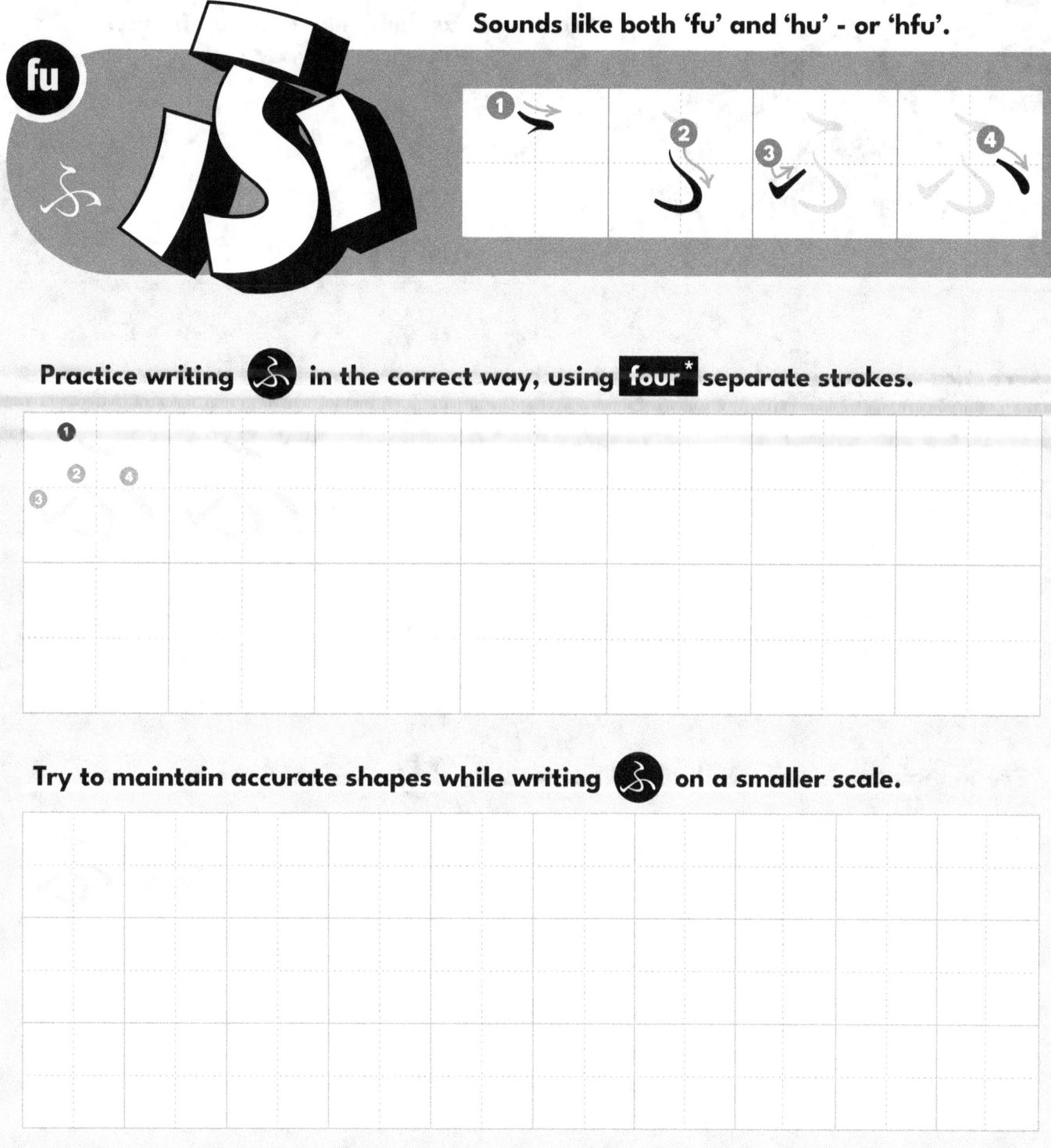

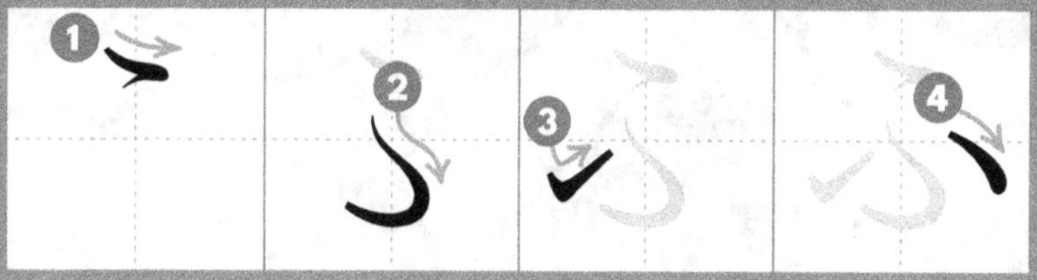

Practice writing ふ in the correct way, using four* separate strokes.

Try to maintain accurate shapes while writing ふ on a smaller scale.

Mnemonic.

Examples.

- Imagine Mount Fuji
- Can you picture a hula dancer?
- Upside-down, who?

Pronounce as 'heh', like the 'he-' in hey!

he

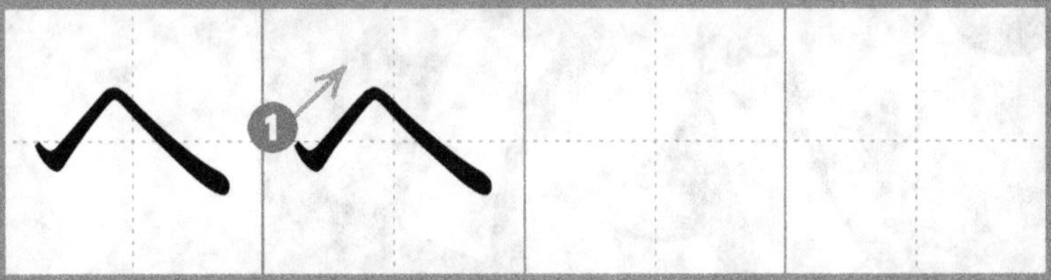

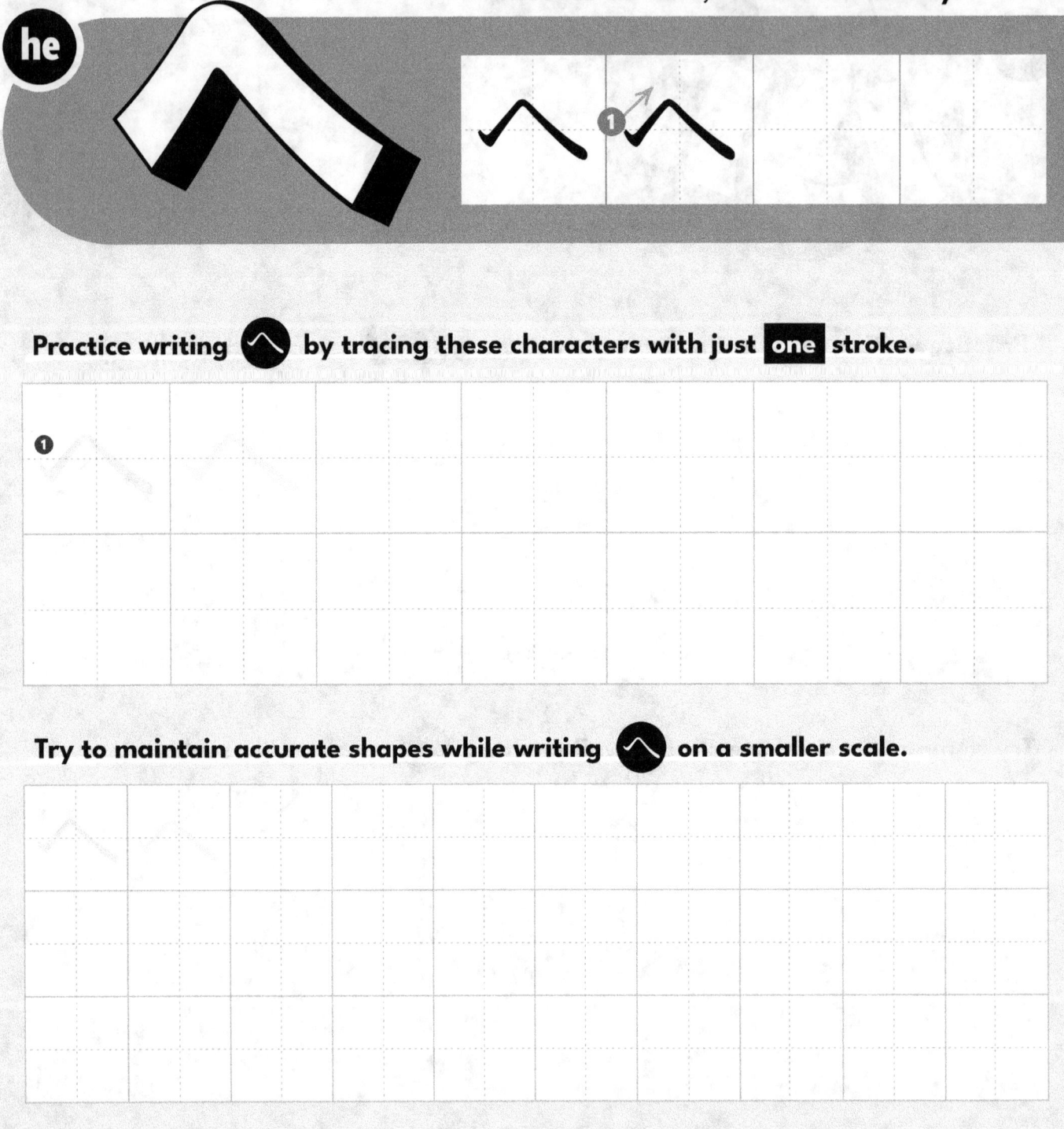

Practice writing へ by tracing these characters with just **one** stroke.

Try to maintain accurate shapes while writing へ on a smaller scale.

Mnemonic.

Examples.

- Points to heaven
- Hey, that's easy to write

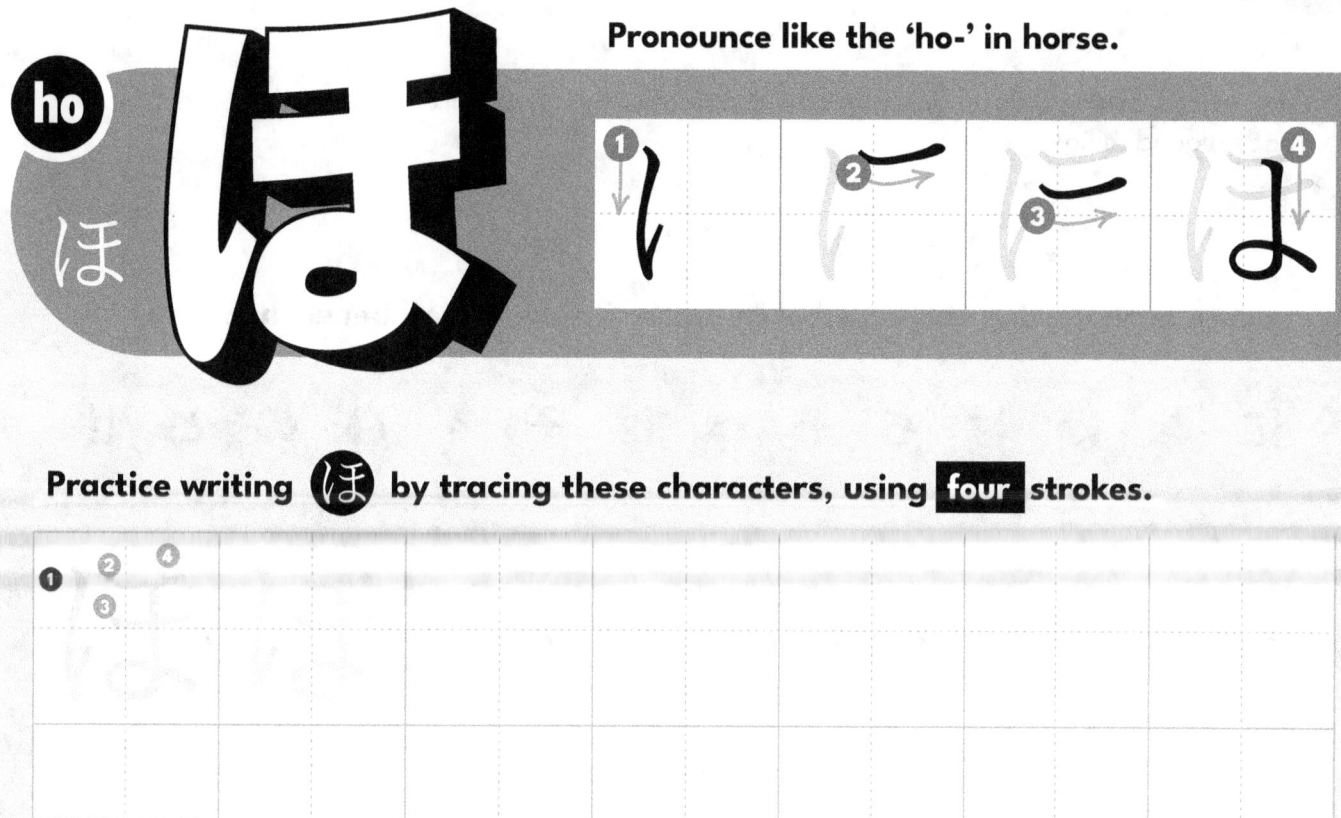

ho ほ ほ

Pronounce like the 'ho-' in horse.

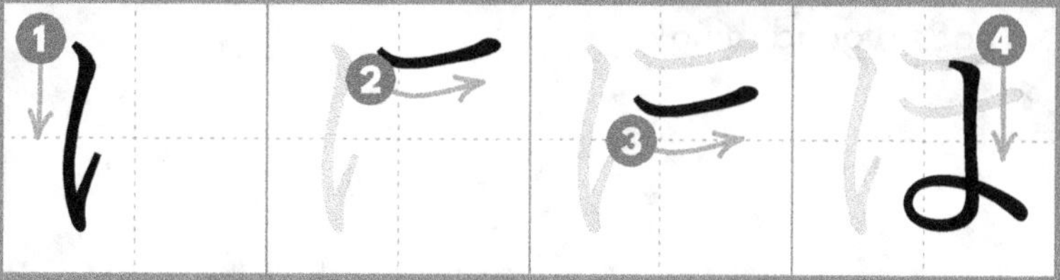

Practice writing ほ by tracing these characters, using **four** strokes.

Try to maintain accurate shapes while writing ほ on a smaller scale.

Mnemonic.

Examples.

- 'ha' with a hat = Santa! Ho ho <u>ho</u>!
- A w<u>hol</u>e lot of lines.

Even after learning a large group of new characters, this may start to feel easier each time. That's a good thing!

Practice pronouncing each symbol as you write the romaji beneath.

に	な	ほ	は	ち	そ	へ	は	そ	す	ひ	の	と	せ
へ	く	つ	ひ	ね	あ	て	こ	な	ふ	し	ほ	へ	は
ぬ	ふ	の	す	ち	ふ	ほ	つ	き	お	ひ	に	た	さ

Take a 5-minute break, and then do the same for these symbols too.

せ	つ	う	へ	き	え	さ	こ	あ	し	す	そ	の	い
な	か	け	ひ	ね	た	は	す	ぬ	く	け	せ	ふ	ほ
に	と	お	い	の	ほ	そ	く	し	あ	え	こ	き	て

You could make this more challenging by introducing a time limit for each group and reducing it for each set. Try to improve from one group to the next.

This time, take a 10-minute break and come back to complete these.

こ	の	な	あ	ぬ	く	つ	た	え	う	に	ほ	ぬ	ね
せ	と	ち	ひ	へ	き	ふ	そ	す	に	ね	け	ひ	は
か	の	お	へ	ほ	ふ	へ	ぬ	さ	は	て	い	な	ほ

After a much longer break, add the romaji for each symbol below.

ふ	の	ぬ	あ	て	ほ	な	へ	そ	へ	た	こ	は	ね
つ	き	に	ひ	せ	と	い	ひ	へ	な	ぬ	な	さ	は
す	ほ	ち	し	ぬ	け	う	に	お	さ	ほ	か	の	ふ

Practice reading and writing words with all the characters so far.

なに	what	きぬ	silk
ほね	bone	ほし	star
ぬの	cloth	ひと	person
ひふ	skin	のき	eaves
へた	unskillful	にし	west
はな	nose/flower	はいく	Haiku
ふね	ship	かたな	Katana
かに	crab	せいふ	government
ひな	doll/fledgling	いのしし	boar
はし	chopsticks/bridge	へいそつ	soldier

H6. The M & Y Columns

Two more columns coming up in this section. The two symbols that seem to be 'missing' from the Y column *(YE and YI)* sounded similar enough to the vowel-only column that the Japanese dropped them altogether (い & え). This just simplified the alphabet, meaning fewer symbols to learn!

Symbols in this learning block.

ま	み	む	め	も
ma	**mi**	**mu**	**me**	**mo**
や		ゆ		よ
ya		**yu**		**yo**

Pronunciation

The *'m-'* sounds are pronounced in virtually the same way as in English, bringing your lips together, voiced *(your vocal chords are used)*, and nasal like *'n-'* sounds.

The *'y-'* sound characters are very much like the English pronunciation and you will notice that there are only three to learn. It is possible to hear the occasional *'ye'* but this is usually limited to foreign words and so isn't a sound that you need to learn for the Japanese language.

ma ま

Sounds like 'ma-' in the word man.

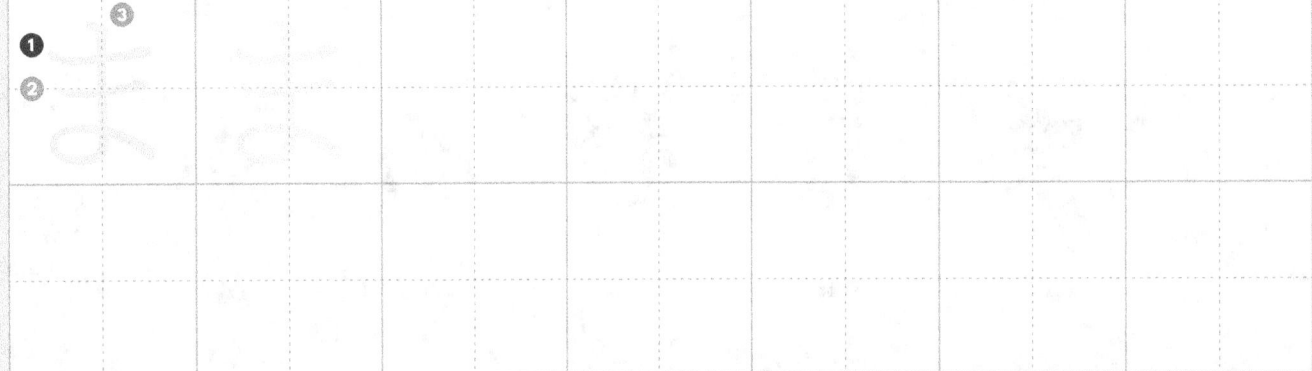

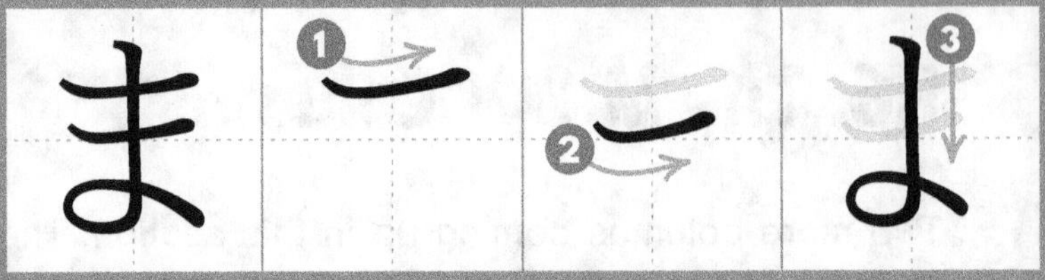

Practice writing ま by tracing these characters, using **three** strokes.

Try to maintain accurate shapes while writing ま on a smaller scale.

Mnemonic.

Examples.

- Magma, exploding from a volcano
- Looks mathematical

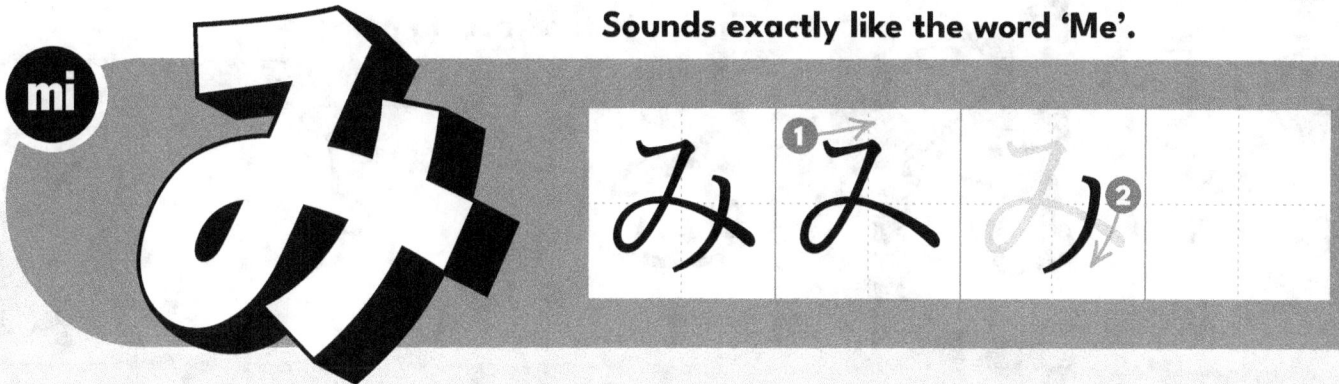

Sounds exactly like the word 'Me'.

mi み

みみみ

Practice writing み by tracing these characters, using **two** strokes.

Try to maintain accurate shapes while writing み on a smaller scale.

Mnemonic.

Examples.

- Looks like 21 to <u>me</u>.
- Who wishes to be aged 21 again? <u>Me</u>!

mu む

Similar to the 'moo' in moon.

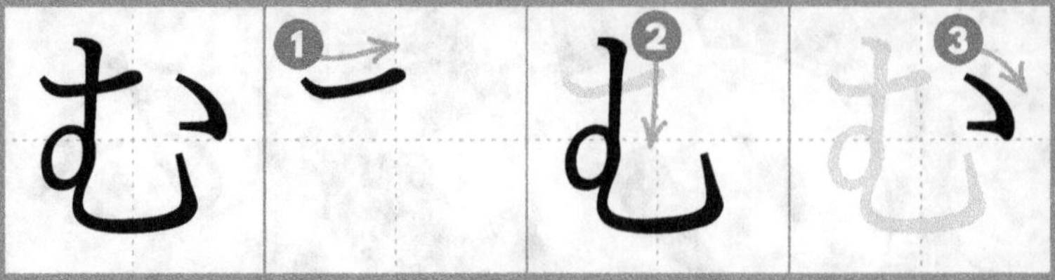

Practice writing む by tracing these characters, using **three** strokes.

Try to maintain accurate shapes while writing む on a smaller scale.

Mnemonic.

Examples.

- Picture the shape of a cow... Moo!
- A projector, showing a movie?

me め

Sounds like the 'me-' in men.

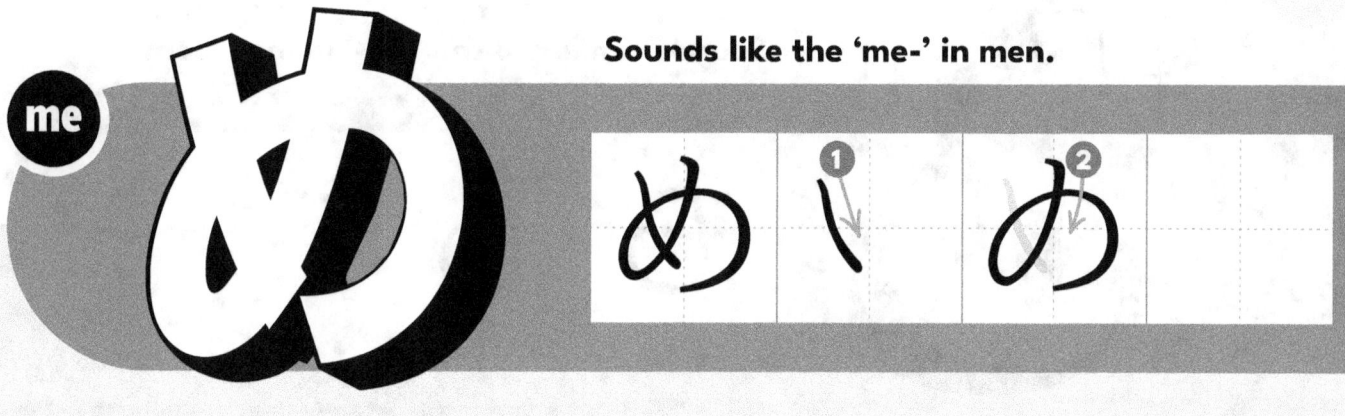

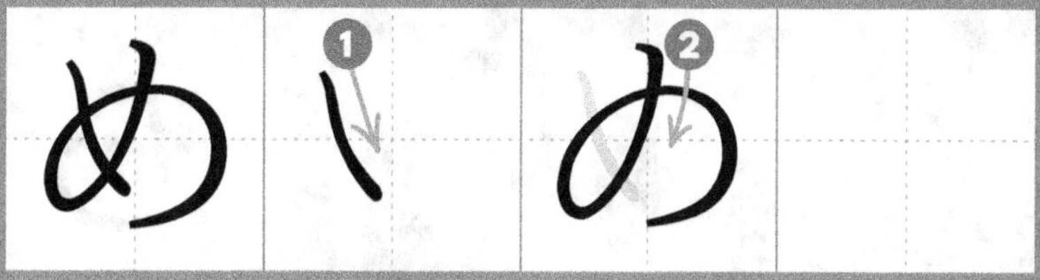

Practice writing め by tracing these characters, using **two** strokes.

Try to maintain accurate shapes while writing め on a smaller scale.

Mnemonic.

Examples.

- Like an eye, which is 'me' in Japanese
- Like 'nu' for noodles, but not as messy.

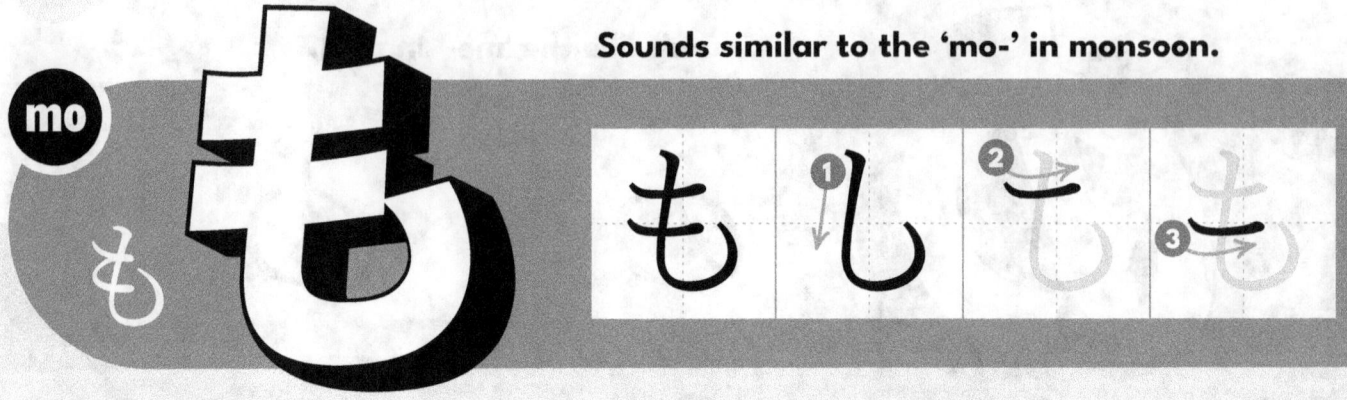

mo も

も

Sounds similar to the 'mo-' in monsoon.

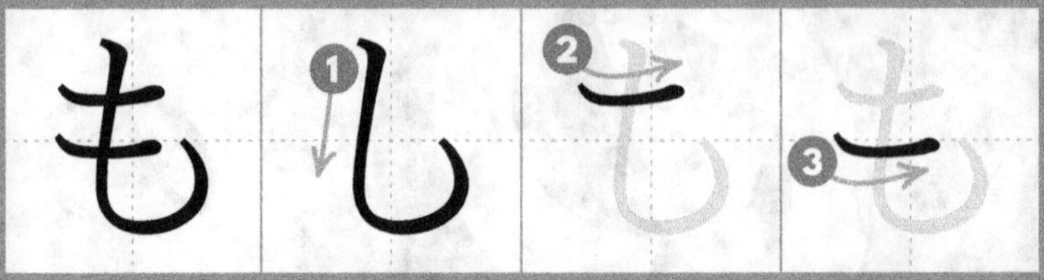

Practice writing も by tracing these characters, using three strokes.

Try to maintain accurate shapes while writing も on a smaller scale.

Mnemonic.

Examples.

- A fishing hook with more worms.
- You will catch more fish with this hook.

Sounds much like the 'ya-' in yak.

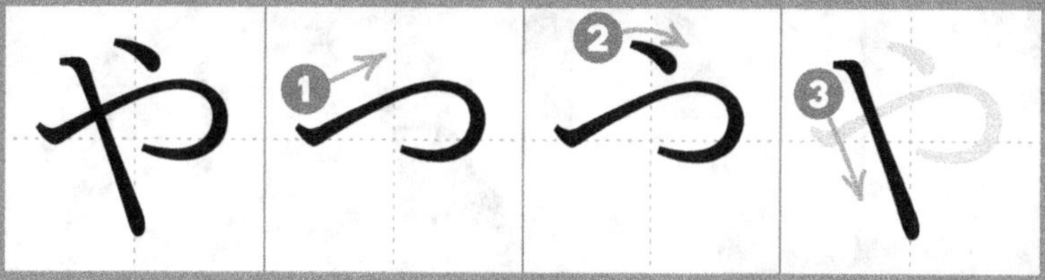

Practice writing や by tracing these characters, using **three** strokes.

Try to maintain accurate shapes while writing や on a smaller scale.

Mnemonic.

Examples.

- Picture the shape of a yak's head
- Maybe the sail from a yacht?

yu ゆ

Sounds just like the word 'You'.

ゆ ① ②

Practice writing ゆ by tracing these characters, using **two** strokes.

Try to maintain accurate shapes while writing ゆ on a smaller scale.

Mnemonic.

Examples.

- Combines letters that spell 'you'
- Picture a new and unique fish

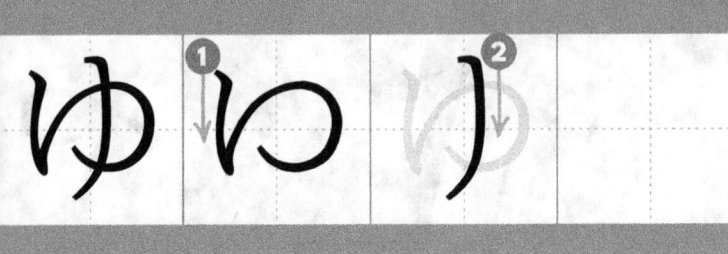

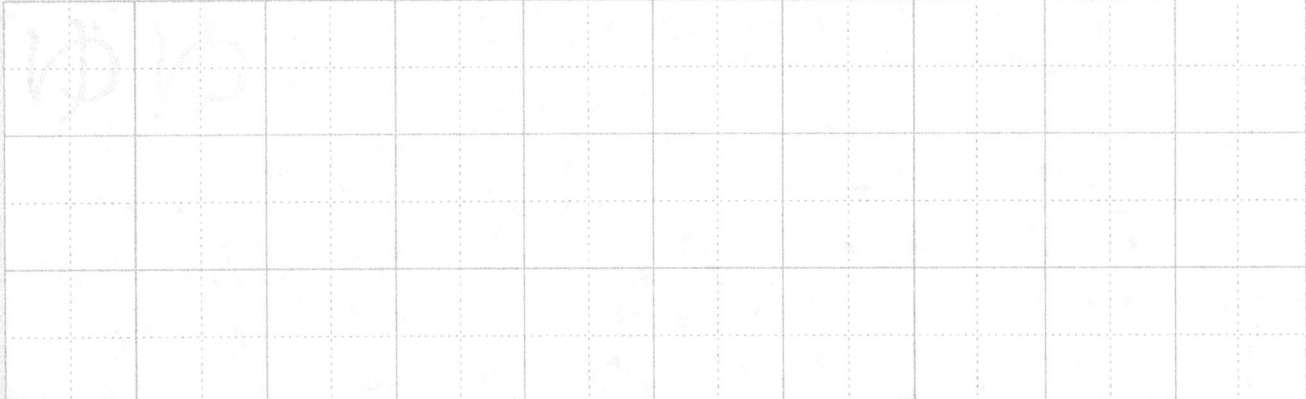

yo よ

Sounds like the informal greeting 'Yo'.

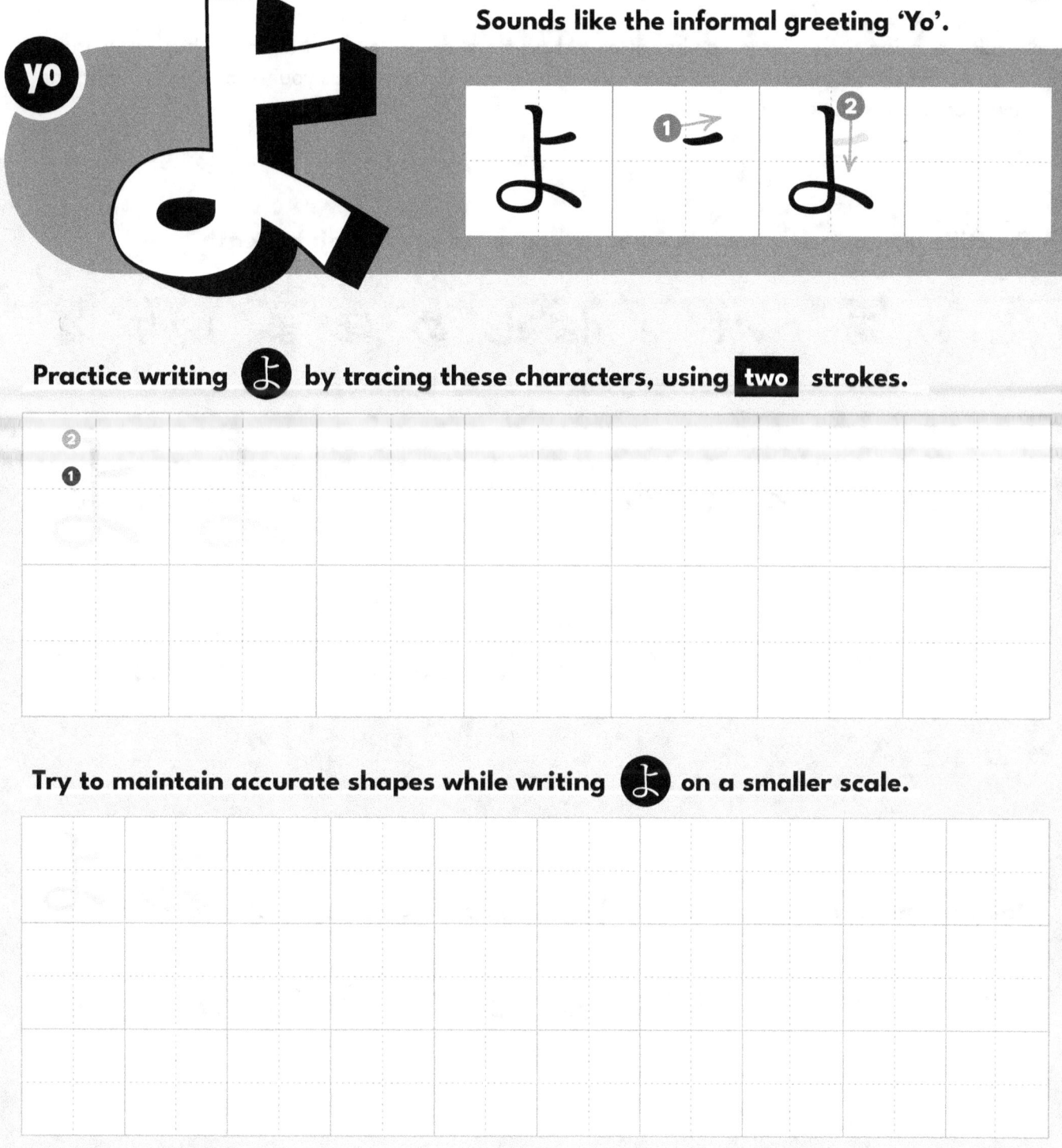

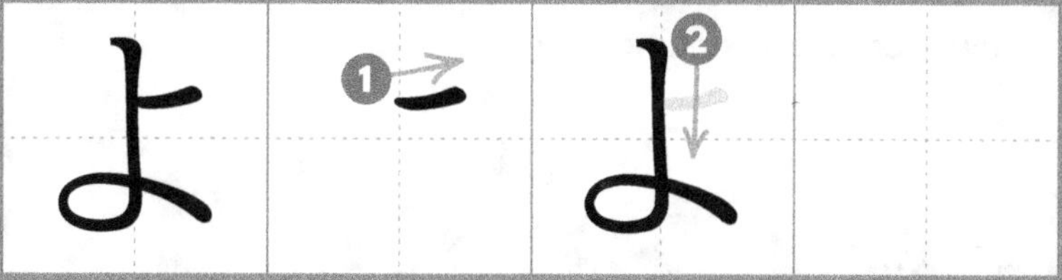

Practice writing よ by tracing these characters, using two strokes.

Try to maintain accurate shapes while writing よ on a smaller scale.

Mnemonic.

Examples.

- A new yo-yo trick?
- A hitch-hiker needs a ride, he yells "yo!"

Despite learning such a large number of new characters, repetition of characters that you learned much earlier should mean they are firmly in your memory. You can focus your efforts on ensuring the newer ones are sinking in too.

Practice pronouncing each symbol as you write the romaji beneath.

と	め	あ	へ	も	よ	は	し	め	ほ	ま	よ	ゆ	な

ひ	の	む	ま	え	ぬ	む	ふ	ま	よ	ち	や	ほ	は

ぬ	や	ね	ゆ	み	に	も	や	ふ	み	ね	な	み	に

Take a 5-minute break, and then do the same for these symbols too.

め	む	き	ほ	や	と	よ	せ	つ	そ	に	も	ゆ	ほ

た	み	て	ね	の	ま	は	お	ひ	す	な	く	ね	も

や	ぬ	よ	む	め	な	ゆ	は	ぬ	う	へ	に	み	ふ

This time, take a 10-minute break and come back to complete these.

し	ね	か	や	と	い	ぬ	す	へ	つ	ゆ	た	そ	さ

ま	ひ	く	せ	え	な	て	め	に	こ	せ	こ	の	よ

み	あ	も	か	し	ち	き	お	う	く	ふ	む	お	い

After a much longer break, add the romaji for each symbol below.

け	め	て	ち	え	ゆ	け	す	お	き	い	か	や	さ

ひ	ぬ	む	も	へ	ふ	せ	の	く	こ	せ	た	み	と

し	は	う	ほ	つ	そ	ま	そ	な	よ	お	に	ね	い

The words below are all written with syllables you have now studied.

やま
mountain

ゆめ
to dream

よむ
to read

もも
peach

みや
shrine

こめ
uncooked rice

つゆ
dew

むし
insect

まつ
to wait/pine tree

うめ
plum

むね
chest, breast

きもの
kimono

さしみ
sashimi

ゆかた
cotton kimono

えまき
picture scroll

みこし
portable shrine

うきよえ
woodblock print

せともの
porcelain

すきやき
sukiyaki

H7. The R Column

The romaji letter *'r'* is a poor substitute for the Japanese *'r-'* sound and pronunciation of characters in this column can be difficult to master. It is a mixture of romaji letter sounds that is only two thirds *'r'*. A quarter of the sound feels like a lower case *'l' (as in 'learn')*, and the remainder almost a lower case *'d'* sound *(like in 'dark')*.

Symbols in this learning block.

ら	り	る	れ	ろ
ra	**ri**	**ru**	**re**	**ro**

Pronunciation

Combining the sounds of three letters in one is tricky. We found the exercise below can help English speakers to understand and produce an accurate Japanese 'r-' sound:

Begin with a regular *'l'* sound, saying *'La'* out loud a few times. Your tongue will point upwards a little so that the bottom of it makes contact with the roof of your mouth. Say *'La'* a few more times, paying attention to the position of your tongue and location that it makes contacts with the top of your mouth. *"La. La. La".*

Now do the same with a *'d'* sound, saying *'Da'* until you can feel exactly where your tongue is touching the inside of your mouth. Your tongue will have a much flatter shape and forward position, touching the back of your upper front teeth. "*Da. Da. Da".*

Finally, alternate between saying *'La'* and *'Da'*, paying attention to the placement of your tongue. Both positions should be the same as in the steps above. As your tongue moves back and forth, you may begin to notice that your it skips over the same spot each time. "*La. Da. La. Da".*

The Japanese *'r'* sound is made by positioning the tongue in that space between *'La'* and *'Da'*. It takes some getting used to but with enough practice, muscle memory will take over. Simply follow these same steps for the other vowel sounds, swapping out the 'a' sound each time. "*Li, Di"... "Lu, Du"... and so on.*

ra ら

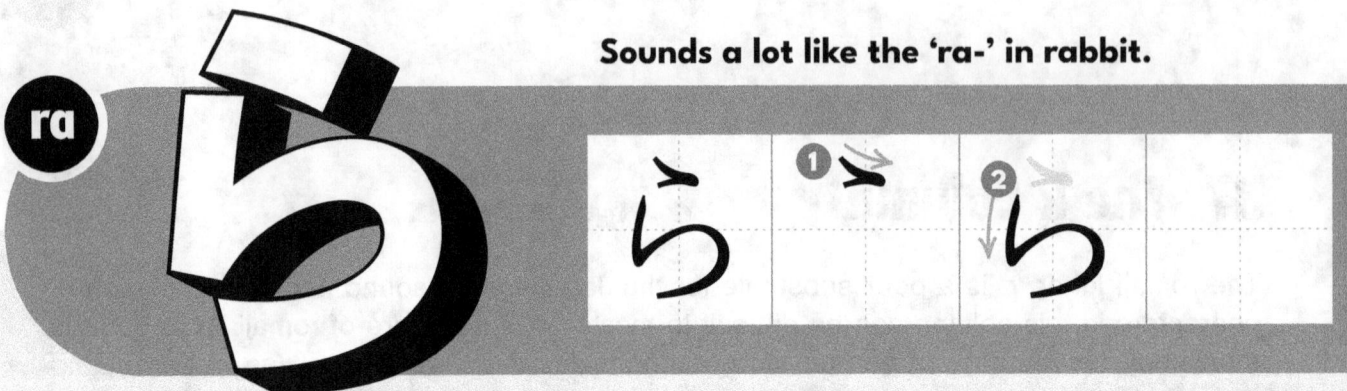

Sounds a lot like the 'ra-' in rabbit.

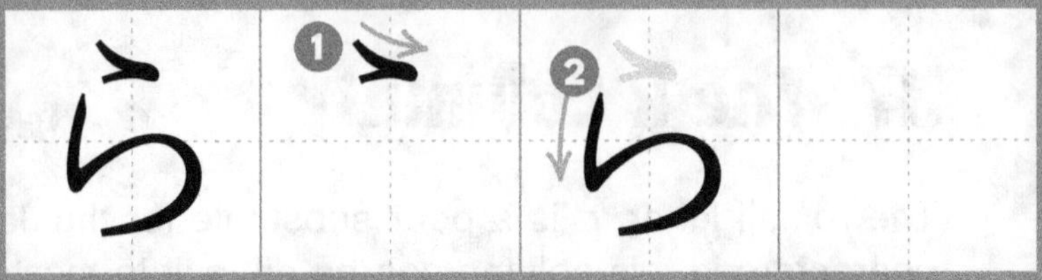

Practice writing ら by tracing these characters, using two strokes.

Try to maintain accurate shapes while writing ら on a smaller scale.

Mnemonic.

Examples.

- Imagine the shape of a rabbit
- Maybe the number 5 but it's a bit rattled

ri り

Sounds a lot like the 'rea-' in reach.

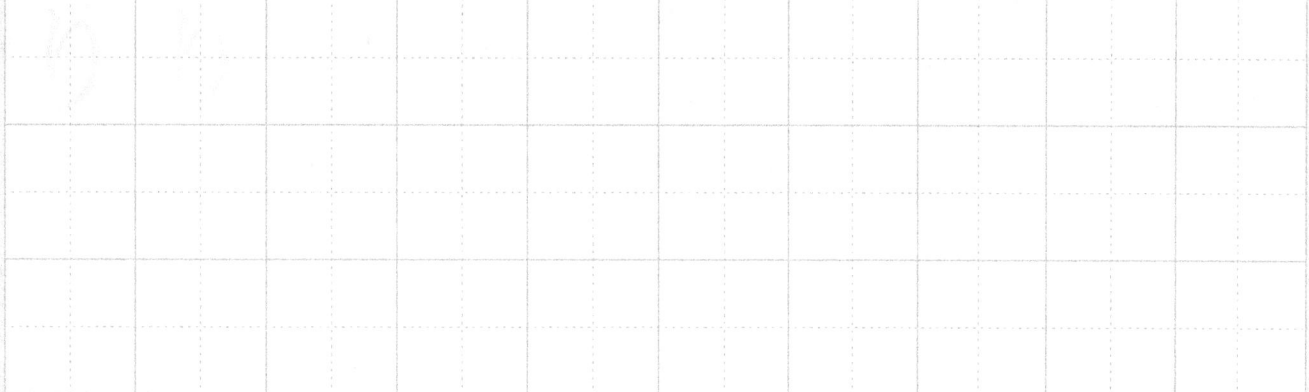

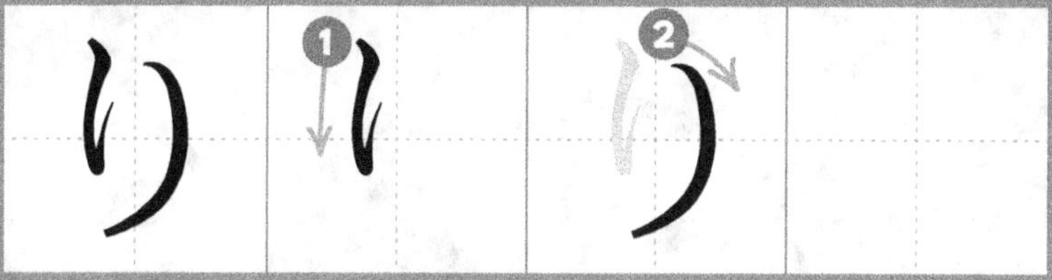

Practice writing り by tracing these characters, using two strokes.

Try to maintain accurate shapes while writing り on a smaller scale.

Mnemonic.

Examples.

- Two reaching arms
- Maybe two reeds

ru

る

Sounds like the '-ru' in guru.

る る

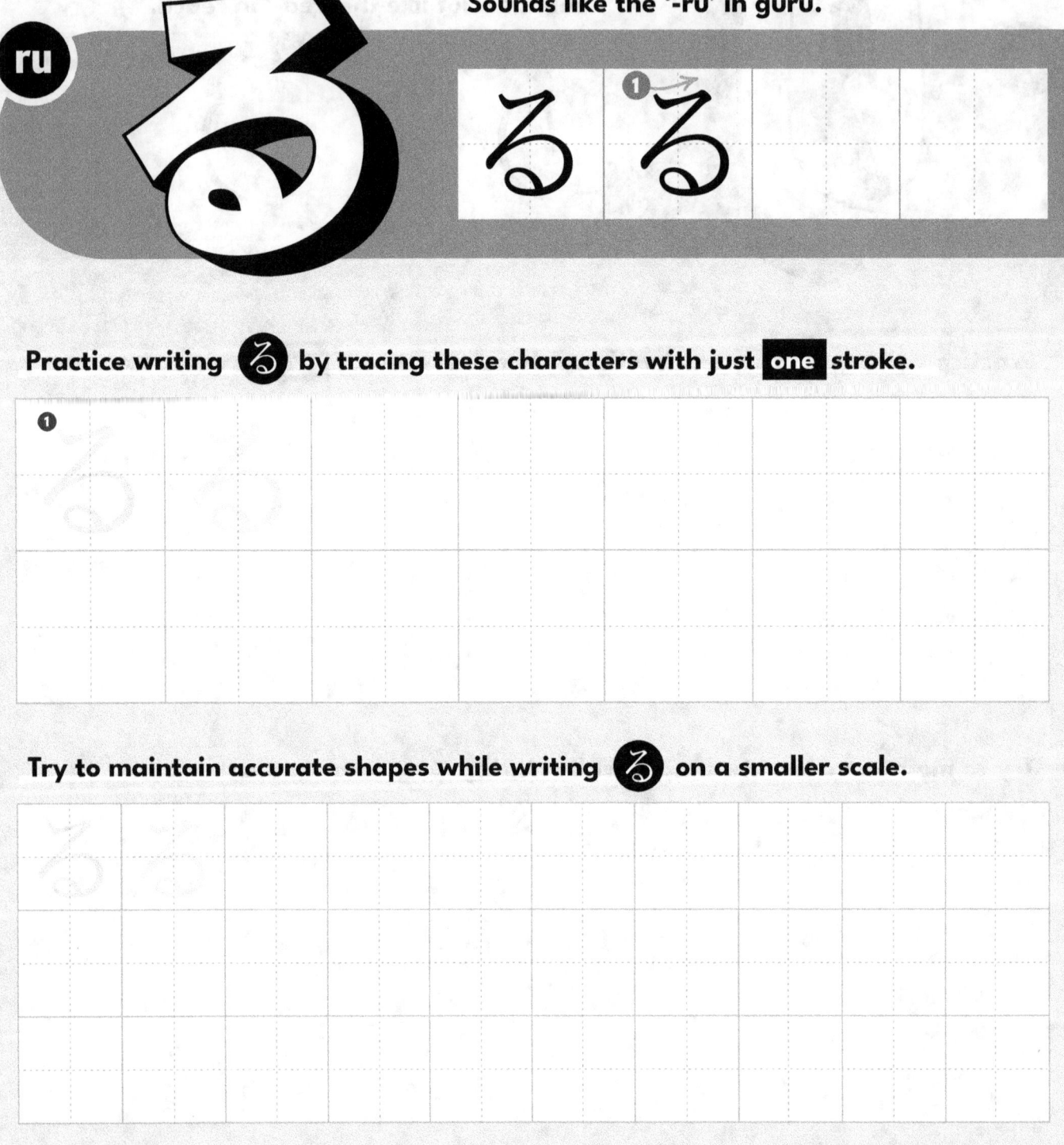

Practice writing る by tracing these characters with just **one** stroke.

Try to maintain accurate shapes while writing る on a smaller scale.

Mnemonic.

Examples.

- Rope, with a loop
- As roads go, this is the scenic route.

re れ

Sounds like the 'ra-' in race, like 'ray'.

れ ① ②

Practice writing れ by tracing these characters, using **two** strokes.

Try to maintain accurate shapes while writing れ on a smaller scale.

Mnemonic.

Examples.

- A race across the finish line
- Picture a snake, resting on a branch

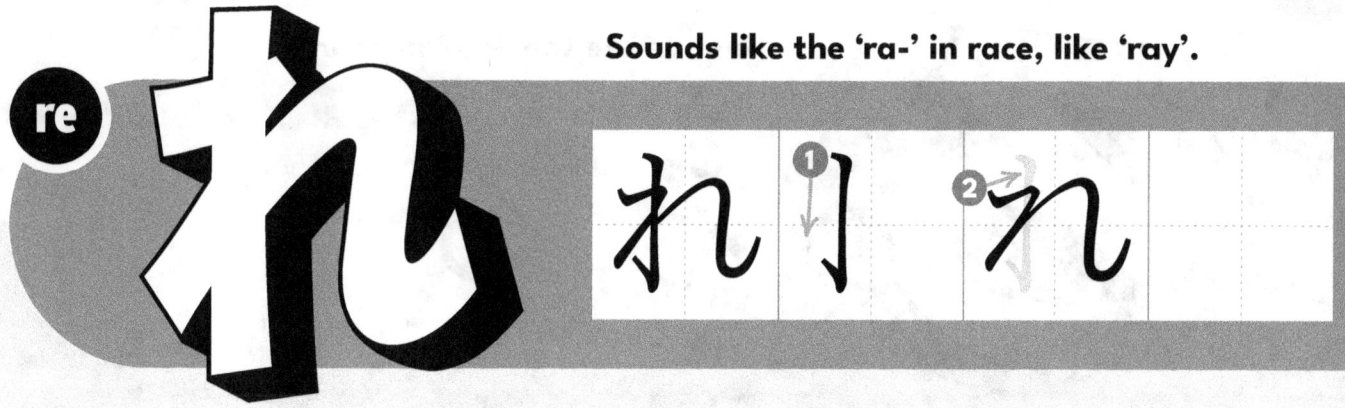

ro

ろ

Sounds like the '-rro' in churro.

ろ ろ

Practice writing ろ by tracing these characters with just **one** stroke.

Try to maintain accurate shapes while writing ろ on a smaller scale.

Mnemonic.

Examples.

- This road is less bendy than in 'ru'
- Rope, but no loop

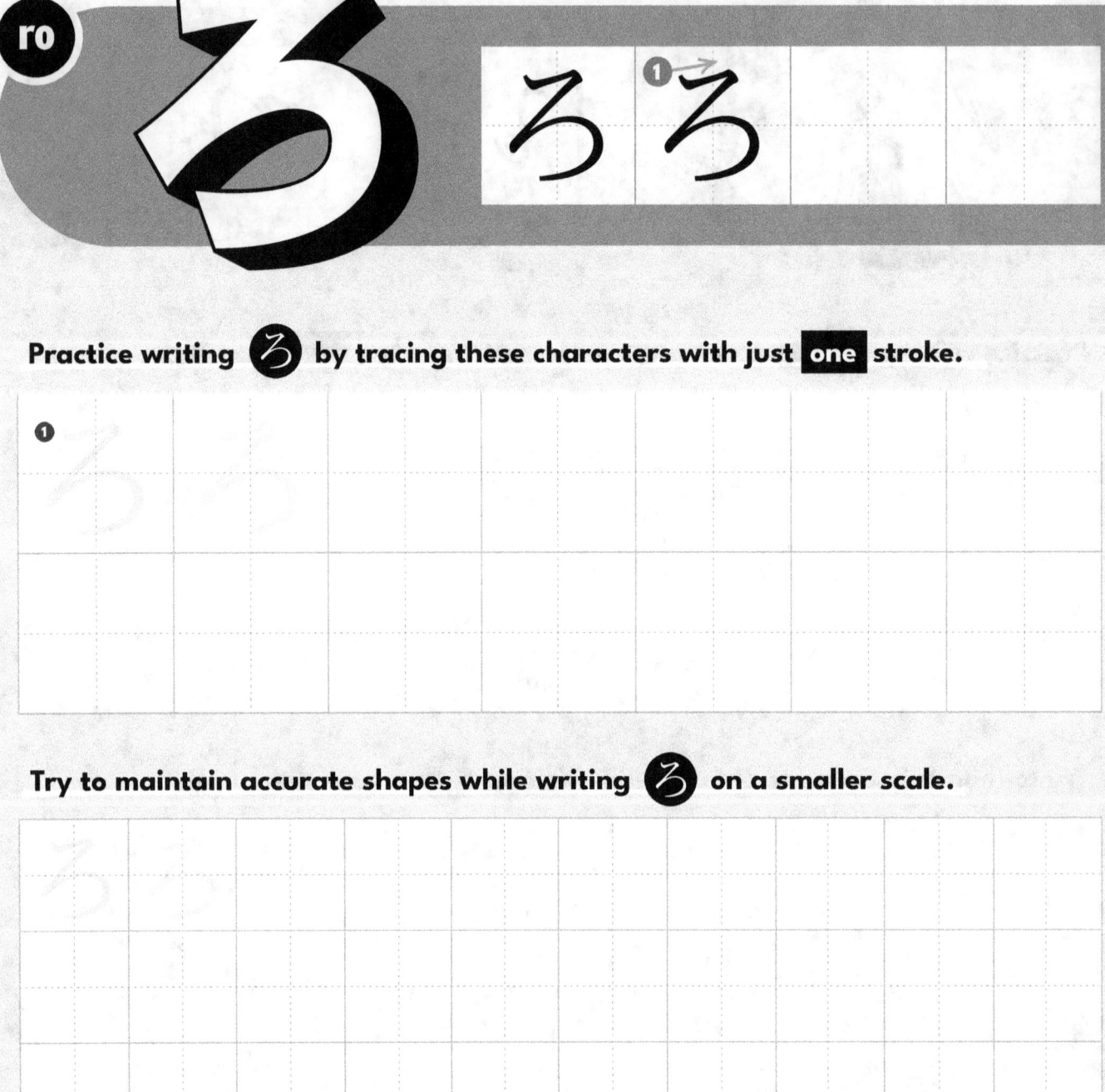

H8. The W Column + N

This last block of hiragana has just three characters to learn. The first is relatively normal but the second and third are a little different. The *'w-'* is quite close to the *'u'*, and should be pronounced this way. The last symbol doesn't actually have any vowel sound but needed to be placed in a group:

Symbols in this learning block:

わ	を	ん
wa	**wo**	**n**

Pronunciation

As mentioned above, the *'w-'* characters are pronounced in a similar way to the vowel sounds for 'u' and less like the letter *'w'* in English. Your lips should not be pushed out as they would if saying *'oo'* but they do need to be compressed. When pronouncing *'wa'*, it should almost sound like *'oo-wah'* and taking the same length of time to say as any other symbol.

The sound of *'wo'* is similar, sounding like *'oo-woh'*. This character is mainly found in use as a particle.

Unlike all the other kana you have learned, the Japanese *'n'* character ん has no vowel sound attached to it. Pronounce this as *'nnn'*, as it sounds in ten or rain.

Sounds like the 'wa-' in wacky or wax.

Practice writing わ by tracing these characters, using two strokes.

Try to maintain accurate shapes while writing わ on a smaller scale.

Mnemonic.

Examples.

- Picture a wasp, crawling up a tree
- Maybe a waiter, and their big, round tray

wo を

With a silent 'w', this sounds like 'Oh?'

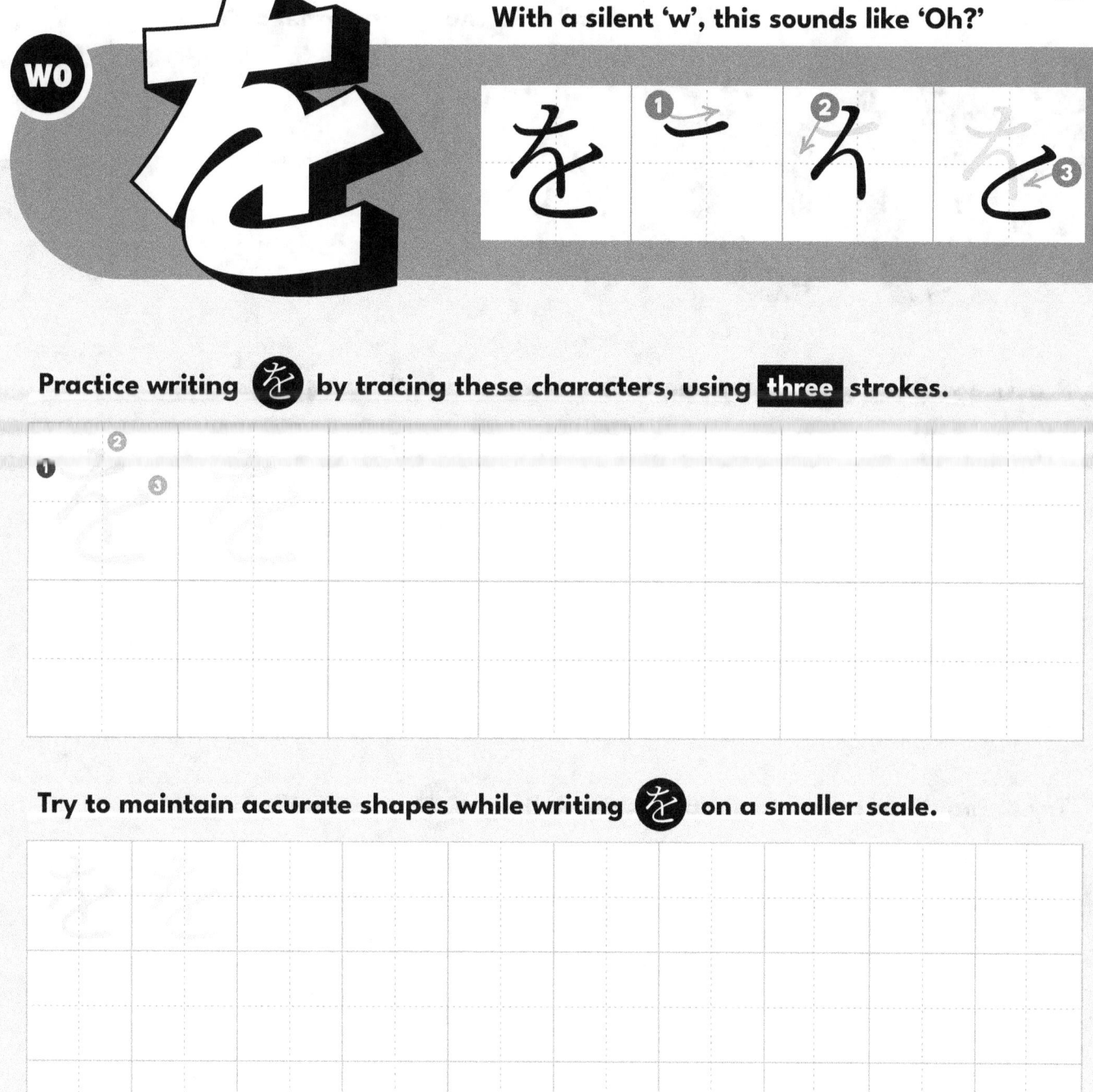

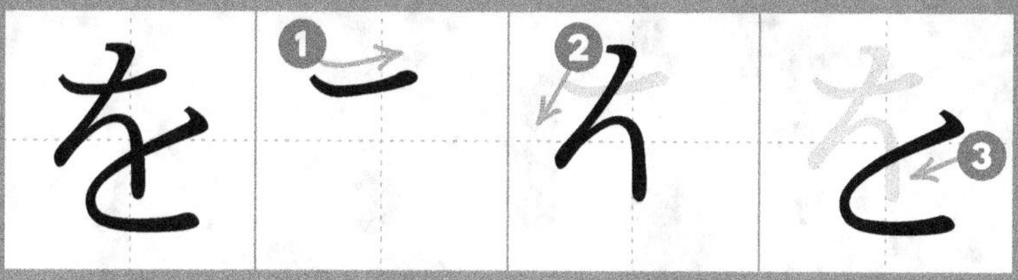

Practice writing を by tracing these characters, using three strokes.

Try to maintain accurate shapes while writing を on a smaller scale.

Mnemonic.

Examples.

- Dipping a toe in a cold pond... "woah"
- Picture a cowboy on a horse... "woah"

n ん

Similar to the '-n' in plane, or 'nnn'.

ん ん

Practice writing ん by tracing these characters with just **one** stroke.

Try to maintain accurate shapes while writing ん on a smaller scale.

Mnemonic.

Examples.

- Lower case letter 'n'
- The last hiragana, at the e<u>n</u>d.

That last group completes the set, meaning this exercise may contain any of the 46 hiragana. Most should be familiar by now; write the romaji below characters from all groups below.

Practice pronouncing each symbol as you write the romaji beneath.

り	む	を	ろ	ほ	み	ん	さ	ま	ゆ	ち	ら	ろ	よ
わ	ろ	も	よ	れ	む	ん	と	ん	り	る	く	み	る
れ	る	ら	り	も	や	ま	め	を	け	れ	わ	め	や

Take a 5-minute break, and then do the same for these symbols too.

て	ゆ	ら	ほ	へ	む	け	は	す	う	ろ	く	ね	や
る	い	の	き	お	か	あ	を	に	ち	も	し	つ	こ
そ	ひ	ら	わ	を	ふ	れ	み	な	り	ま	え	さ	め

This time, take a 10-minute break and come back to complete these.

ひ	ら	ん	そ	り	ぬ	た	む	わ	る	れ	ろ	に	ら

み	め	ゆ	る	や	へ	え	も	よ	す	く	む	ま	ん

ろ	を	め	も	ま	ほ	つ	の	み	は	ふ	あ	れ	わ

After a much longer break, add the romaji for each symbol below.

ゆ	よ	や	を	ね	た	ん	せ	と	ゆ	ら	わ	あ	を

ほ	よ	に	む	も	る	り	み	つ	ら	れ	ろ	を	す

は	を	ひ	ん	や	ね	わ	の	る	ゆ	く	め	も	ふ

These final word lists may contain characters from all hiragana study blocks.

わん
bay/bowl

てら
temple

つる
crane / to fish

これ
this

ふろ
bath

のり
seaweed/glue

はる
to stretch

れい
example/soul

しろ
castle/white

にほん
Japan

さくら
cherry blossom

うちわ
round fan

まつり
festival

ほたる
firefly

ふとん
futon

れきし
history

わふく
Japanese clothing

りろん
theory

ひのまる
Rising Sun flag

さむらい
Samurai

////////////////////////////////////// **PART 3**

Katakana

カタカナ

The *letters* in this alphabet ***represent the same sounds as hiragana,*** and we pronounce them the same way. While it might seem strange to have two alphabets for the same syllable sounds, we use them differently. You could almost think of katakana as having a similar role to a Japanese speaker, as romaji has for you.

Katakana is mainly for reading and writing foreign *'loanwords,'* though. The terms to describe ideas or objects originating from outside of Japan. Pronunciations transcribed in katakana often sound similar *(but with a Japanese twist)*, and these spellings become the Japanese word for that *'thing.'* Some of the most common examples are the names for certain foodstuffs from abroad, such as chocolate, hamburger, or pizza. In written Japanese, this script also represents sound effects (onomatopoeia). Essentially, it spells words for which there is not already a Japanese equivalent. The English language also has loanwords, such as 'karaoke' imported from Japan, funnily enough.

It's important to mention that loanwords originate from non-English-speaking countries too. The Japanese word for bread derives from the Portuguese word *'pão,'* written in katakana as **パン** *(pan)*, for example. This everyday food item was entirely new to the Japanese people when it was first introduced, shipped over by traders from Portugal in the 1500s. Katakana loanwords are a sort of placeholder for words that don't exist.

Foreign loanwords can often sound quite similar to the original word in Japanese. The easiest way to understand this concept is to look at an example or two. Here are some loanwords in katakana, shown with romaji and the original English word:

アメリカ	**タクシー**	**クリスマス**
A-me-ri-ka	*ta-ku-shii*	*Ku-ri-su-ma-su*
America	Taxi	Christmas
カメラ	**ホテル**	**フライドポテト**
Ka-me-ra	*Ho-te-ru*	*fu-ra-i-do-po-te-to*
Camera	Hotel	French fries

Certain English syllable sounds are difficult to reproduce in kana, much like how romaji cannot transcribe Japanese accurately. You can see in the examples above that there is no *'X'* sound in the word *'taxi'*. Instead, a relatively close equivalent must be used, further illustrating how the two languages don't share all of the same syllable sounds.

The following chart displays the ***46 primary katakana characters*** you are about to learn. They are organized similarly to the hiragana, with romaji transcriptions below. The vowel sounds are on the right side, shown with romaji vowels, and each consonant sound shown across the top row. Pronunciations follow the pattern where both sounds are combined - a vowel sound is added to the end of a consonant sound - and the same exception applies to 'n' sounds.

Notes:

* ン iis the only character in this table that we pronounce as a syllable without adding any of the vowel sounds.

** ヲ is a *"particle"* and is used for grammar. We write it as *"wo"*, but it is transcribed in romaji as either *"o"* or *"wo"*.

Katakana

w	r	y	m	h	n	t	s	k		
ワ wa	ラ ra	ヤ ya	マ ma	ハ ha	ナ na	タ ta	サ sa	カ ka	ア a	a
	リ ri		ミ mi	ヒ hi	ニ ni	チ chi	シ shi	キ ki	イ i	i
ン * n	ル ru	ユ yu	ム mu	フ fu	ヌ nu	ツ tsu	ス su	ク ku	ウ u	u
	レ re		メ me	ヘ he	ネ ne	テ te	セ se	ケ ke	エ e	e
ヲ ** wo	ロ ro	ヨ yo	モ mo	ホ ho	ノ no	ト to	ソ so	コ ko	オ o	o
p. 155	p. 149	p. 144	p. 138	p. 131	p. 125	p. 117	p. 111	p. 104	p. 098	

K1. The Vowel & K Columns

As the symbols in katakana represent the same syllable sounds as hiragana, they will be learned in the same order. The first column contains the characters that represent the basic vowel sounds, followed by the K column with exactly the same *[consonant + vowel]* pattern of pronunciation.

Symbols in this learning block.

ア	イ	ウ	エ	オ
a	i	u	e	o

カ	キ	ク	ケ	コ
ka	ki	ku	ke	ko

Pronunciation

There are no differences in sound between the first ten hiragana that you learned and the way in which you should pronounce these characters.

a ア

Pronounce as 'ah' like the 'a' in car.

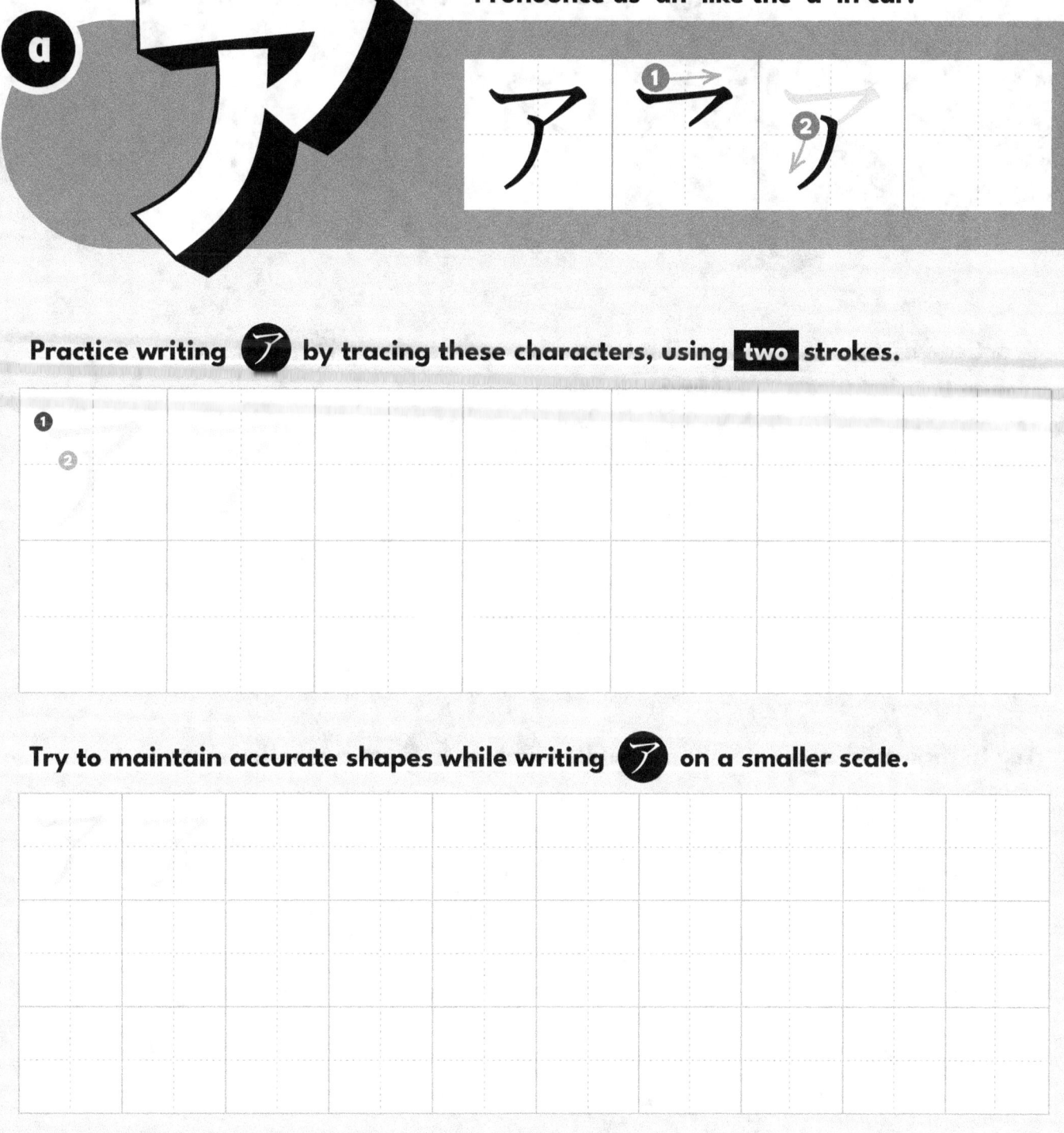

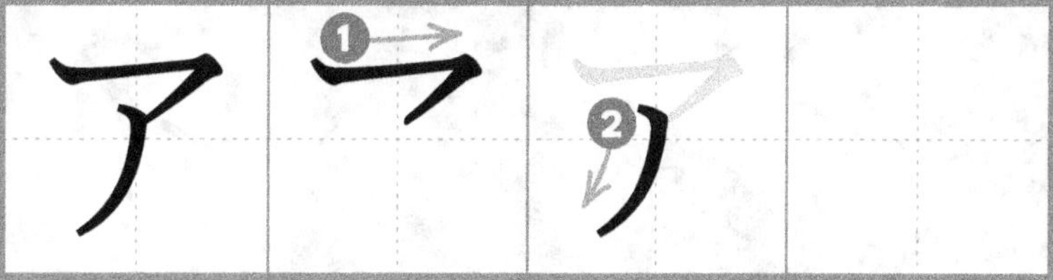

Practice writing ア by tracing these characters, using two strokes.

Try to maintain accurate shapes while writing ア on a smaller scale.

Mnemonic.

Examples.

- The letter 'A' rotated to the right.

i イ

Sounds like 'i' in king, or 'ee' in cheek.

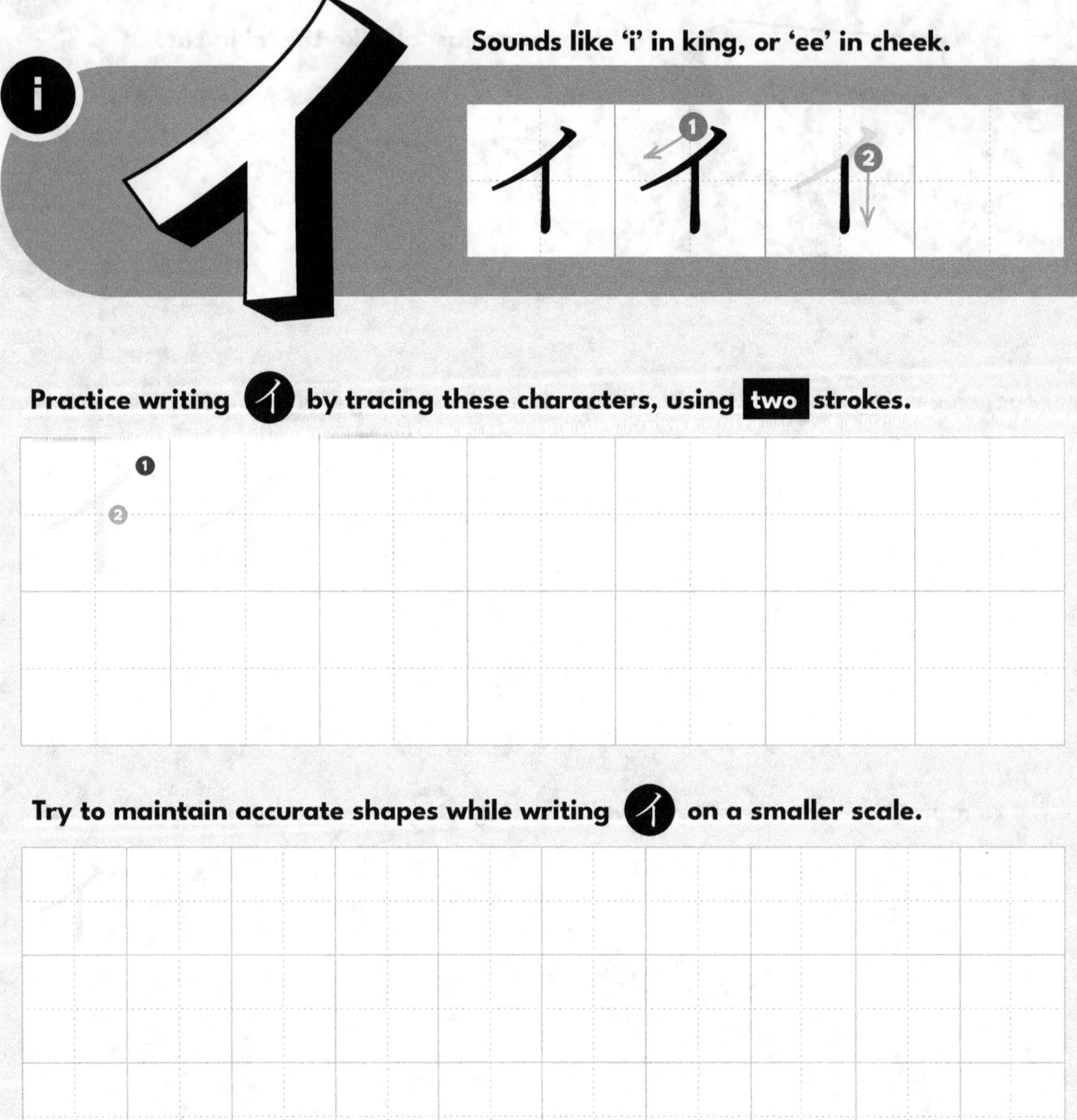

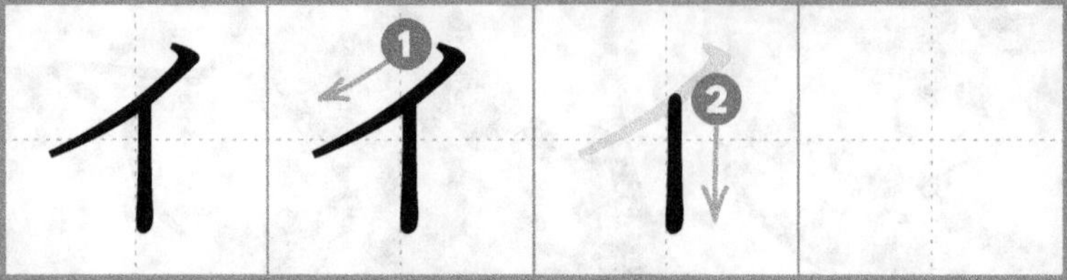

Practice writing イ by tracing these characters, using **two** strokes.

Try to maintain accurate shapes while writing イ on a smaller scale.

Mnemonic.

Examples.

- An artist would paint on their easel
- Letter 'i' with a hat

u ウ

Similar to ‘oo’ but like the ‘ue’ in true.

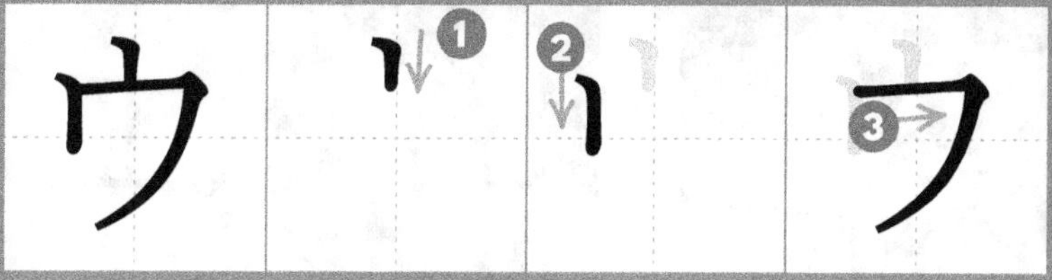

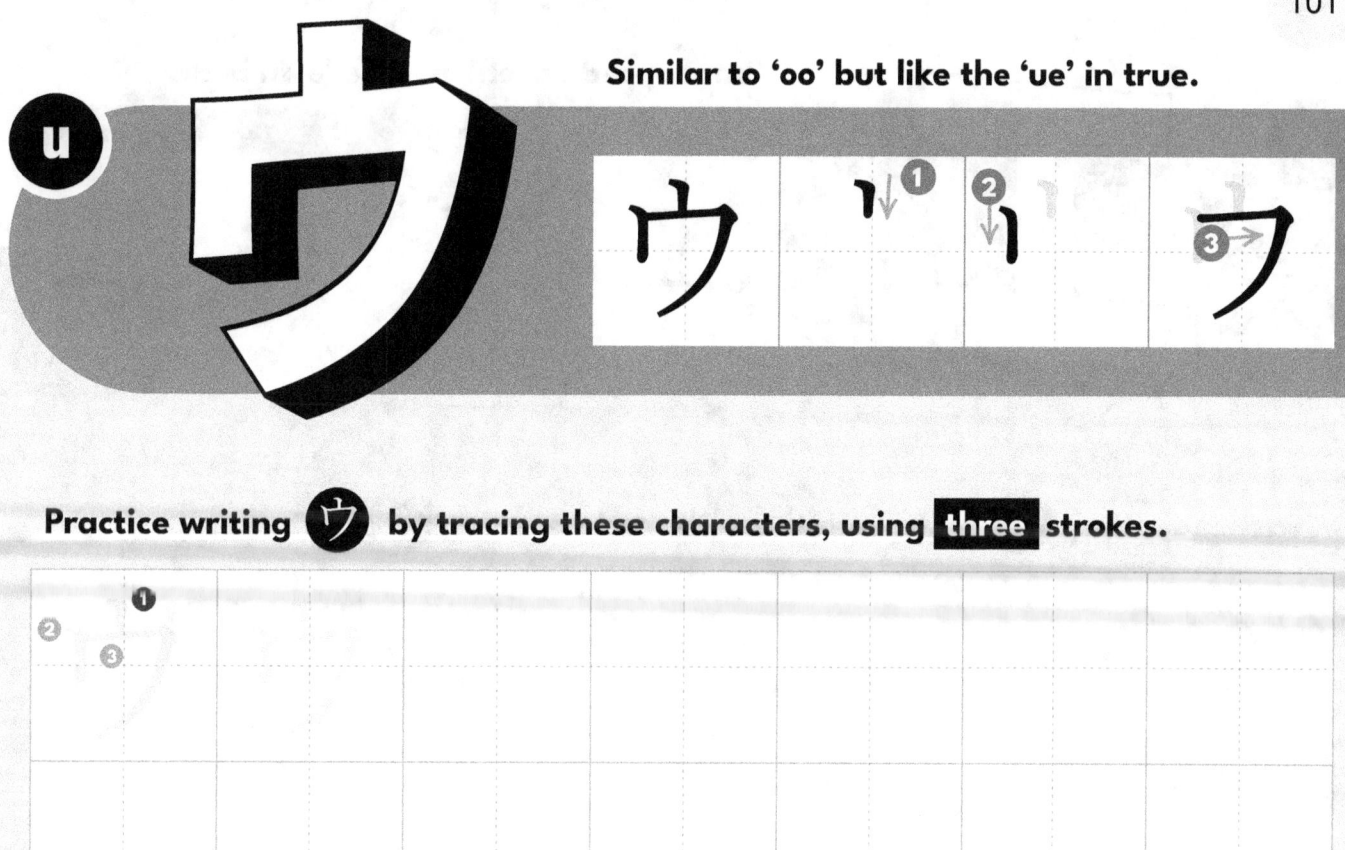

Practice writing ウ by tracing these characters, using **three** strokes.

Try to maintain accurate shapes while writing ウ on a smaller scale.

Mnemonic.

Examples.

- Similar to hiragana
- Upside down ‘u’

Pronounced as 'eh' like the 'e' in bed.

e エ

エ ① ② ③

Practice writing エ by tracing these characters, using **three** strokes.

Try to maintain accurate shapes while writing エ on a smaller scale.

Mnemonic.

Examples.

- Picture a set of elevator doors
- Engineers use steel girders to build

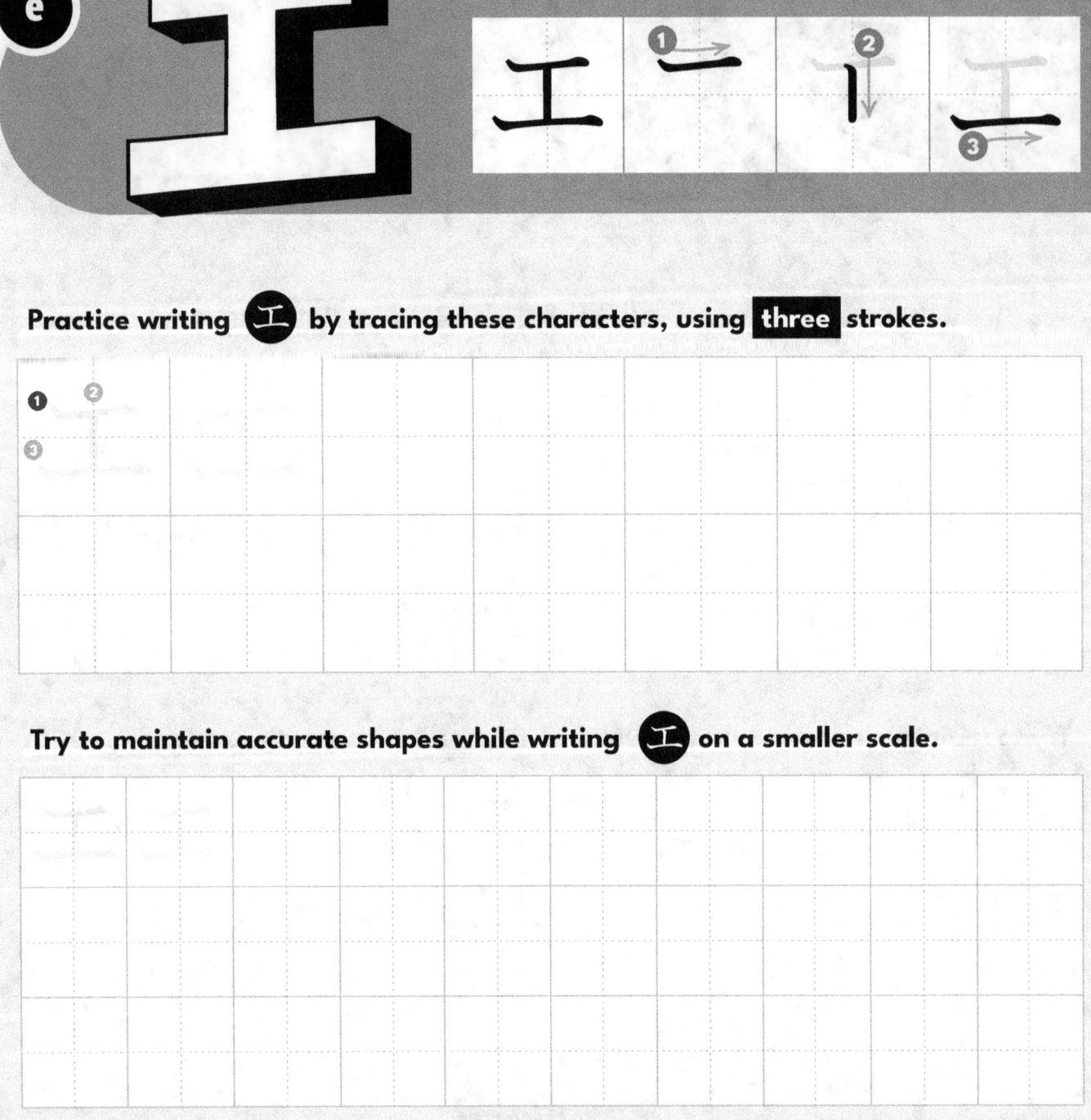

O オ

Sounds like the ‘o’ in box.

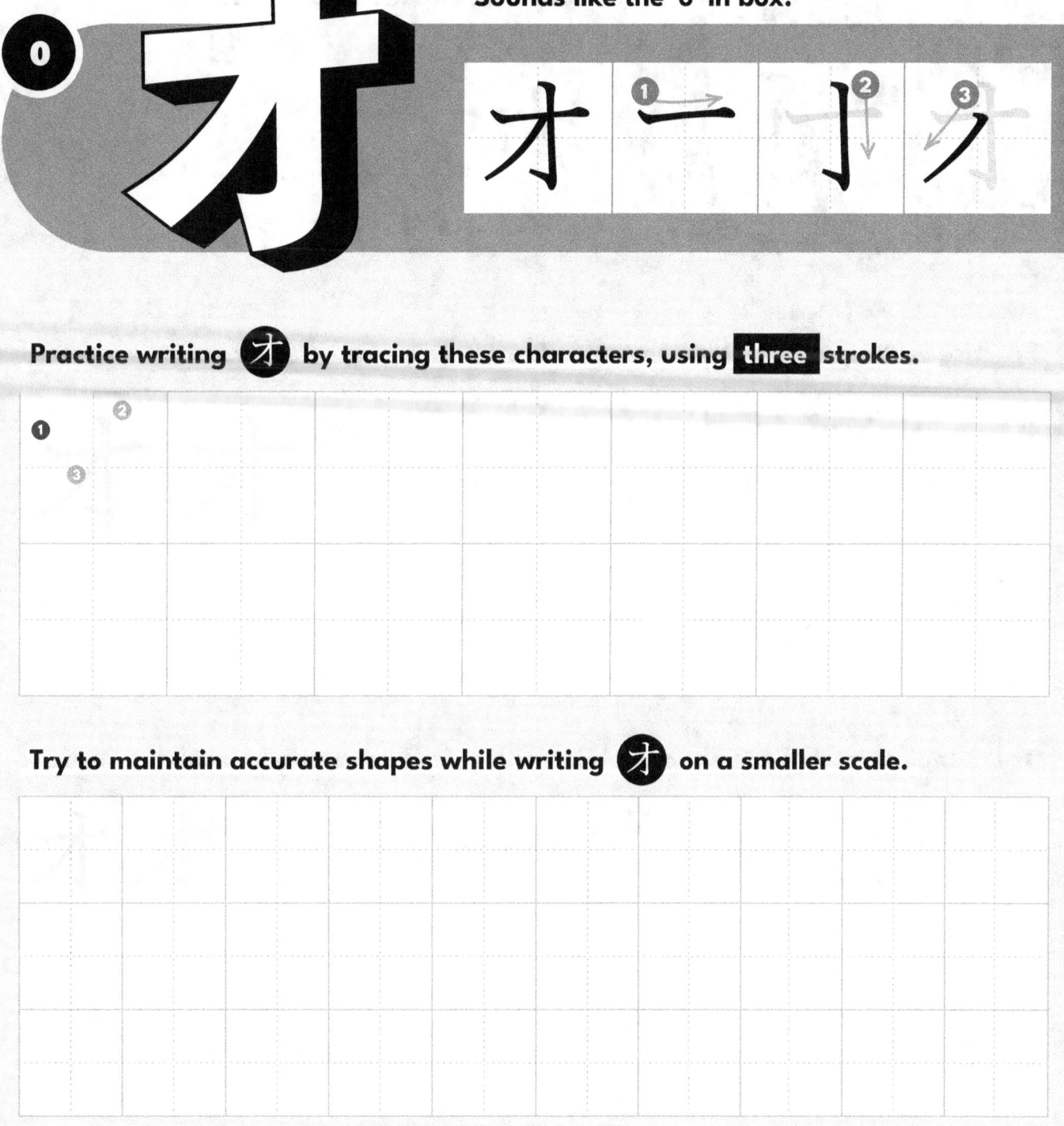

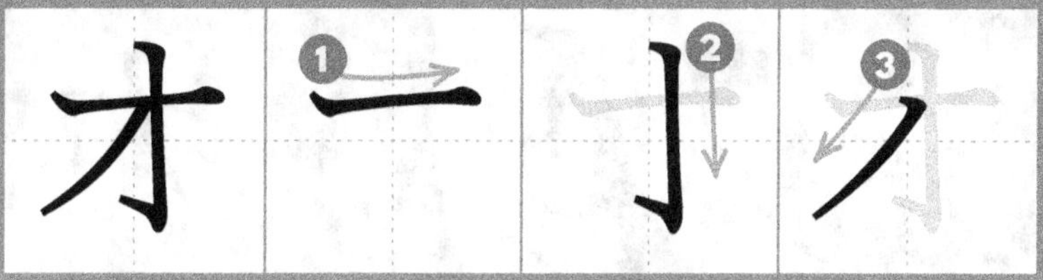

Practice writing オ by tracing these characters, using **three** strokes.

Try to maintain accurate shapes while writing オ on a smaller scale.

Mnemonic.

Examples.

- A person falling backwards, “<u>oh</u> no!”
- Superhero with a cape, “<u>oh</u> wow!”

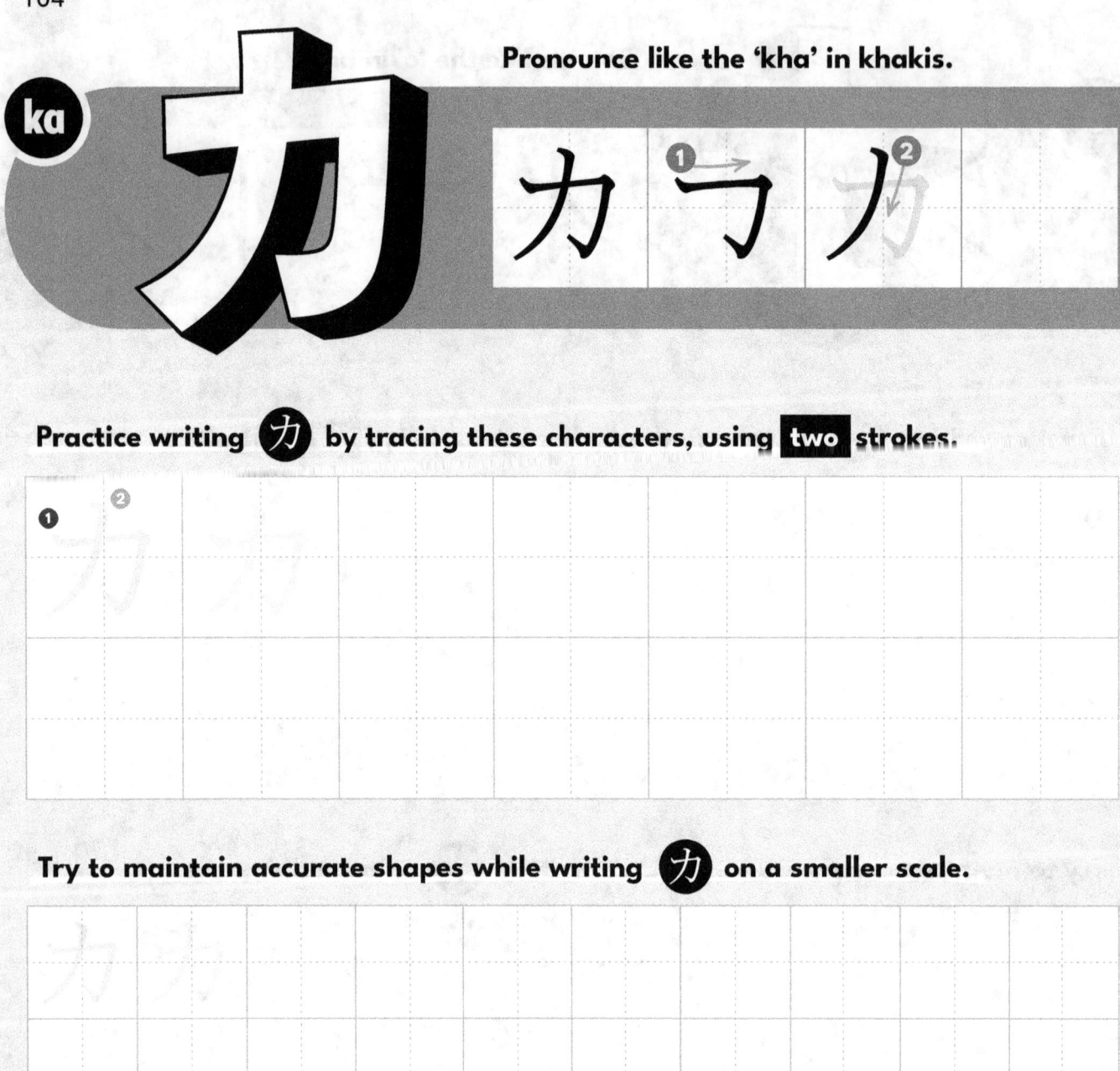

ka カ

Pronounce like the 'kha' in khakis.

カ ① ②

Practice writing カ by tracing these characters, using two strokes.

① ② カ カ

Try to maintain accurate shapes while writing カ on a smaller scale.

カ カ

Mnemonic.

Examples.

- Very similar to the hiragana

ki キ

This kana looks and sounds like a 'key'.

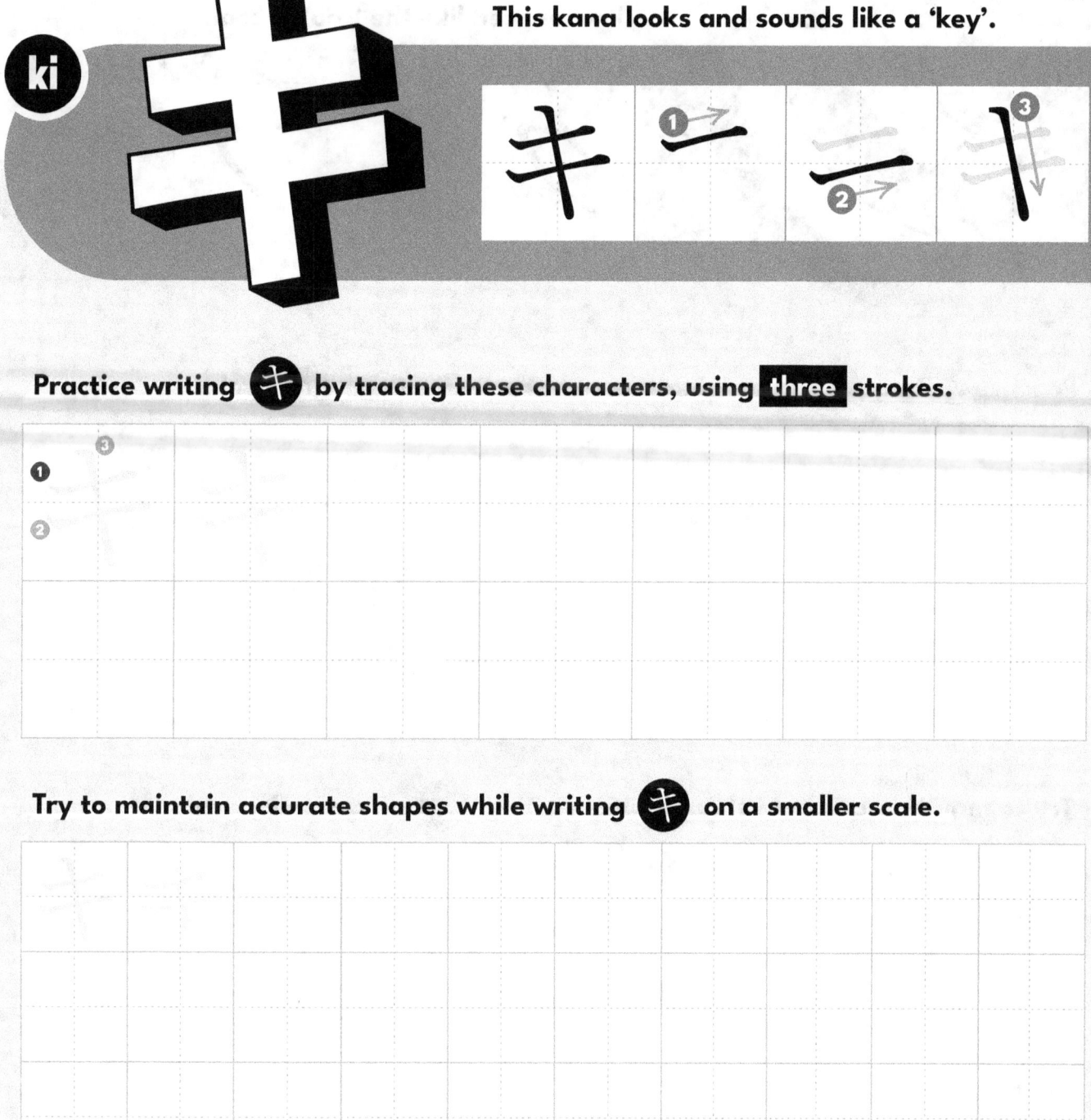

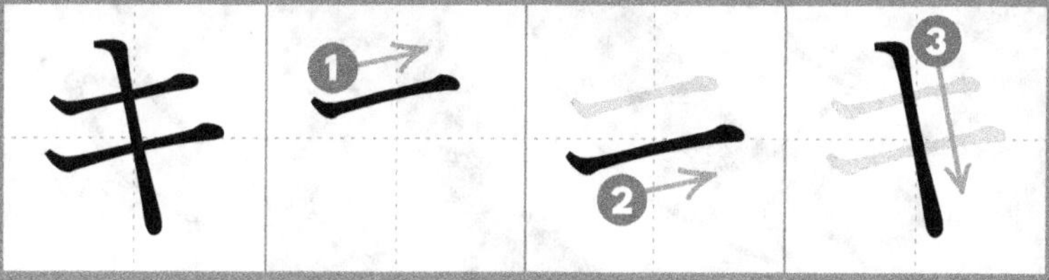

Practice writing キ by tracing these characters, using **three** strokes.

Try to maintain accurate shapes while writing キ on a smaller scale.

Mnemonic.

Examples.

- Similar to hiragana
- A slightly different key this time.

ku ク

Pronounced like the ‘coo’ in cool.

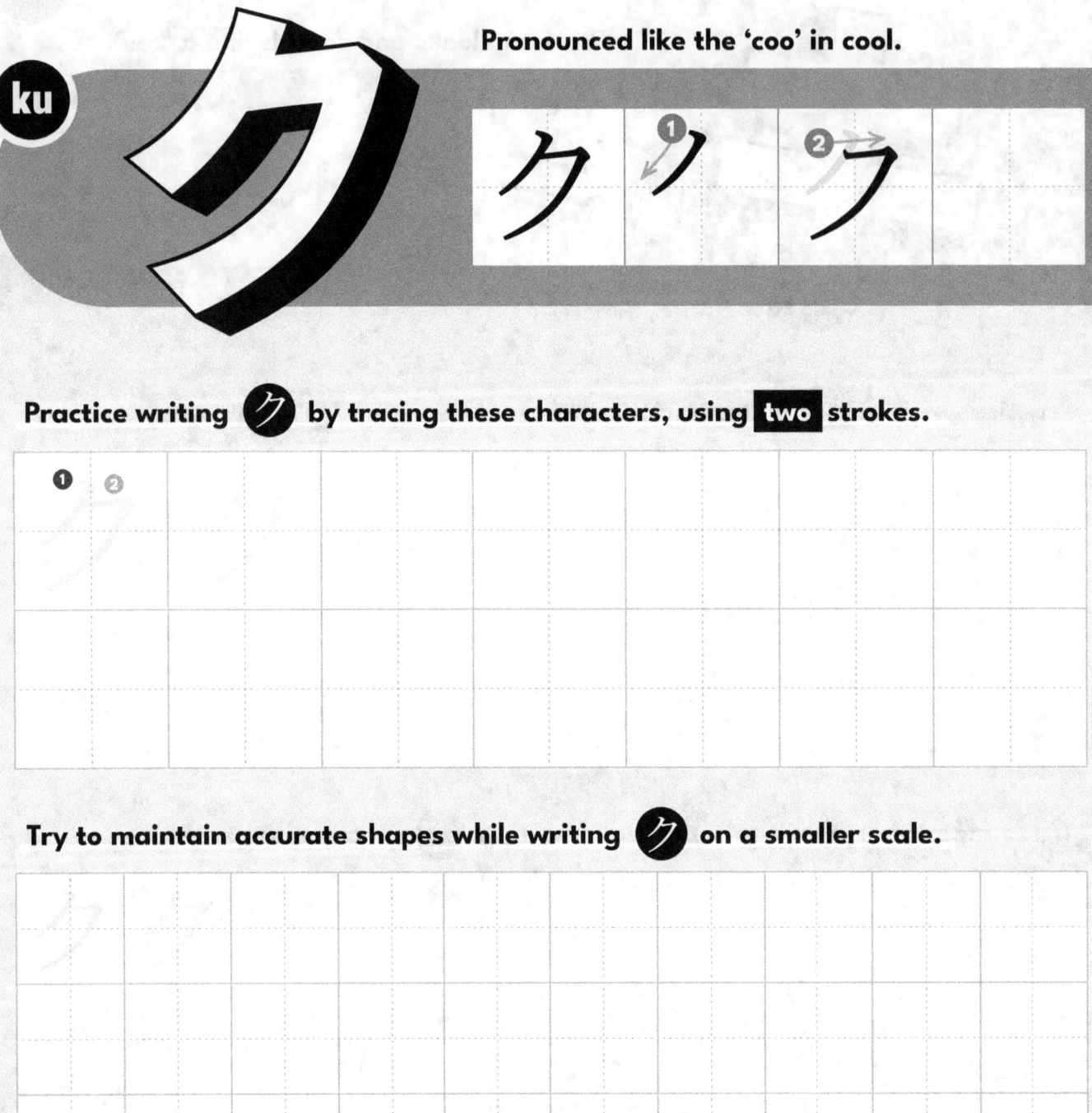

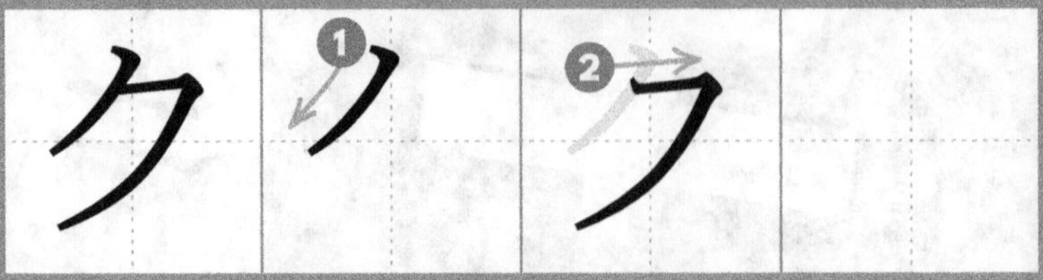

Practice writing ク by tracing these characters, using two strokes.

Try to maintain accurate shapes while writing ク on a smaller scale.

Mnemonic.

Examples.

- Picture a cook’s hat
- Number 7, with a cool hat

ke ケ

Sounds like the 'ke' in kettle.

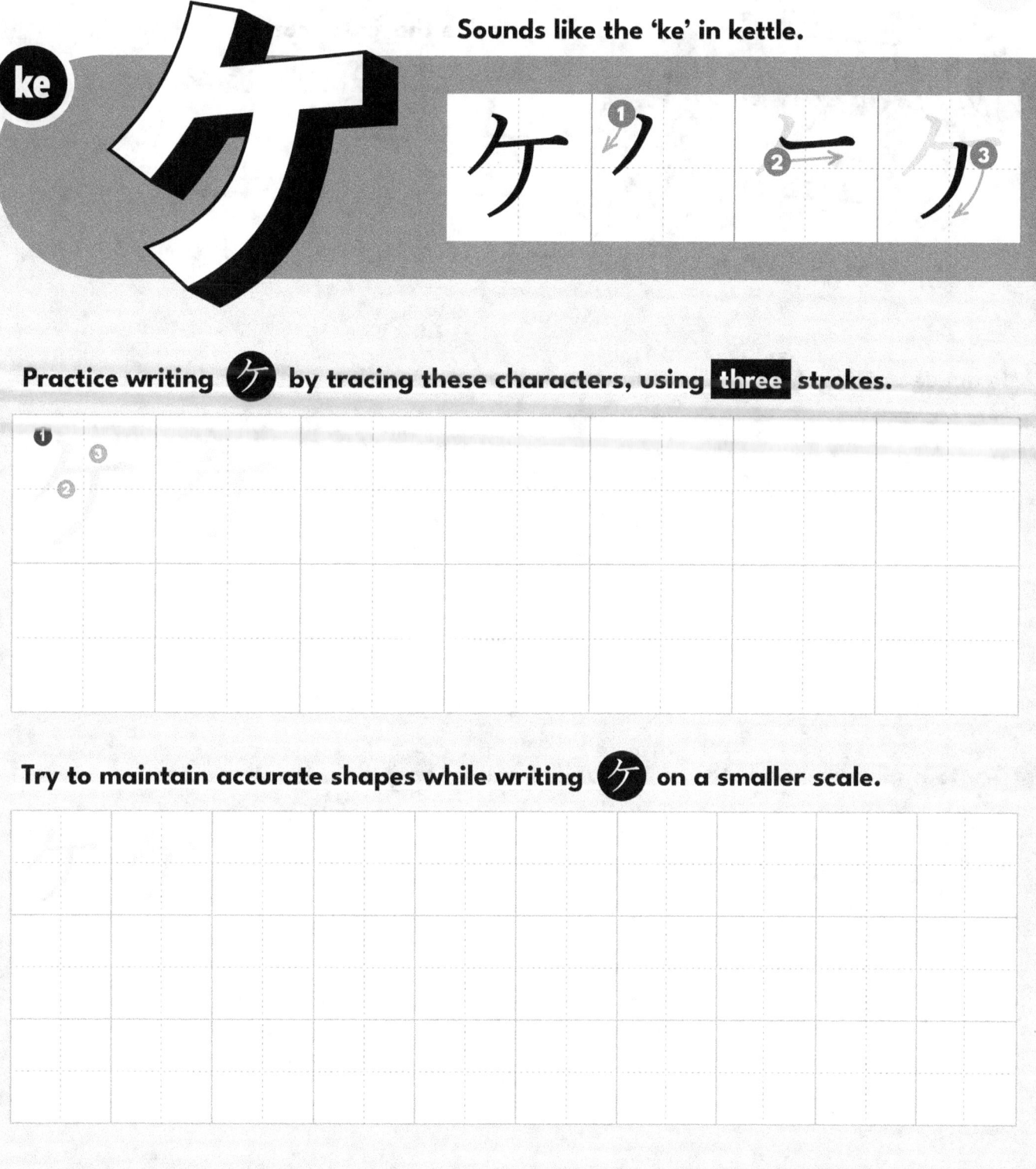

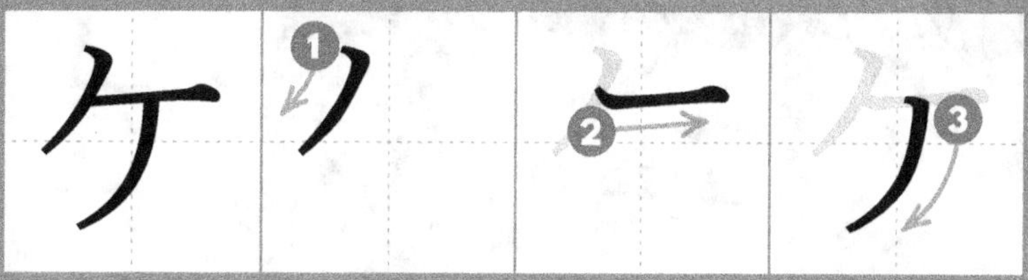

Practice writing ケ by tracing these characters, using three strokes.

Try to maintain accurate shapes while writing ケ on a smaller scale.

Mnemonic.

Examples.

- Letter 'k' tilting to the right

ko コ

Sounds like the 'co' in comb.

Practice writing コ by tracing these characters, using two strokes.

Try to maintain accurate shapes while writing コ on a smaller scale.

Mnemonic.

Examples.

- This katakana has two corners

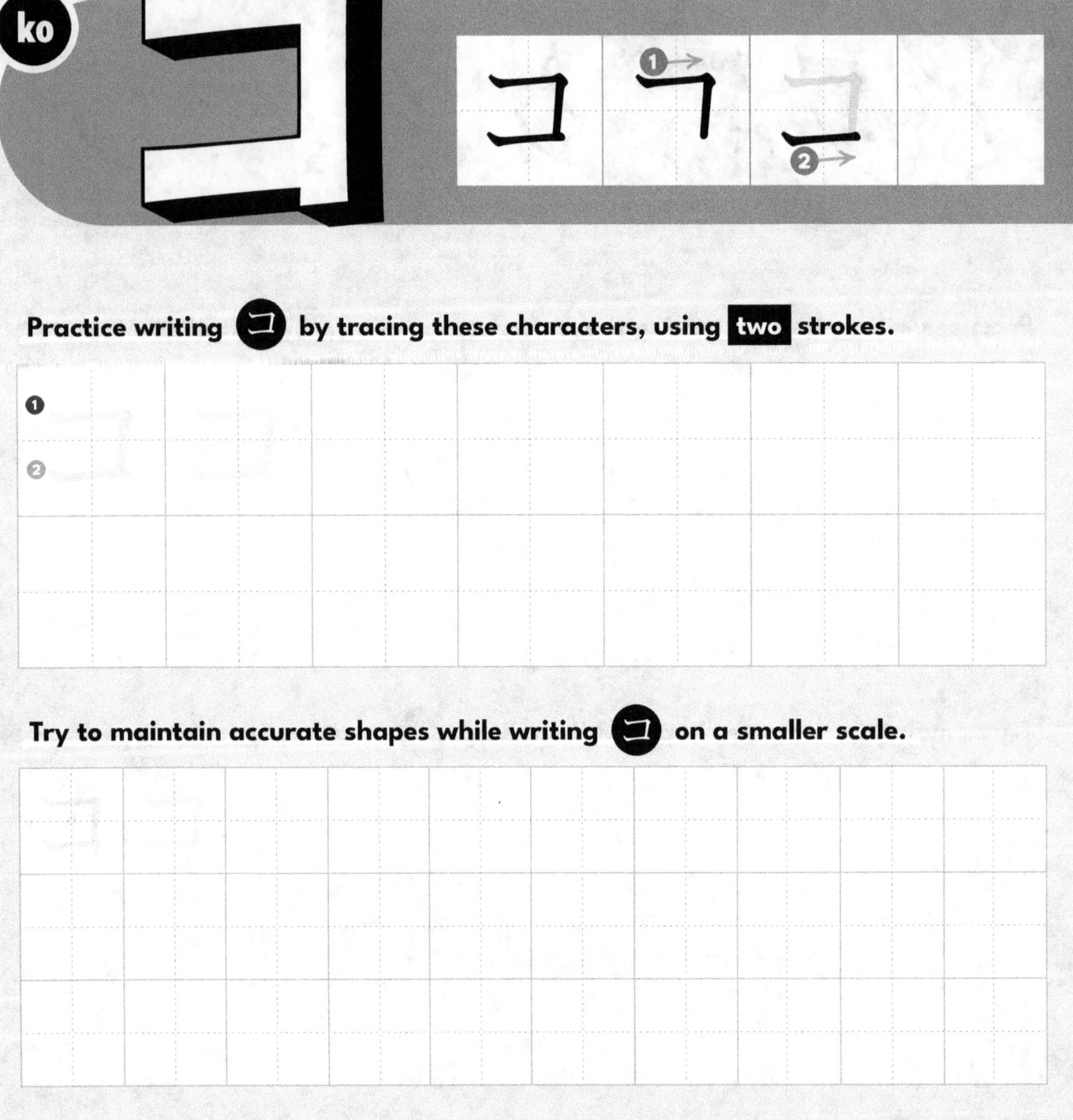

This first set of exercises will test how well you can attach the shape of the new katakana symbol to the same sound as its hiragana counterpart.

Practice pronouncing each symbol as you write the romaji beneath.

ア ウ ア イ オ エ オ イ ア エ オ エ オ ア

ウ イ オ ウ イ エ イ オ ア ウ ア エ ウ ア

ウ イ オ ア エ ウ オ ア エ イ ウ ア エ イ

Take a break for 5 minutes, and then do the same for these symbols too.

ア オ カ オ キ ケ ク ウ エ イ ア ク ウ ア

ク イ オ エ イ カ エ ウ ケ カ オ カ イ ウ

キ ウ カ ク オ イ エ キ カ ケ ア キ オ カ

It may feel easy, but the difficulty is going to ramp up as you learn larger groups of characters.

This time, take a 10-minute break and come back to complete these.

コ	ウ	ク	カ	イ	キ	ケ	ク	エ	キ	ア	イ	オ	ク

ウ	カ	エ	イ	コ	イ	ウ	ケ	ア	キ	オ	コ	キ	カ

ア	ウ	オ	ク	エ	ク	カ	ケ	コ	オ	ア	ウ	ケ	エ

After a much longer break, add the romaji for each symbol below.

キ	ケ	オ	イ	コ	ク	キ	ウ	コ	イ	エ	ア	オ	ク

ク	コ	ウ	カ	オ	ア	ケ	エ	キ	ク	ア	ケ	カ	イ

カ	エ	ウ	ケ	カ	ア	ウ	キ	ク	コ	オ	イ	ウ	エ

K2. The S & T Columns

Once more, pronunciation of this set mirrors the hiragana. The characters in this section are taken from both the S and T columns in the basic katakana table.

Symbols in this learning block.

サ	シ	ス	セ	ソ
sa	**shi**	**su**	**se**	**so**

タ	チ	ツ	テ	ト
ta	**chi**	**tsu**	**te**	**to**

Pronunciation

The same pronunciation rules apply to the exceptions for *'shi', 'chi',* and *'tsu'.*

sa サ

Sounds like the 'sa-' in sarcasm.

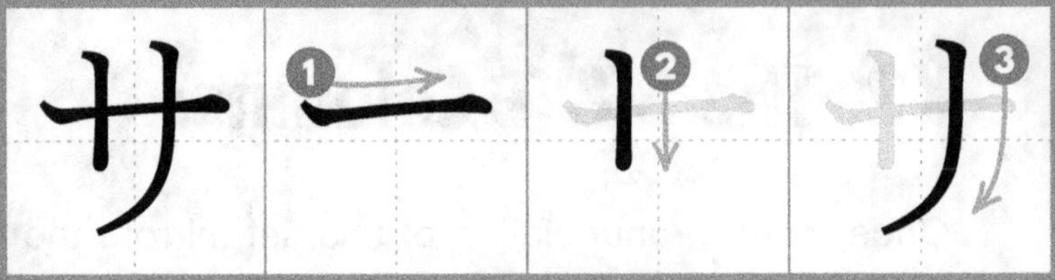

Practice writing サ by tracing these characters, using three strokes.

Try to maintain accurate shapes while writing サ on a smaller scale.

Mnemonic.

Examples.

- Imagine the shape of a saddle

shi シ

Sounds exactly like the 'shi' in sashimi.

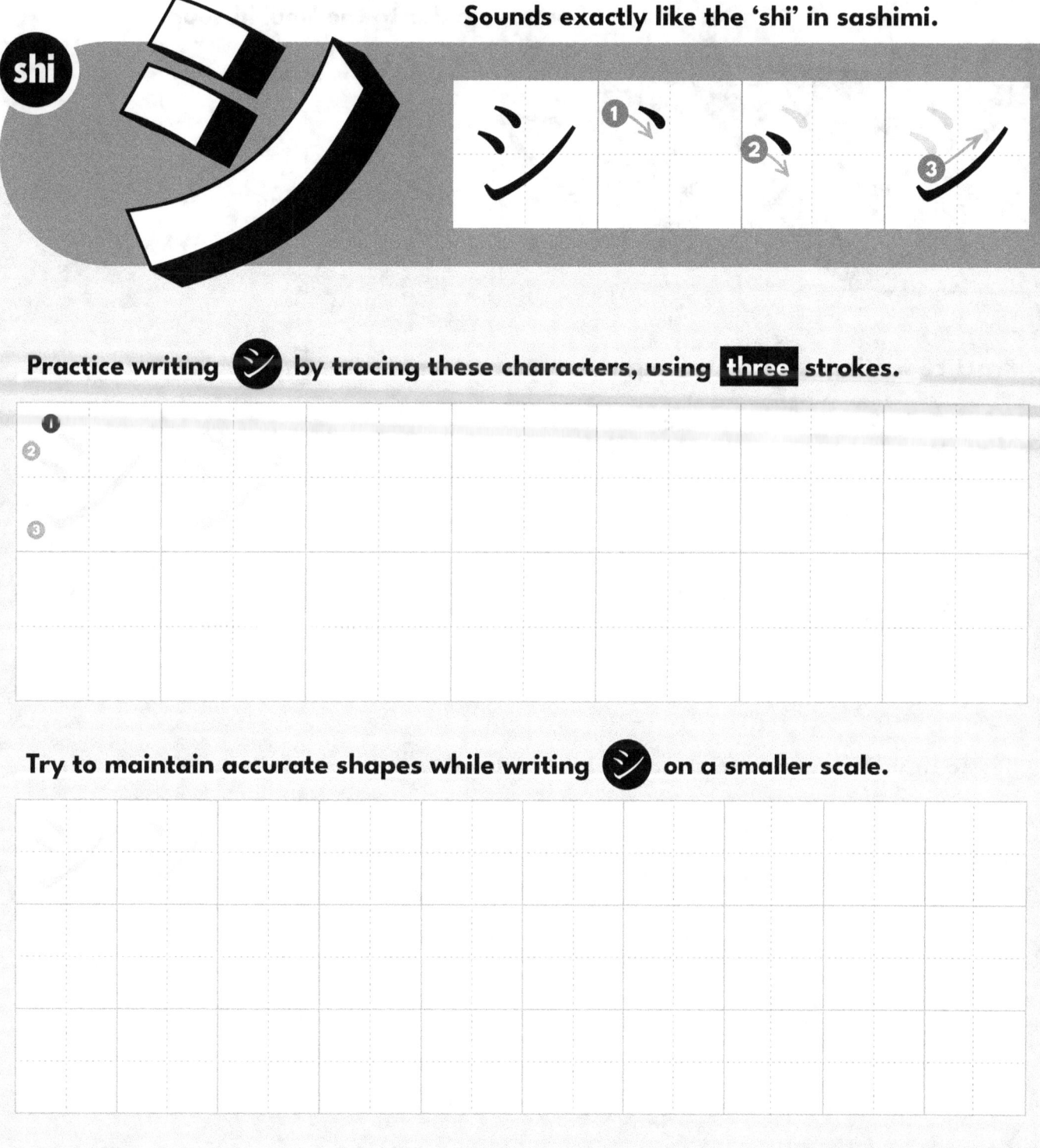

Practice writing シ by tracing these characters, using three strokes.

Try to maintain accurate shapes while writing シ on a smaller scale.

Mnemonic.

Examples.

- She has a crooked smile

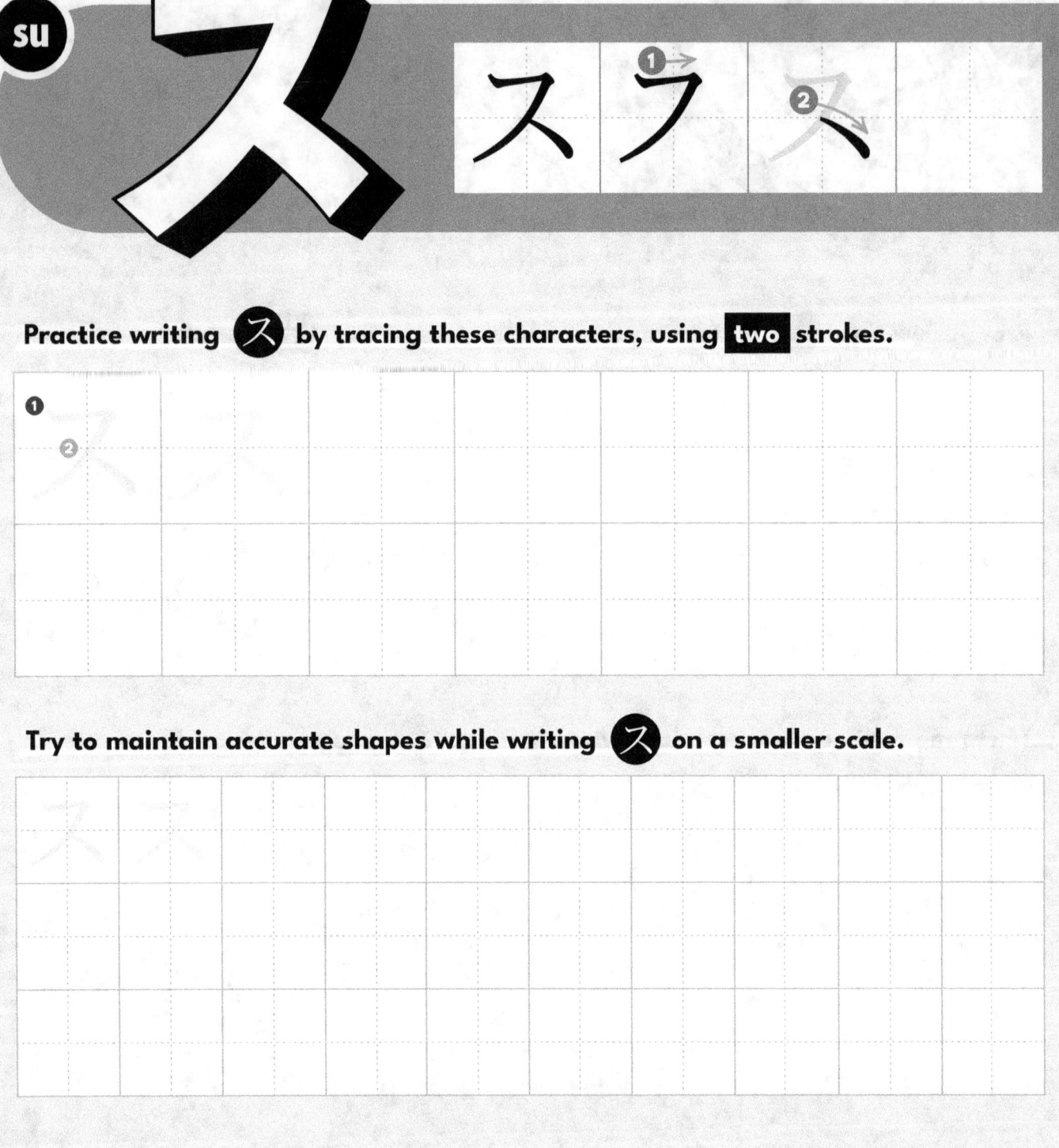

su

ス

Sounds similar to the 'sou' in soup.

ス フ ス

Practice writing ス by tracing these characters, using **two** strokes.

Try to maintain accurate shapes while writing ス on a smaller scale.

Mnemonic.

Examples.

- You hang suits on a coathanger

se セ

Pronounced 'seh' (almost like say).

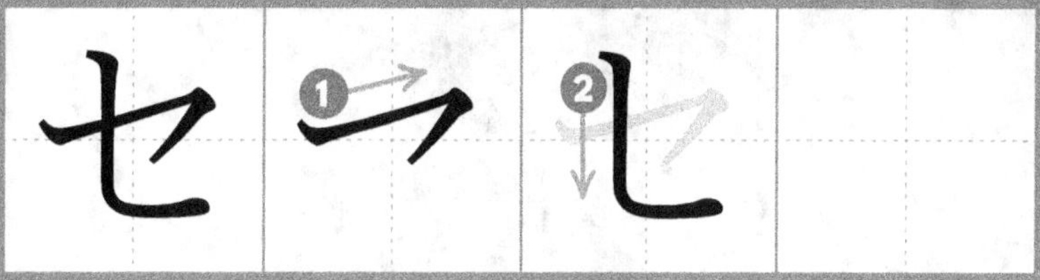

Practice writing セ by tracing these characters, using two strokes.

1 2

Try to maintain accurate shapes while writing セ on a smaller scale.

Mnemonic.

Examples.

- Picture a big mouth, saying something
- Similar to hiragana

SO ソ

Sounds like the 'so-' in soccer or sorry.

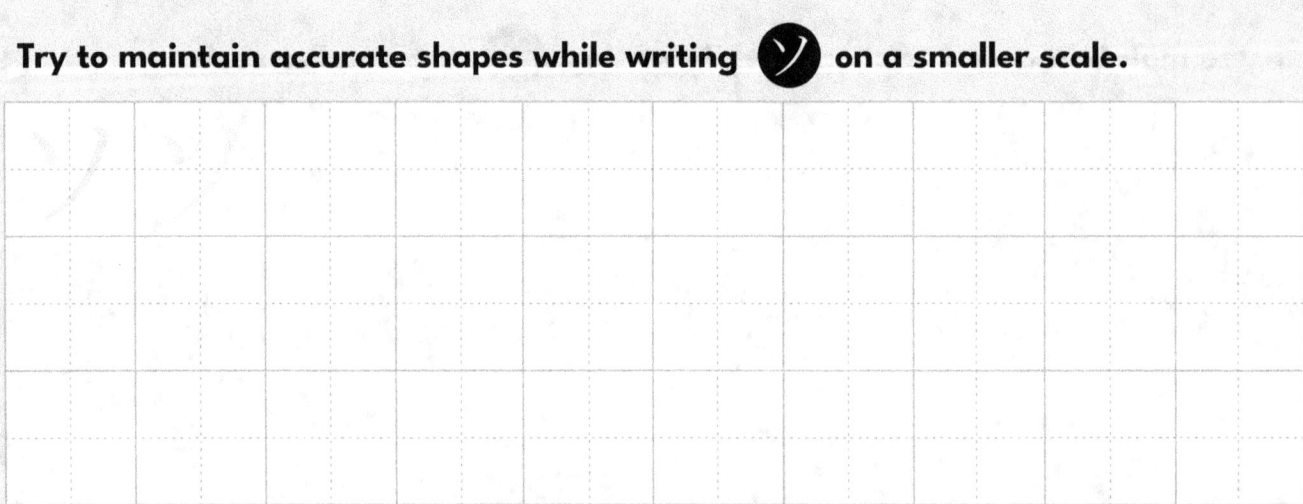

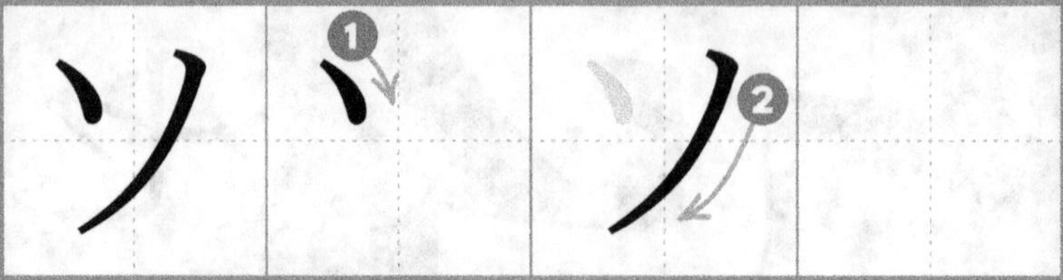

Practice writing ソ by tracing these characters, using two strokes.

Try to maintain accurate shapes while writing ソ on a smaller scale.

Mnemonic.

Examples.

- One sew-ing needle, pulling a thread (notice the small line is vertical)

ta タ

Sounds like the '-ta' in Santa.

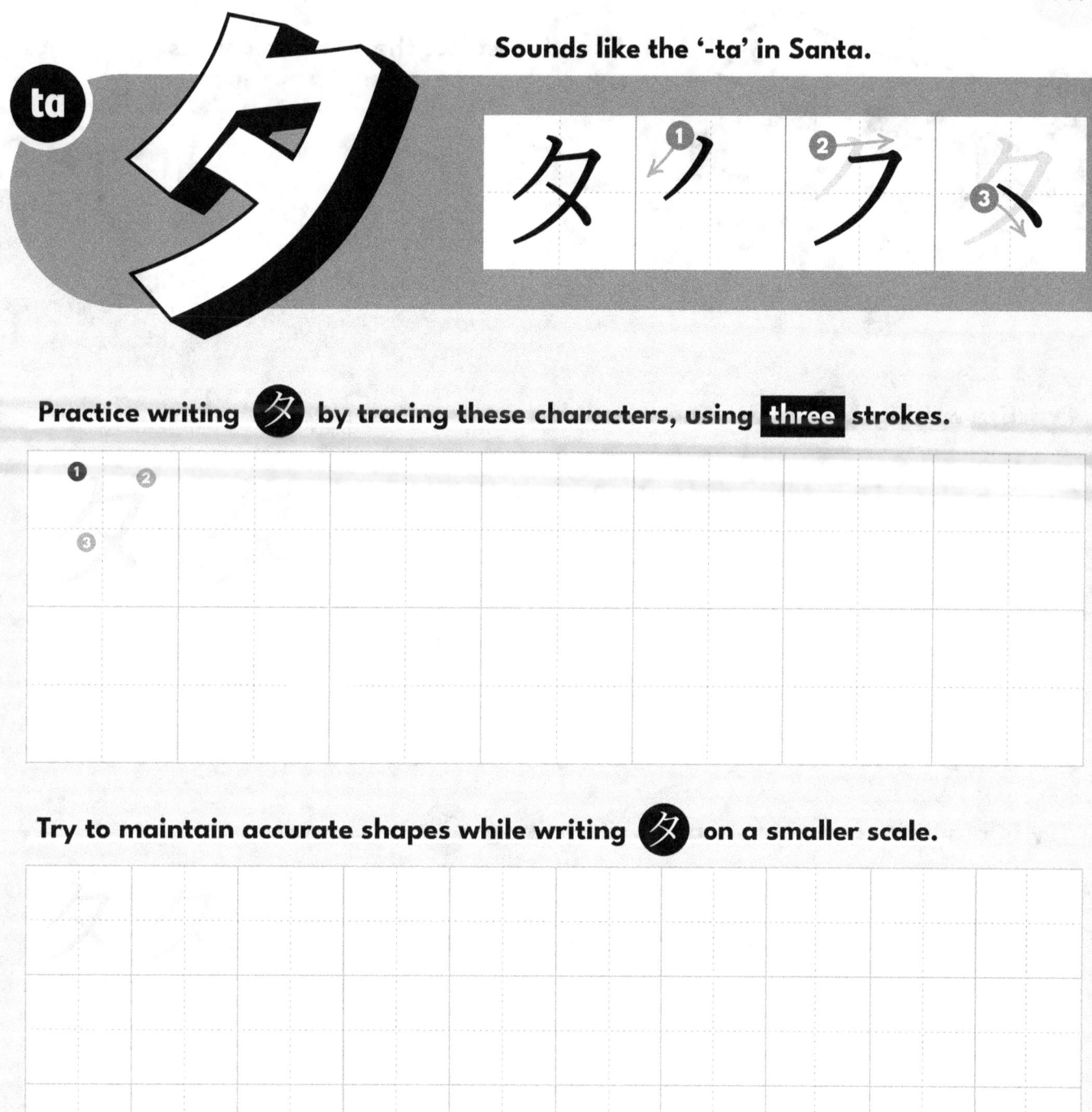

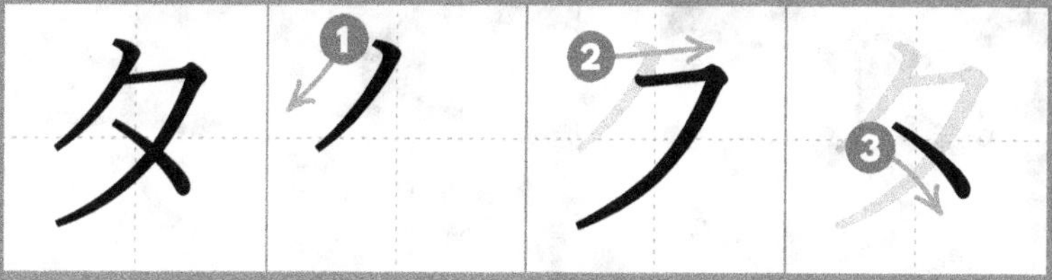

Practice writing タ by tracing these characters, using three strokes.

Try to maintain accurate shapes while writing タ on a smaller scale.

Mnemonic.

Examples.

- The letters 't' and 'A' are hidden inside
- A tidal wave

chi チ

Sounds just like the 'chee' in cheeks.

チ ① ② ③

Practice writing チ by tracing these characters, using **three** strokes.

Try to maintain accurate shapes while writing チ on a smaller scale.

Mnemonic.

Examples.

- The same shape as a cheerleader

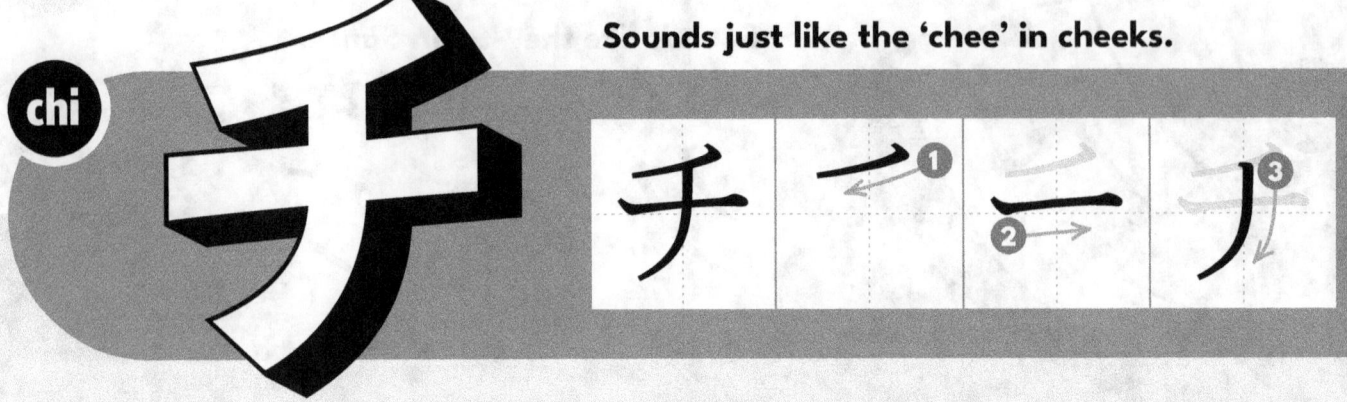

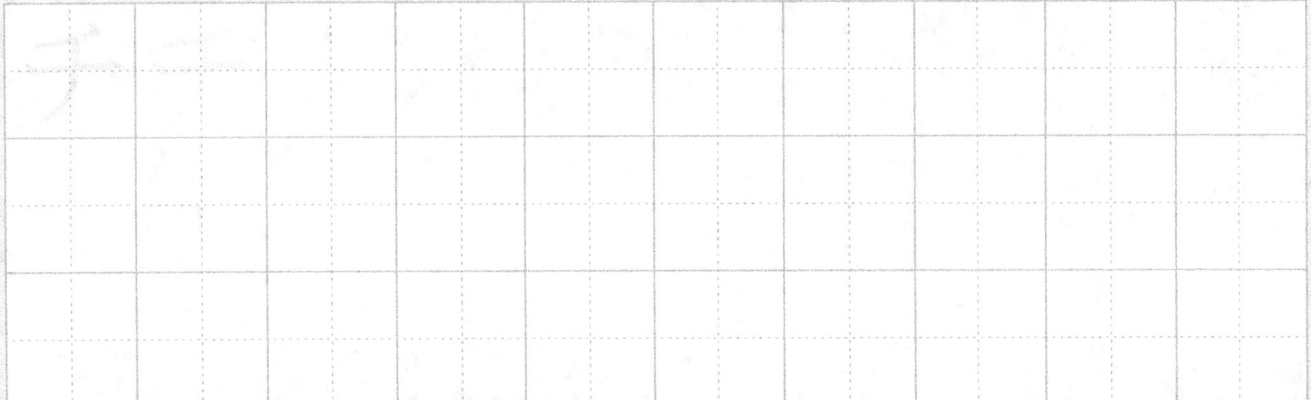

tsu ツ

Sounds like 'two' and the name 'Sue'.

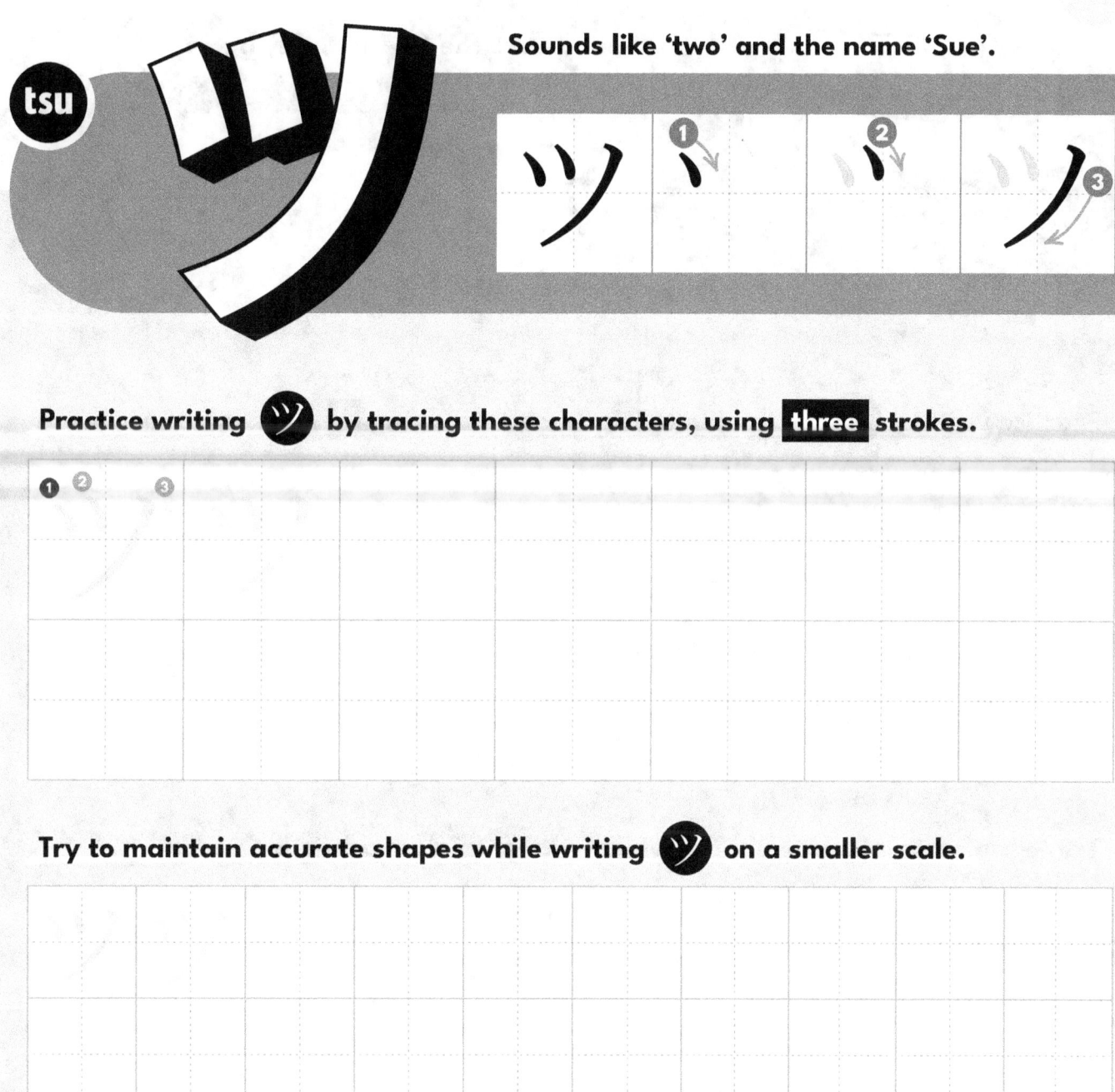

Practice writing ツ by tracing these characters, using **three** strokes.

Try to maintain accurate shapes while writing ツ on a smaller scale.

Mnemonic.

Examples.

- Two needles pulling the same thread (vertical lines just like in kana 'so')

te テ

Sounds like the 'te-' in teddy bear.

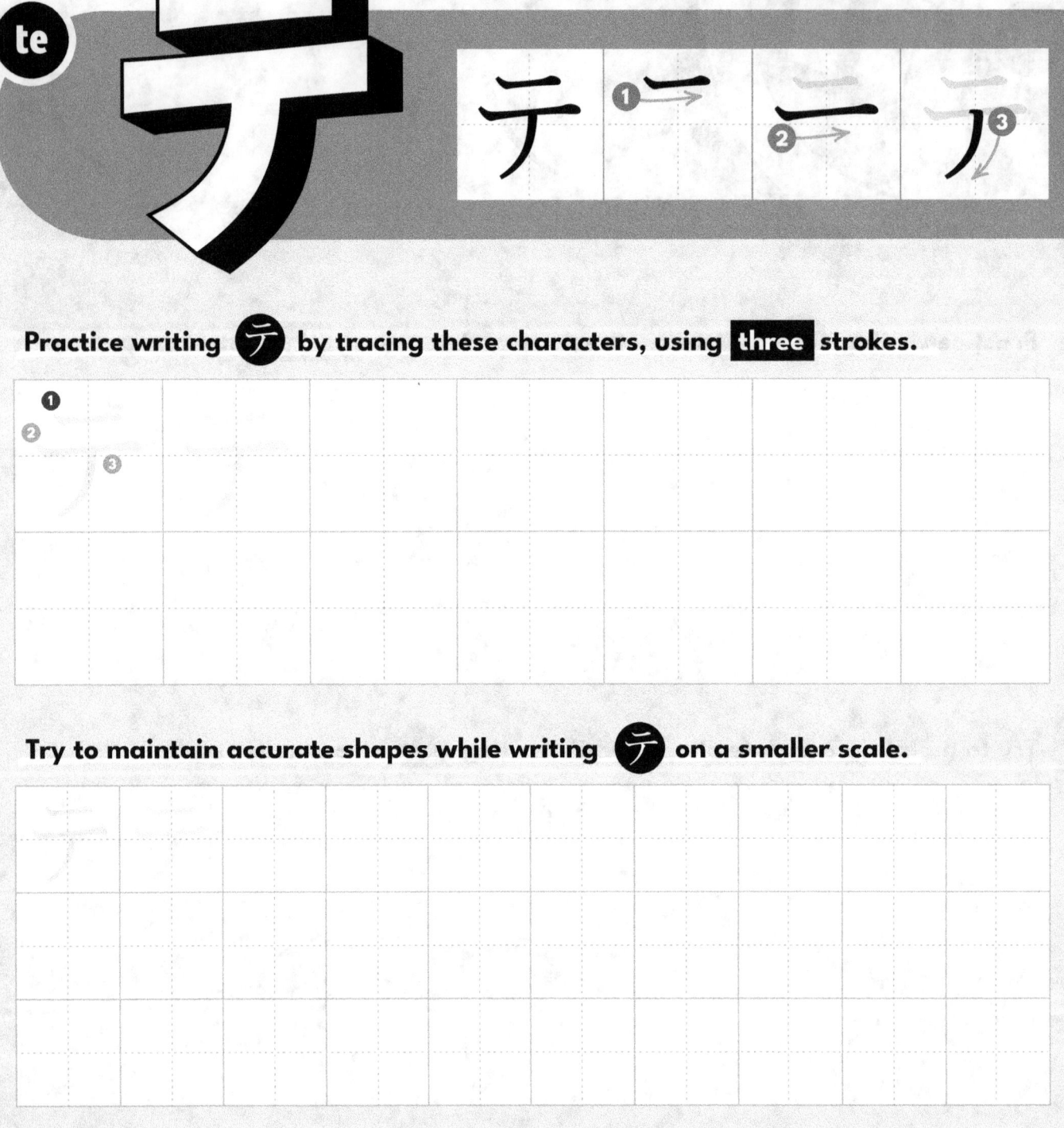

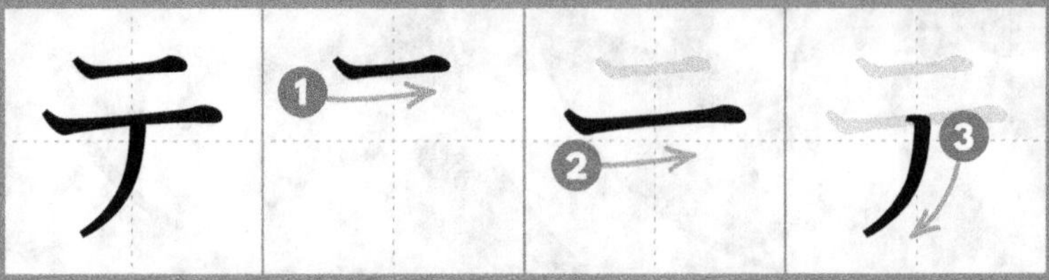

Practice writing テ by tracing these characters, using three strokes.

Try to maintain accurate shapes while writing テ on a smaller scale.

Mnemonic.

Examples.

- Picture the shape of telegraph poles

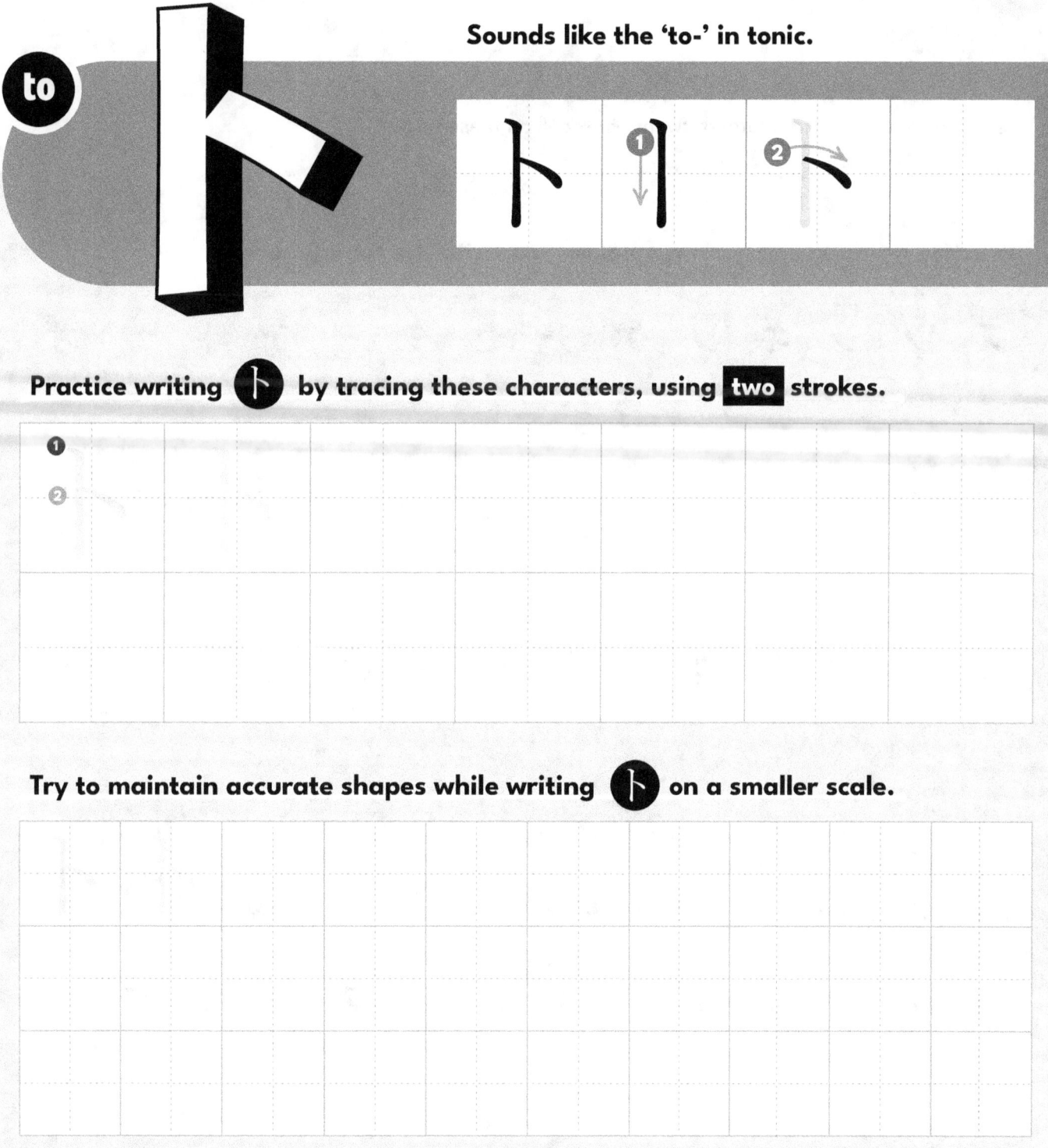

to ト

Sounds like the 'to-' in tonic.

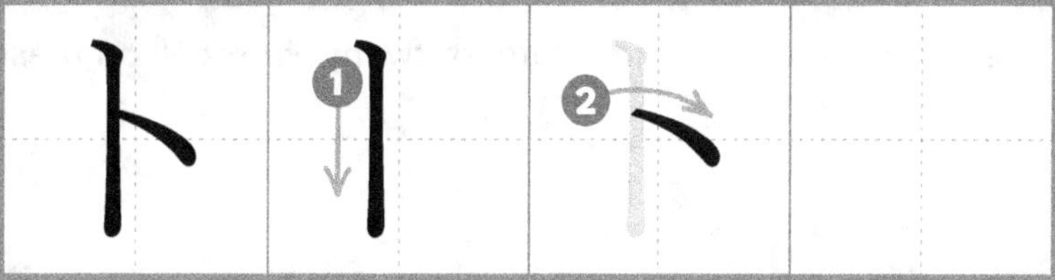

Practice writing ト by tracing these characters, using **two** strokes.

1
2

Try to maintain accurate shapes while writing ト on a smaller scale.

Mnemonic.

Examples.

- Lower case 't'
- Imagine this as a <u>to</u>tem pole

Ten more symbols, and a total of twenty to recall on these pages.

Practice pronouncing each symbol as you write the romaji beneath.

ス ツ シ キ ソ ケ チ セ タ イ ア ト ソ オ

テ エ サ ス タ エ ウ セ コ テ イ カ ト ク

タ テ ツ サ キ ト コ ウ チ オ ス カ シ エ

Take a 5-minute break, and then do the same for these symbols too.

シ チ セ テ ソ タ ツ ス テ ス サ ツ タ セ

サ カ タ ト キ テ ケ サ チ ソ エ セ シ ソ

タ ス ツ ト イ セ ウ ソ コ サ テ ス オ ト

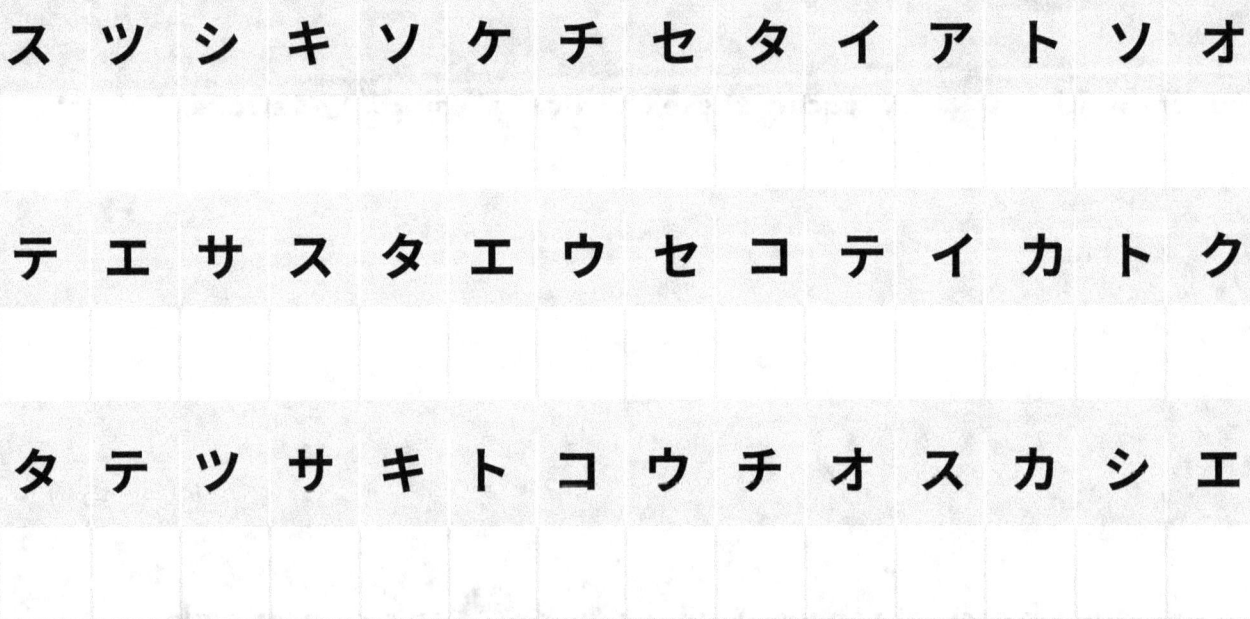

This time, take a 10-minute break and come back to complete these.

エ タ チ セ サ コ チ オ エ ウ イ ツ セ サ

ソ シ テ ス イ ト シ イ サ セ オ ア ク チ

テ ス ウ ア ト タ ソ ツ タ オ キ ウ エ シ

After a much longer break, add the romaji for each symbol below.

ソ チ タ サ エ サ チ ア テ セ ツ セ ソ オ

イ セ ス ト オ ク シ ス シ エ ア ウ タ ト

エ シ イ オ コ キ テ ツ サ チ タ ウ イ ウ

Practice reading the katakana you have learned so far with these examples.

Note: It is common for words in katakana to have horizontal lines. They show that the vowel sound from the previous character should be doubled in length. For example: **カ** *= ka , and* **カー** *= ka-a. (You will learn more about this later)*

カツ cutlet		**コーチ** coach	
アイス ice		**ソース** sauce	
ケーキ cake		**スキー** skiing	
アウト out		**タクシー** taxi	
サーチ search		**ステーキ** steak	
コート coat		**セーター** sweater	
ツアー tour		**サーカス** circus	
テスト test		**オーケー** ok	
シーツ sheet		**エーカー** acre	

K3. The N & H Columns

Another block of ten symbols to learn. This time, we are looking at katakana from both the N and H columns. One exception to the usual pattern is again *'fu'* in place of *'hu'*. The sound is somewhere between *'hu'* and *'fu'*, like *'hfu'*.

Symbols in this learning block.

ナ	ニ	ヌ	ネ	ノ
na	**ni**	**nu**	**ne**	**no**
ハ	ヒ	フ	ヘ	ホ
ha	**hi**	**fu**	**he**	**ho**

Pronunciation

There are no differences in sound between the first ten hiragana that you learned and the way in which you should pronounce these characters. Remember to pay attention to your pronunciation of *'fu'.*

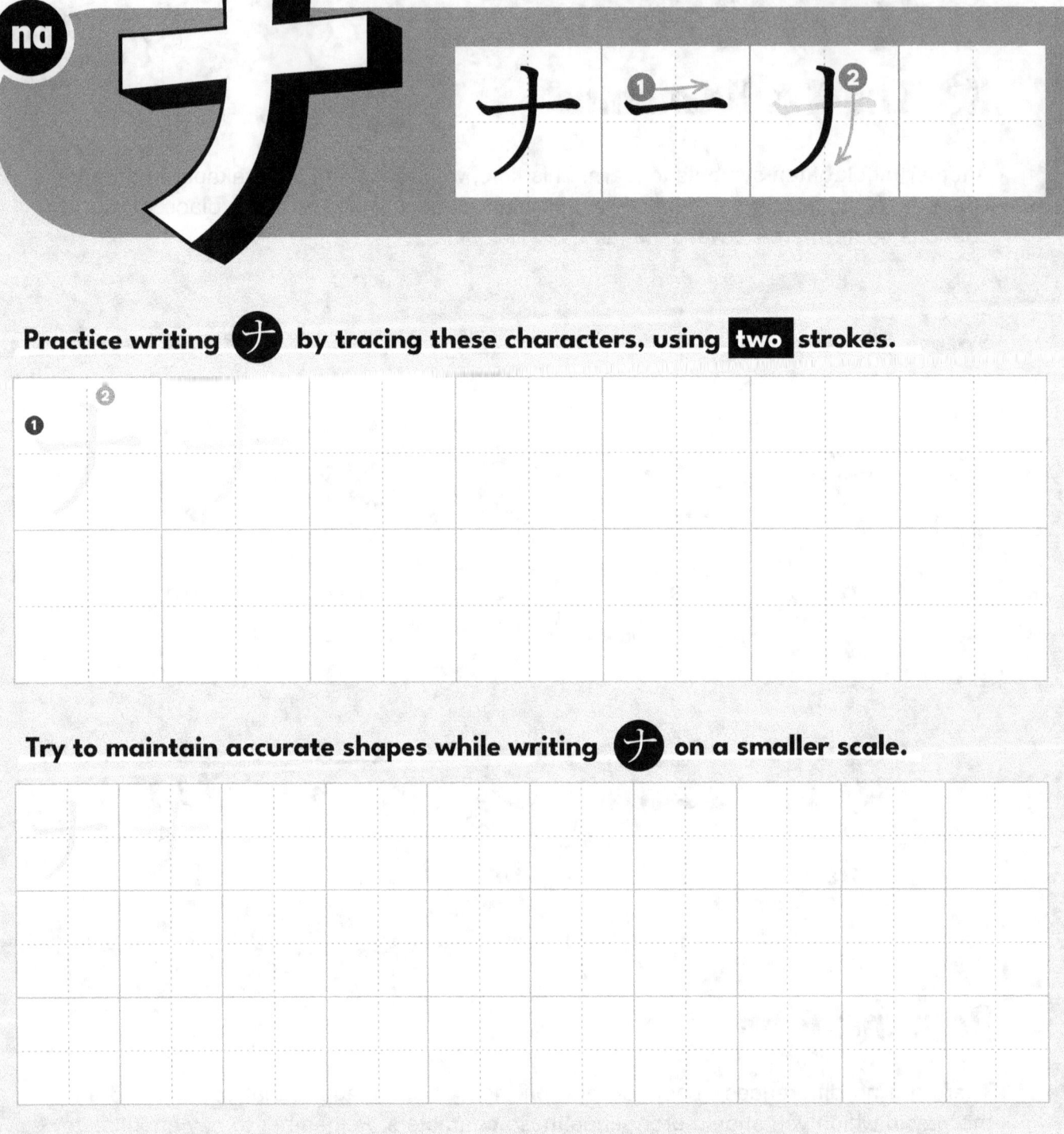

na ナ

Sounds just like the '-na's in banana

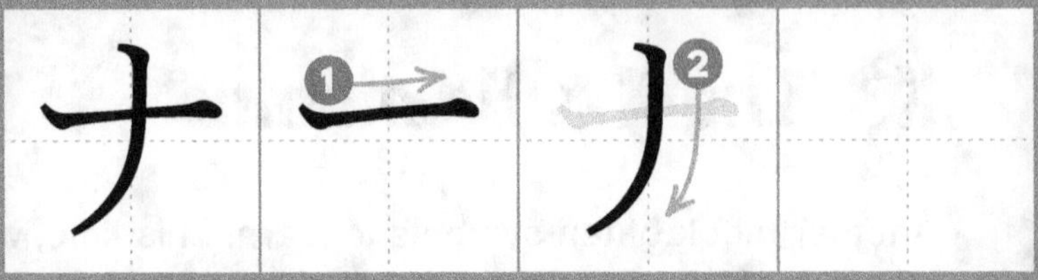

Practice writing ナ by tracing these characters, using two strokes.

Try to maintain accurate shapes while writing ナ on a smaller scale.

Mnemonic.

Examples.

- The shape of a knife
- A peeled banana
- Narwhal with horn

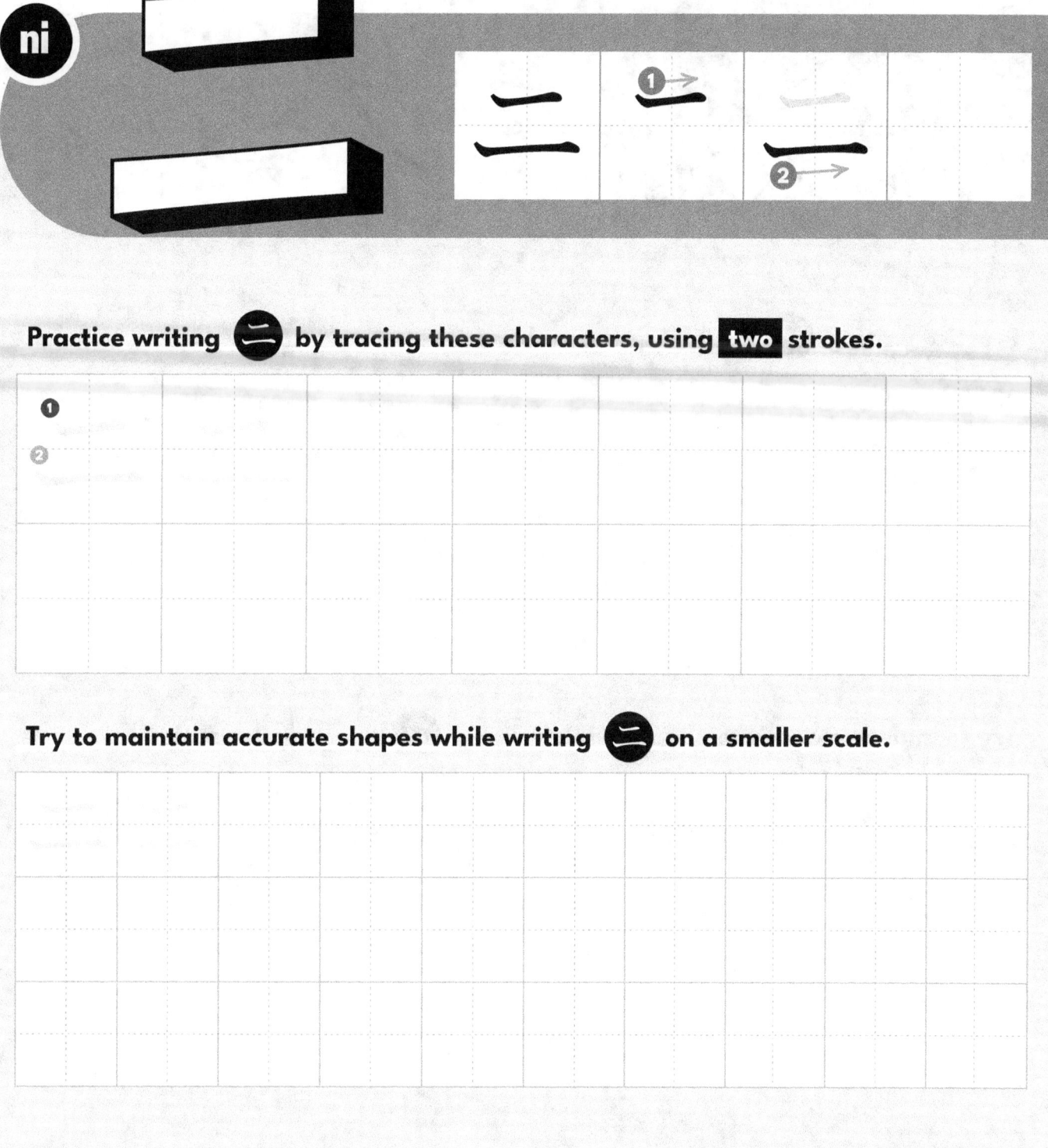

ni

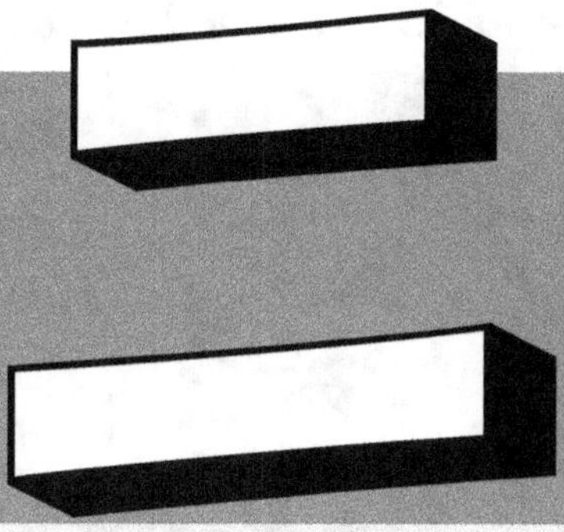

Sounds similar to the word 'knee'.

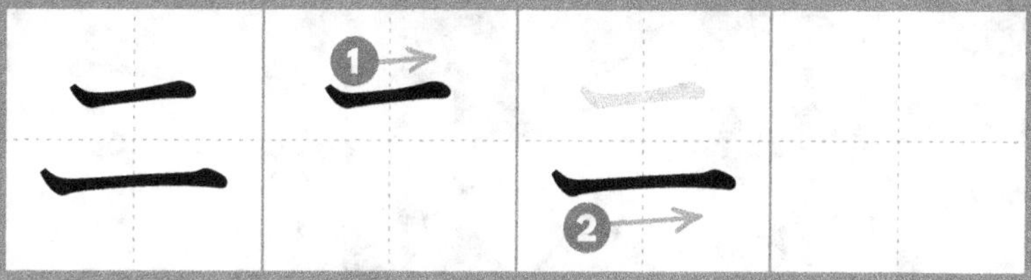

Practice writing ニ by tracing these characters, using two strokes.

Try to maintain accurate shapes while writing ニ on a smaller scale.

Mnemonic.

Examples.

- Two needles

nu ヌ

Sounds like the 'noo' in the word noon.

ヌ フ ヌ

Practice writing ヌ by tracing these characters, using **two** strokes.

Try to maintain accurate shapes while writing ヌ on a smaller scale.

Mnemonic.

Examples.

- Chopsticks, picking up one noodle
- A new type of scythe

ne ネ

Sounds similar to ‘nay’ or ‘neigh’.

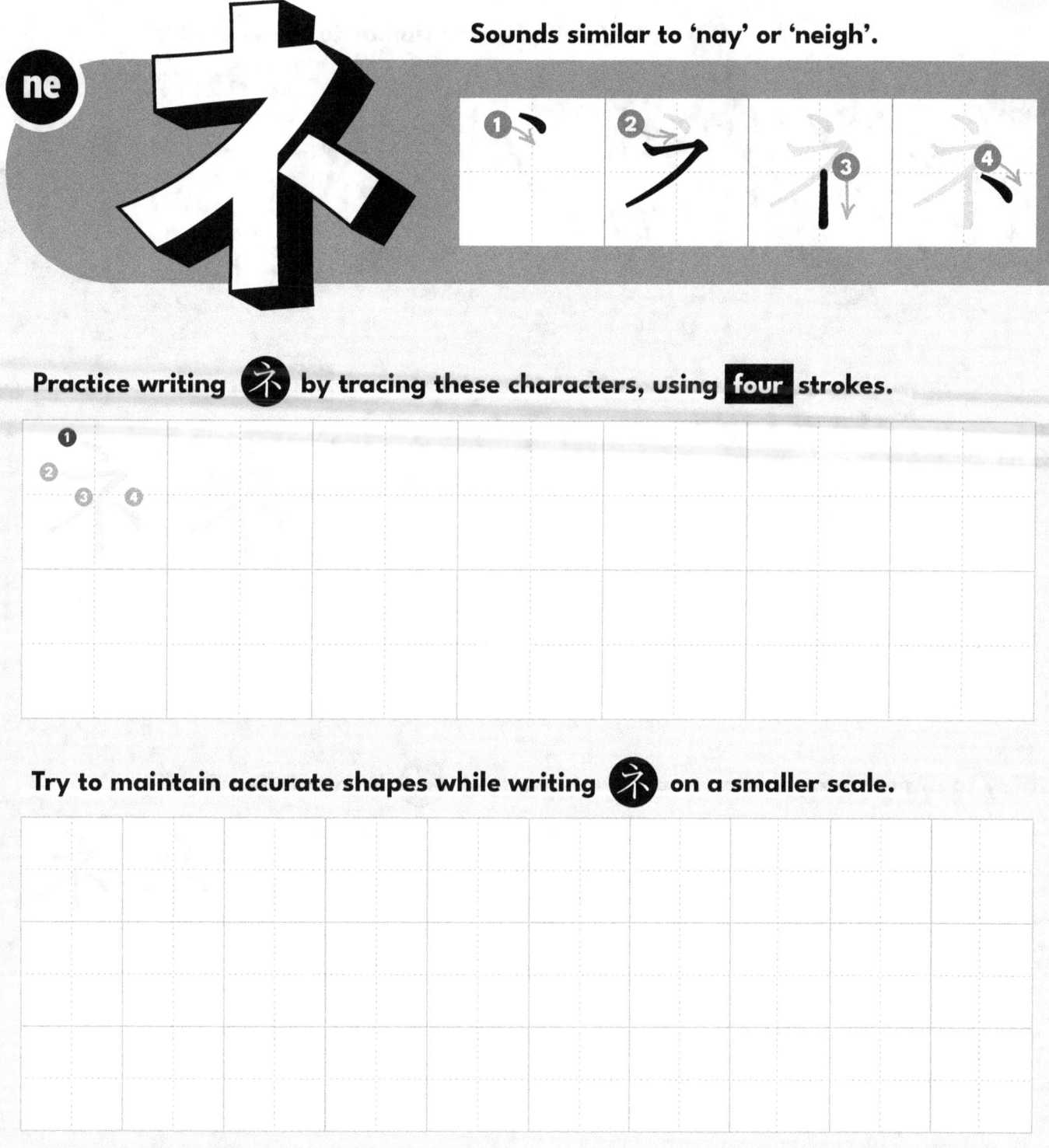

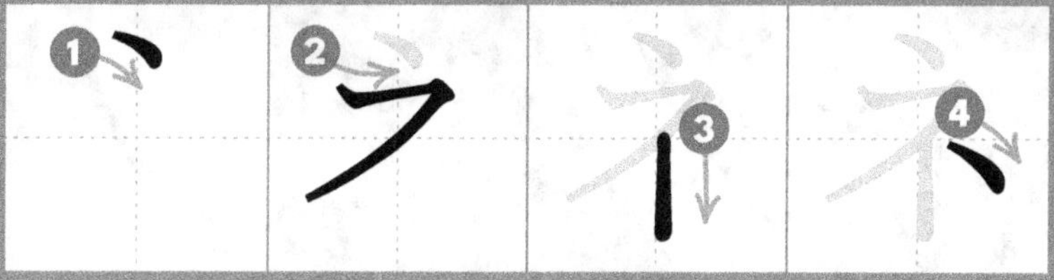

Practice writing ネ by tracing these characters, using **four** strokes.

Try to maintain accurate shapes while writing ネ on a smaller scale.

Mnemonic.

Examples.

- Nelly has grown tusks and charges towards you!

no ノ

Sounds very similar to the word 'No'.

ノ ノ ①

Practice writing ノ by tracing these characters, using one stroke.

①

Try to maintain accurate shapes while writing ノ on a smaller scale.

Mnemonic.

Examples.

- The first part of the 'No Smoking sign' in hiragana.
- A very long nose.

ha ハ

Pronounce as 'ha' like in hand.

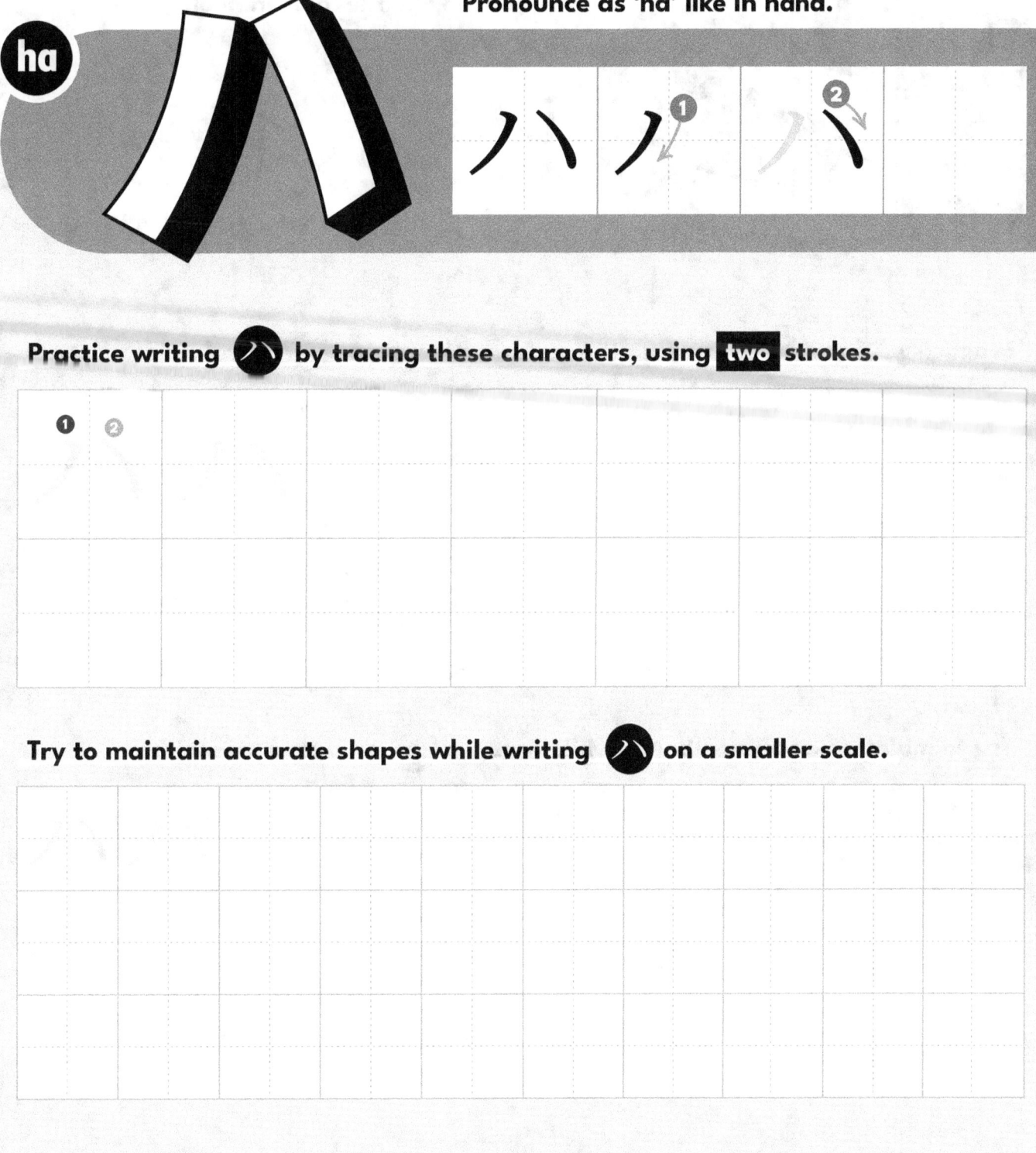

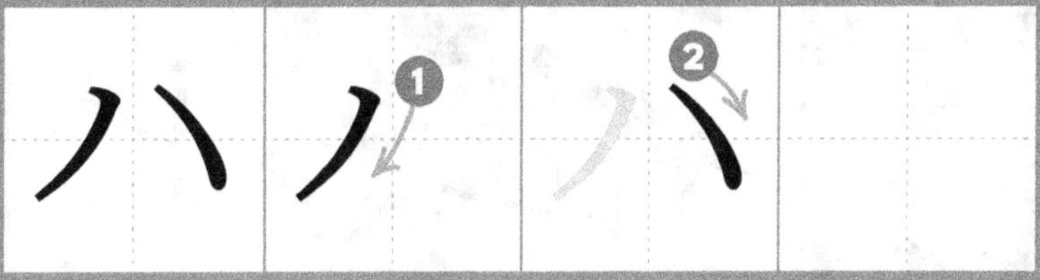

Practice writing ハ by tracing these characters, using two strokes.

1 2

Try to maintain accurate shapes while writing ハ on a smaller scale.

Mnemonic.

Examples.

- The shape of a hat

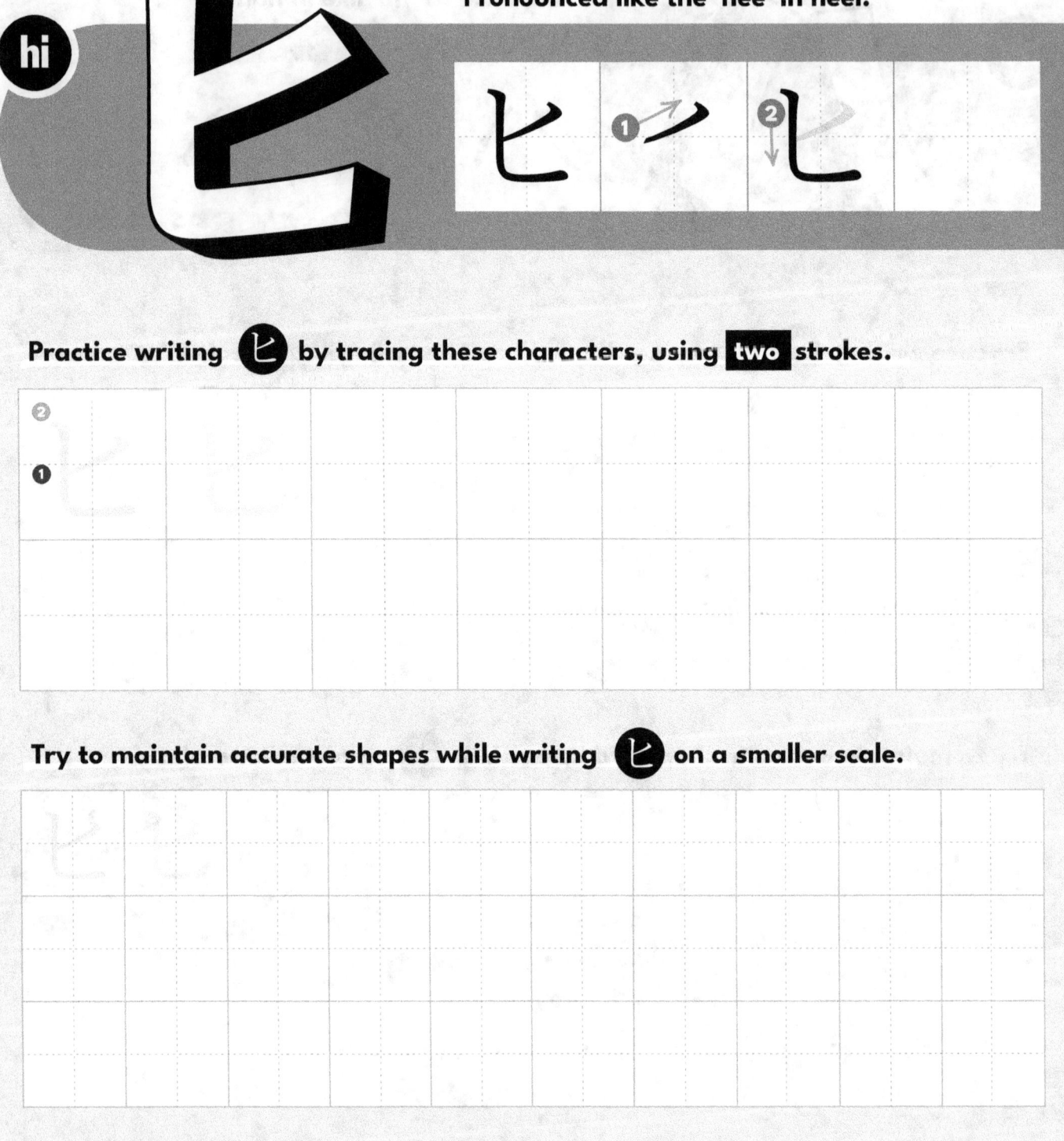

hi ヒ

Pronounced like the 'hee' in heel.

ヒ ① ノ ② L

Practice writing ヒ by tracing these characters, using **two** strokes.

Try to maintain accurate shapes while writing ヒ on a smaller scale.

Mnemonic.

Examples.

- He is sitting down at the table.
- A grinning mouth, "hee hee!"

fu フ

Sounds like both 'fu' and 'hu' - or 'hfu'.

フ フ

Practice writing フ by tracing these characters, using one stroke.

Try to maintain accurate shapes while writing フ on a smaller scale.

Mnemonic.

Examples.

- Who said 7 is lucky?
- A huge beak. Maybe an owl... "hu hu!" (or "fu fu!")

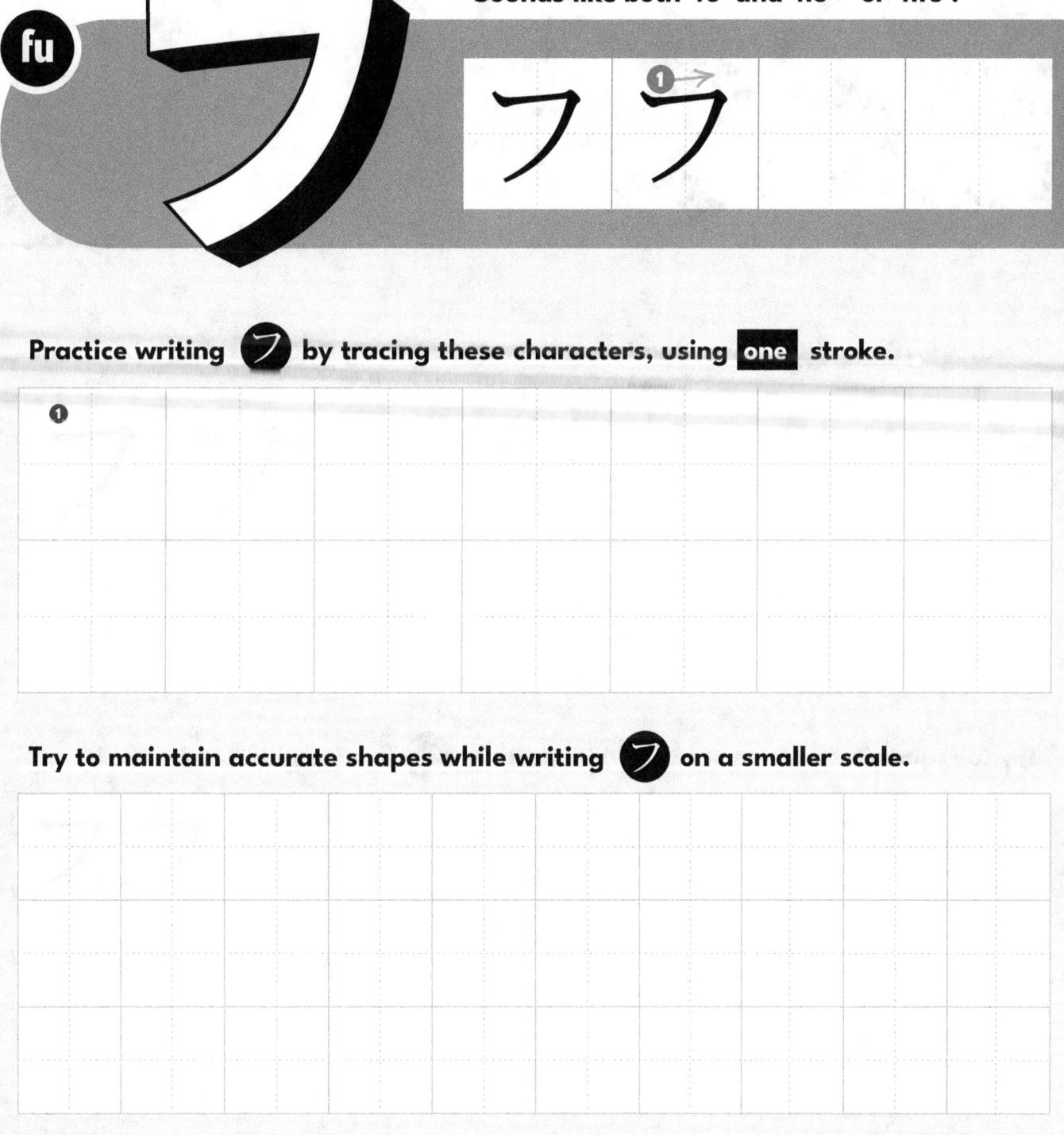

Pronounce as 'heh', almost like 'hey'.

he

ヘ

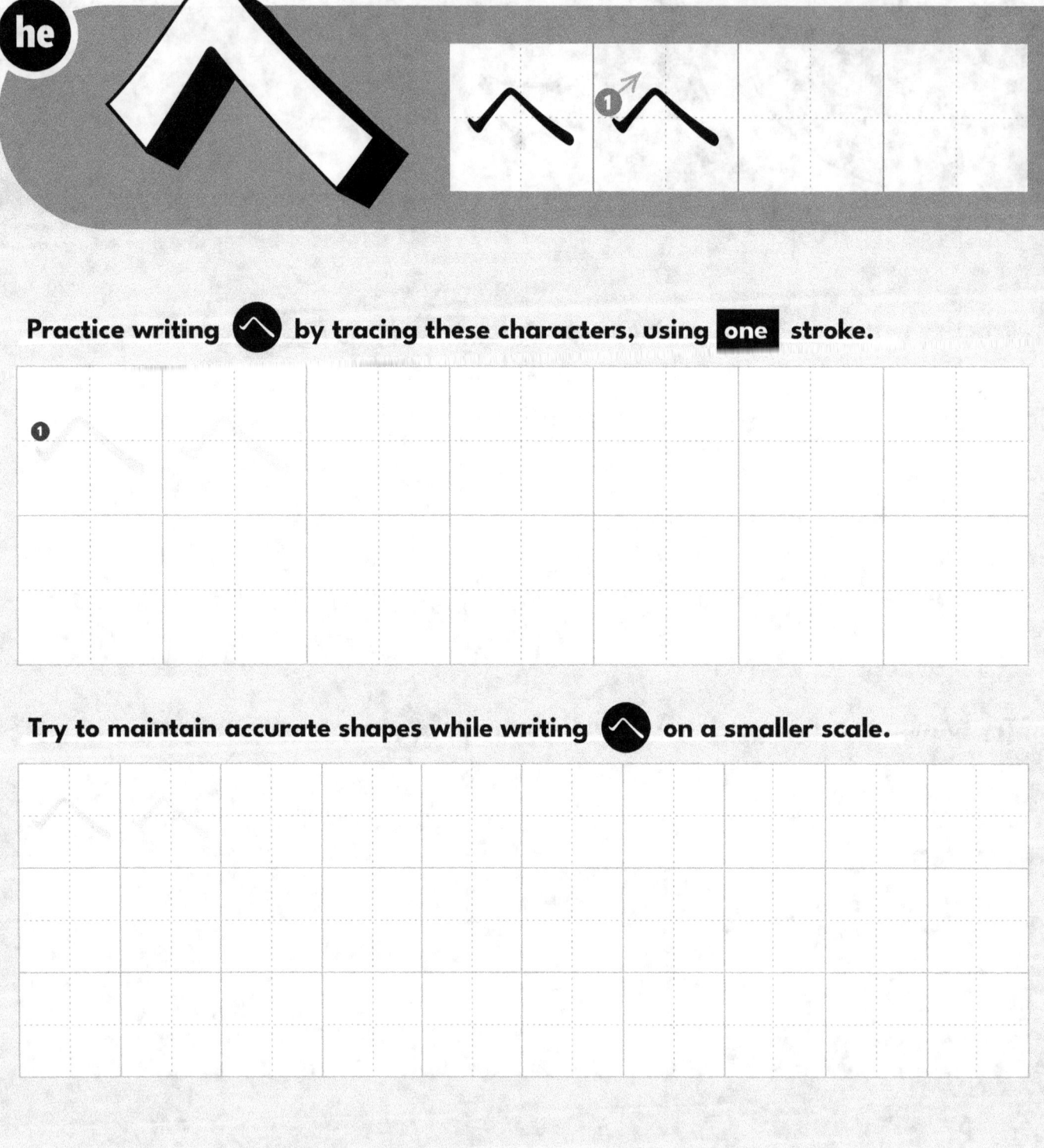

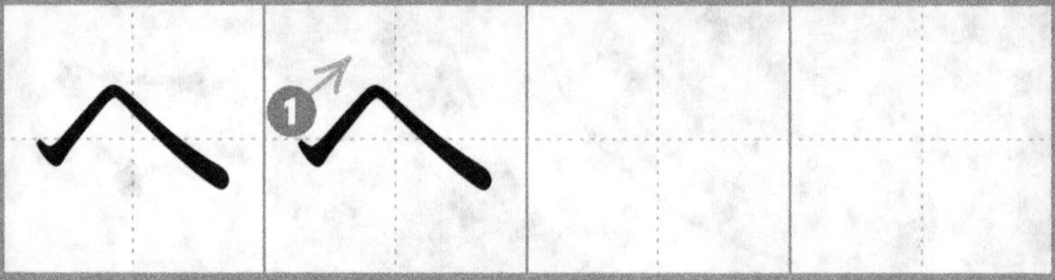

Practice writing ヘ by tracing these characters, using one stroke.

Try to maintain accurate shapes while writing ヘ on a smaller scale.

Mnemonic.

Examples.

- Same as hiragana

ho ホ

Pronounce like the 'ho-' in horse.

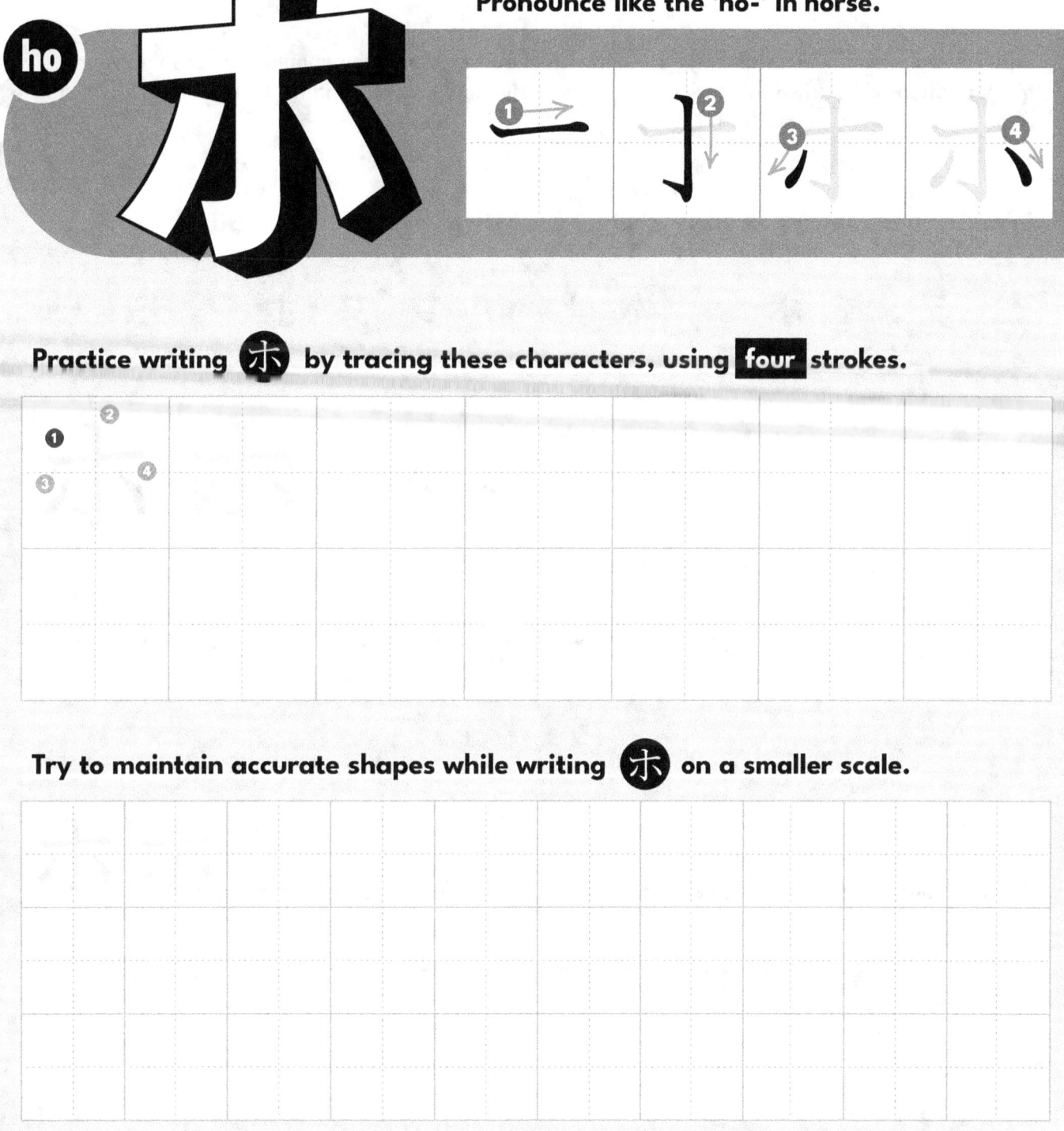

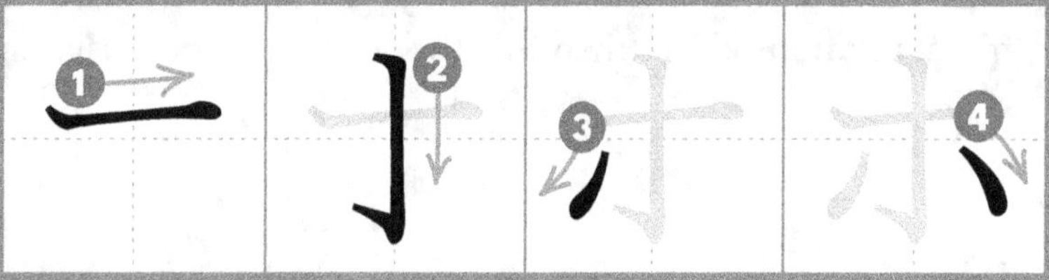

Practice writing ホ by tracing these characters, using **four** strokes.

Try to maintain accurate shapes while writing ホ on a smaller scale.

Mnemonic.

Examples.

- A holy cross
- Outstretch arms, holding a cross.

With several similar shapes amongst the characters in the groups, this should start pushing your memorization skills. When this task becomes too easy, time yourself and try to improve.

Practice pronouncing each symbol as you write the romaji beneath.

ニ	テ	ネ	ホ	ヘ	ネ	ヒ	ト	フ	ヌ	ホ	ヘ	ヌ	チ

ヘ	ホ	ヌ	ネ	ス	ニ	ヒ	コ	フ	ニ	ヌ	ハ	ナ	ソ

フ	ハ	ノ	ハ	オ	ノ	ナ	ヒ	ハ	ヒ	ホ	ネ	タ	ナ

Take a 5-minute break, and then do the same for these symbols too.

セ	ノ	オ	コ	オ	ツ	キ	ナ	ス	フ	シ	チ	ヒ	ク

ア	ケ	テ	ツ	エ	ハ	カ	ニ	サ	ヌ	ケ	シ	ソ	タ

セ	ソ	キ	ホ	ト	コ	ウ	ネ	イ	ク	ウ	チ	サ	ア

This time, take a 10-minute break and come back to complete these.

ツ	テ	チ	ト	キ	エ	ホ	ノ	サ	イ	ヒ	フ	ニ	シ
セ	ソ	ス	テ	コ	ニ	ハ	ネ	ヌ	ヘ	ツ	ネ	ヌ	ウ
ナ	シ	サ	タ	セ	タ	ヘ	ナ	チ	ス	ノ	ホ	ア	ハ

After a much longer break, add the romaji for each symbol below.

エ	ハ	ヒ	チ	テ	ホ	ヘ	ツ	セ	イ	ト	ヌ	ソ	ウ
ナ	ヘ	タ	サ	ツ	ス	テ	タ	ノ	ネ	ヌ	ス	セ	ニ
ニ	コ	ホ	ノ	シ	ネ	ア	ハ	ナ	サ	チ	フ	シ	キ

K4. The M & Y Columns

This group of eight katakana symbols represent the sounds in both the M and Y columns of the basic katakana table. Pronunciations will be familiar but with characters that look completely different.

Symbols in this learning block.

マ	ミ	ム	メ	モ
ma	mi	mu	me	mo
ヤ		ユ		ヨ
ya		yu		yo

Pronunciation

There are no new exceptions to the pronunciation of these characters.

ma マ

Sounds like the 'ma-' in the word man.

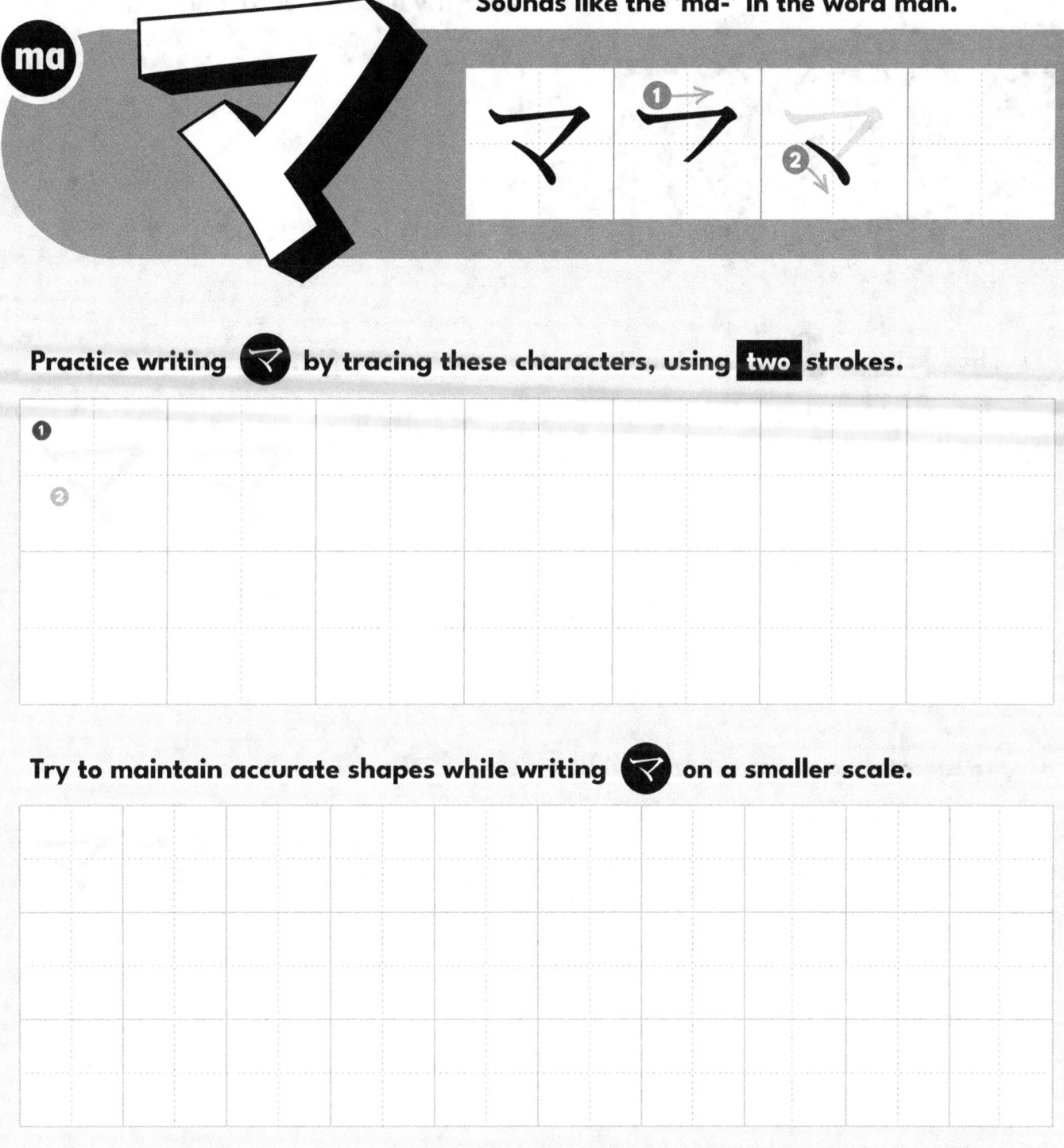

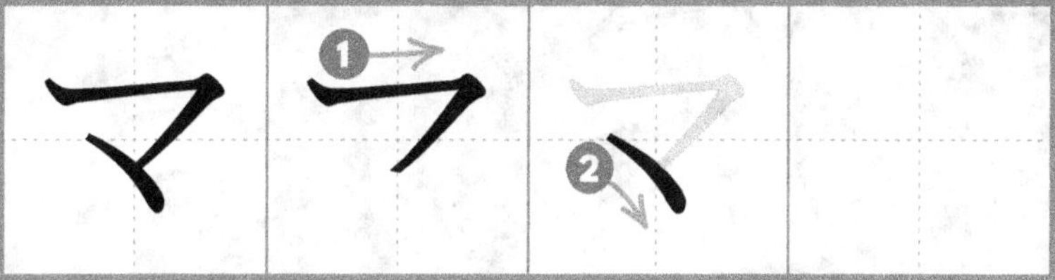

Practice writing マ by tracing these characters, using **two** strokes.

Try to maintain accurate shapes while writing マ on a smaller scale.

Mnemonic.

Examples.

- Imagine a martini cocktail glass
- Maths, angles et.
- Marathon medal

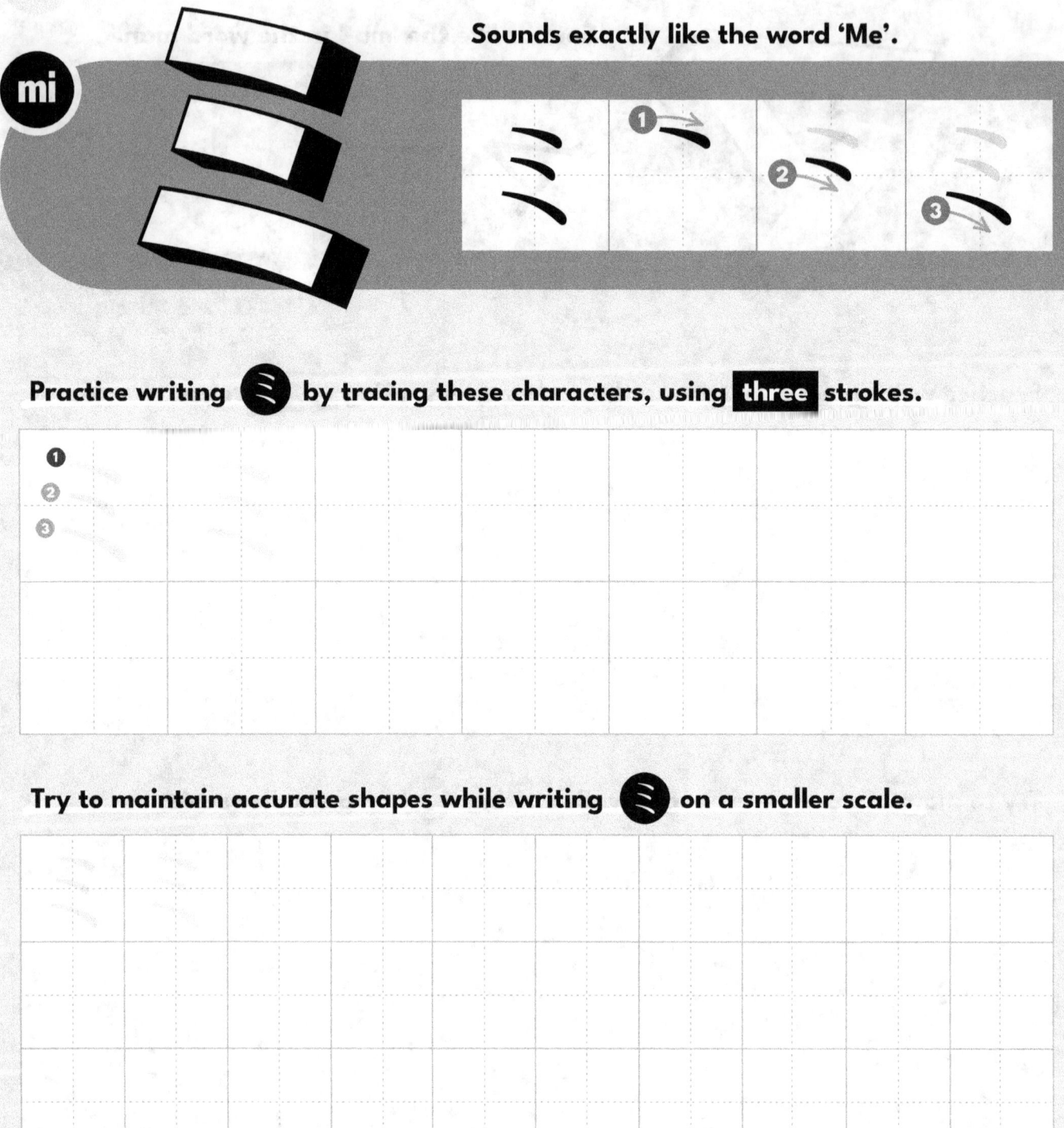

mi

Sounds exactly like the word 'Me'.

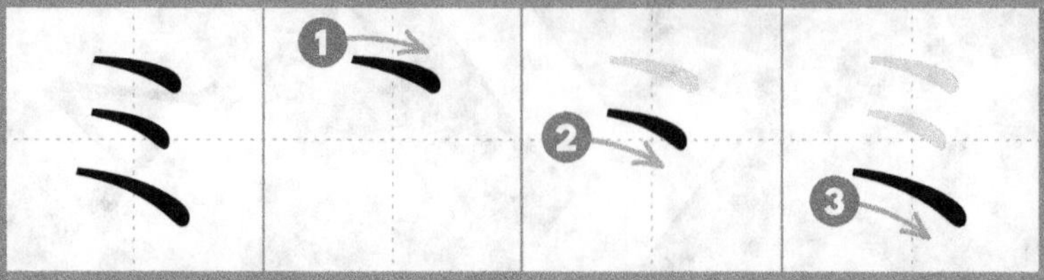

Practice writing ミ by tracing these characters, using three strokes.

Try to maintain accurate shapes while writing ミ on a smaller scale.

Mnemonic.

Examples.

- The letter 'm' on its side, now 'E'... "me!"
- Three <u>mi</u>ssiles

mu ム

Similar to the 'moo' in moon.

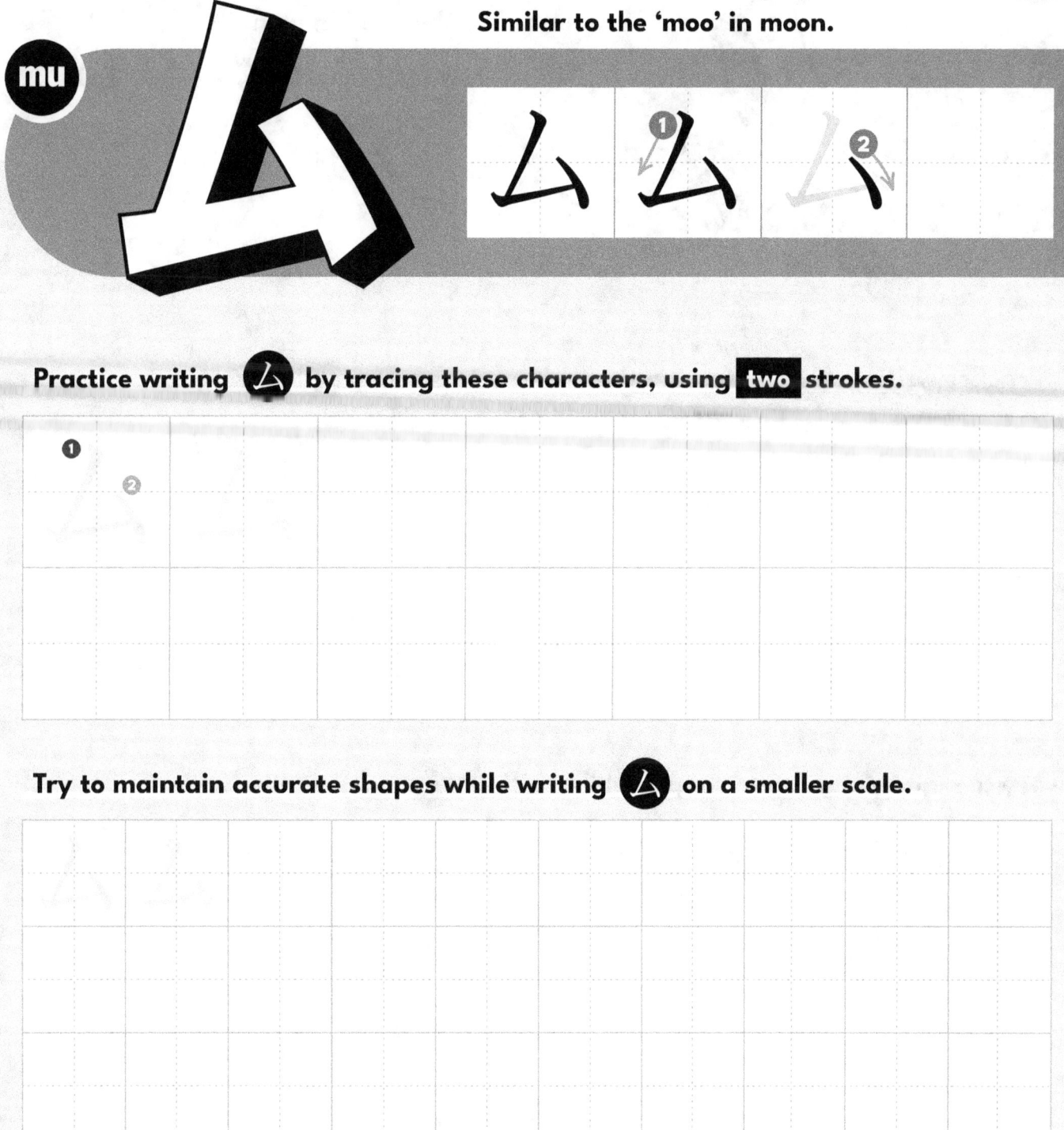

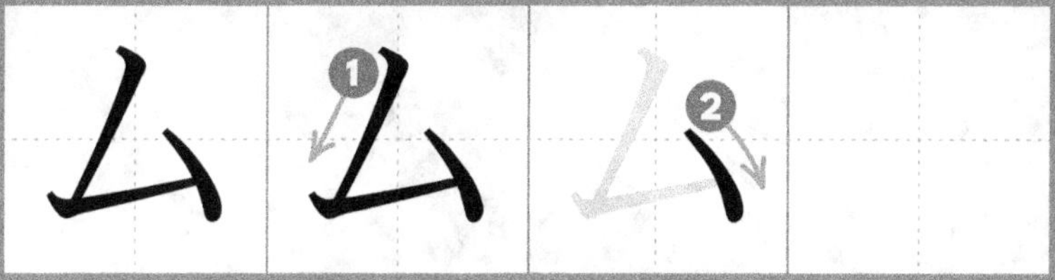

Practice writing ム by tracing these characters, using two strokes.

Try to maintain accurate shapes while writing ム on a smaller scale.

Mnemonic.

Examples.

- An arm, flexing to show off <u>mu</u>scles

me メ

Sounds like the 'me-' in men.

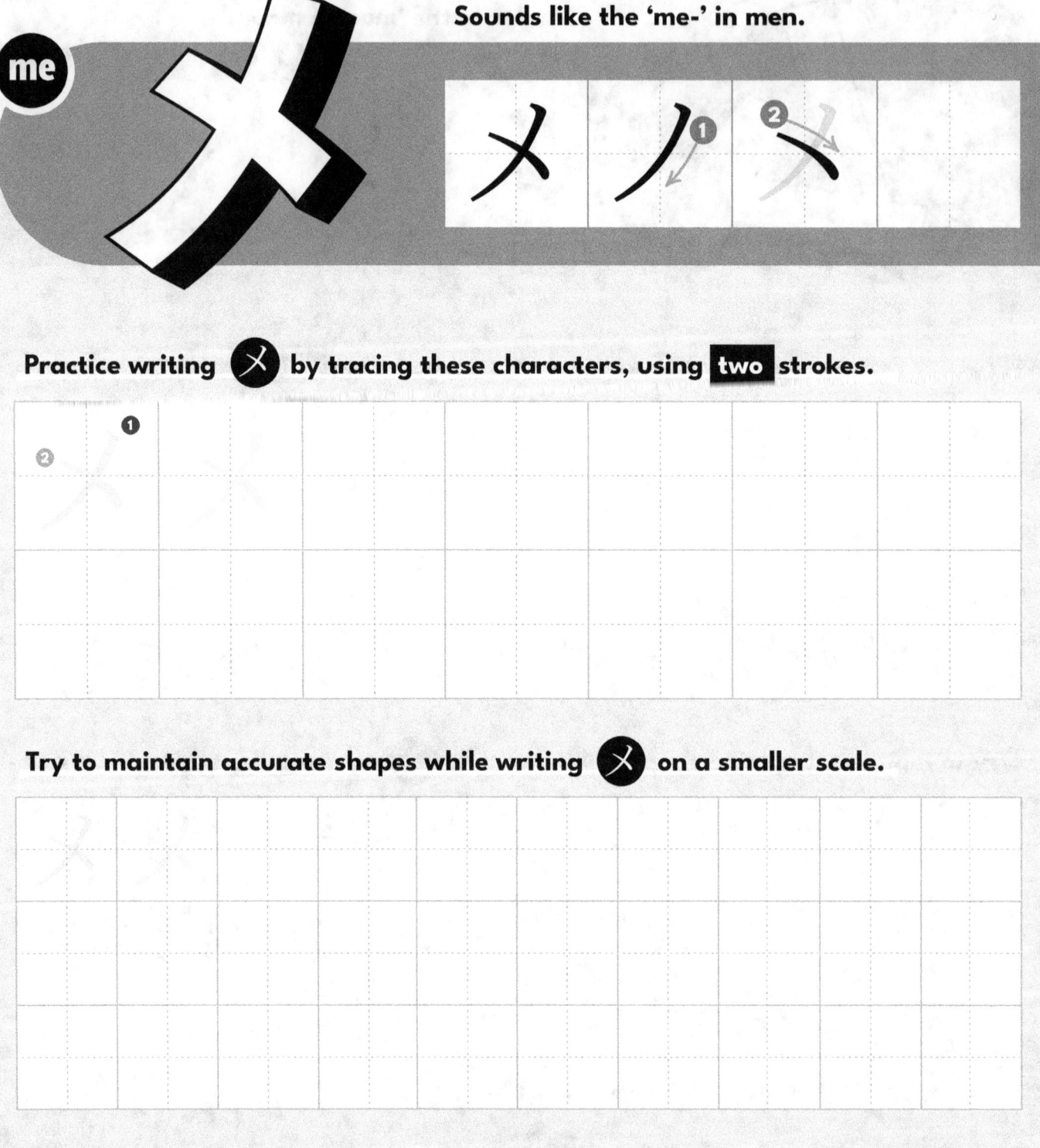

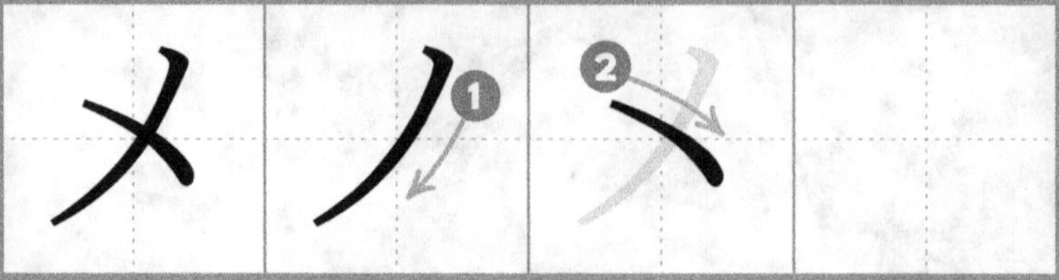

Practice writing メ by tracing these characters, using two strokes.

Try to maintain accurate shapes while writing メ on a smaller scale.

Mnemonic.

Examples.

- **Simplified version of hiragana 'Me', the Japanese for eye. Picture X on an eye**

mo モ

Sounds similar to the 'mo-' in monsoon.

モ ① ② ③

Practice writing モ by tracing these characters, using three strokes.

Try to maintain accurate shapes while writing モ on a smaller scale.

Mnemonic.

Examples.

- Similar to hiragana
- More worms on a hook shape.

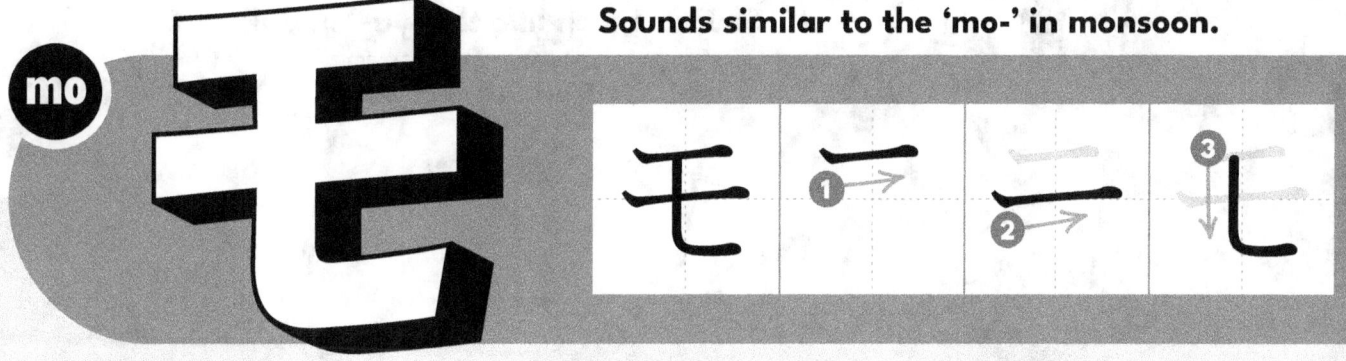

ya ヤ

Sounds much like the 'ya-' in yak.

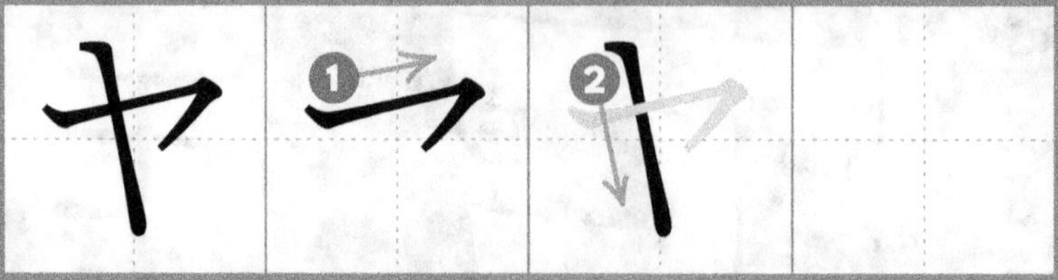

Practice writing ヤ by tracing these characters, using two strokes.

Try to maintain accurate shapes while writing ヤ on a smaller scale.

Mnemonic.

Examples.

- Similar to hiragana
- Yak with one horn

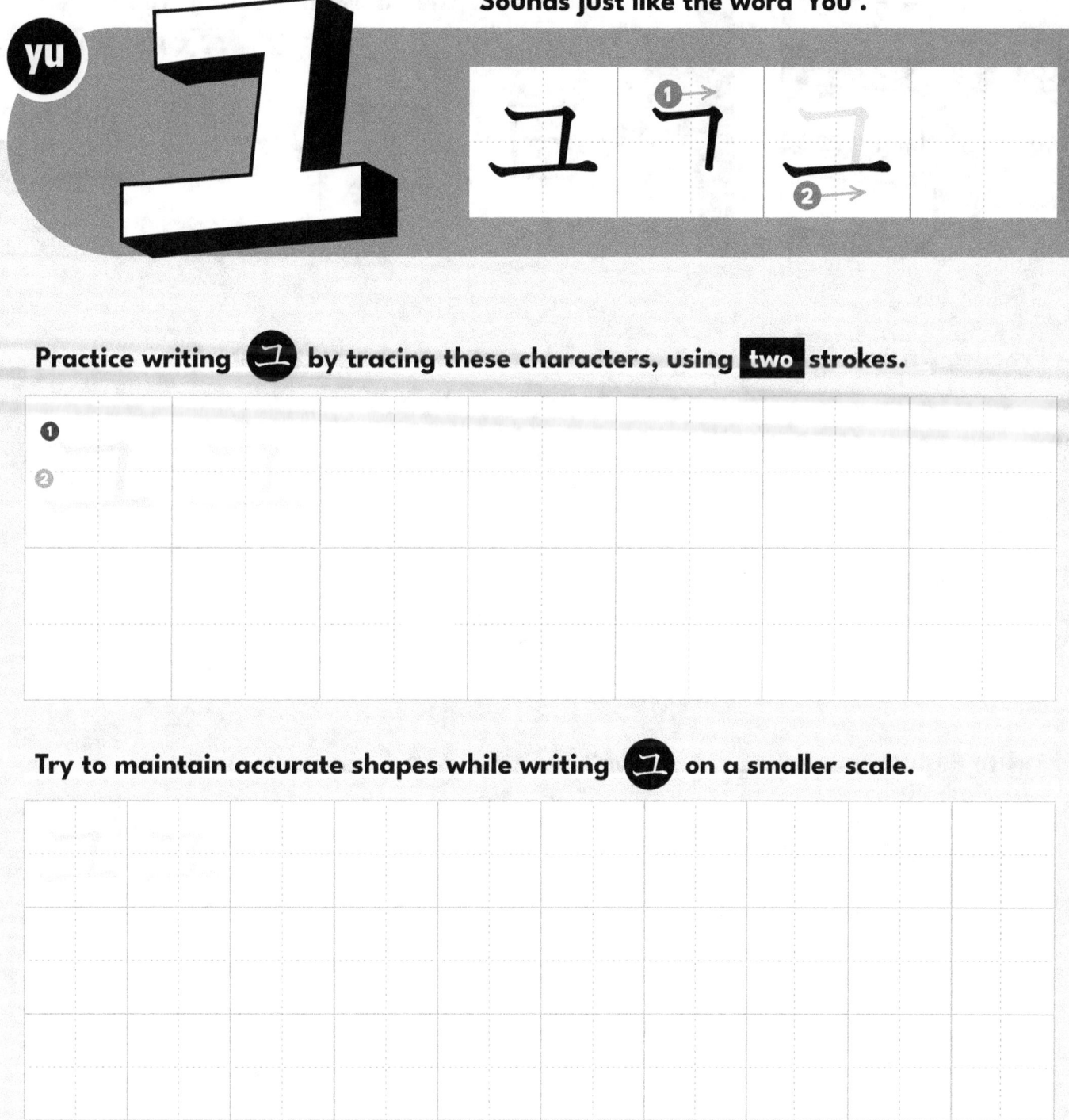

yu

ㅠ

Sounds just like the word 'You'.

ㅠ ㅜ ㅠ

Practice writing ㅠ by tracing these characters, using **two** strokes.

Try to maintain accurate shapes while writing ㅠ on a smaller scale.

Mnemonic.

Examples.

- Like a submarine, or YU-boat (u-boat)

yo ㅋ

Sounds like the informal greeting 'Yo'.

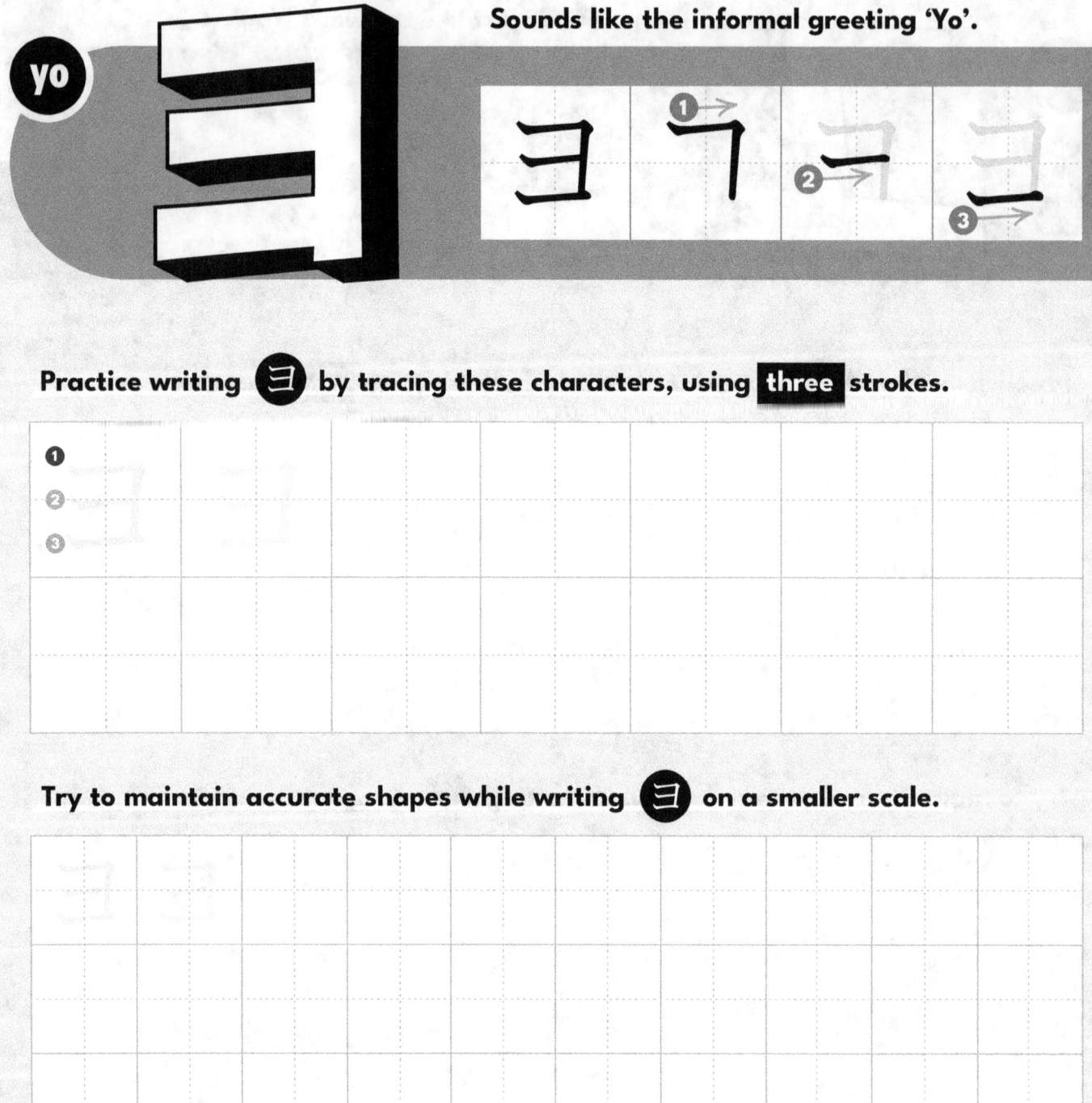

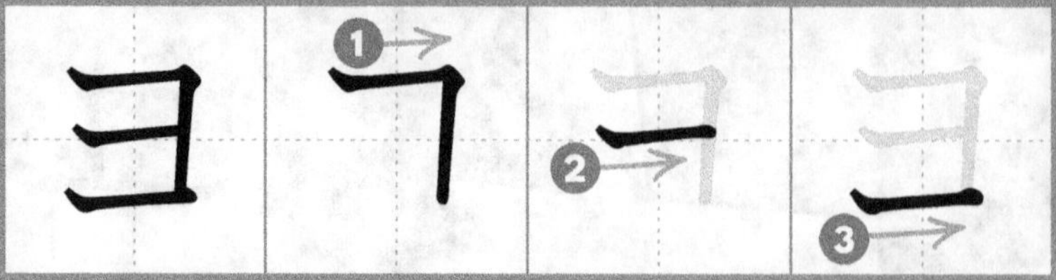

Practice writing ㅋ by tracing these characters, using three strokes.

Try to maintain accurate shapes while writing ㅋ on a smaller scale.

Mnemonic.

Examples.

- **Backwards 'E'... "Yo, what happened?"**
- **Awkward yoga pose.**

The gaps between each group are helping to teach your brain that you will need to recall this new information again in the future - and that it should store it in your longer-term memory.

Practice pronouncing each symbol as you write the romaji beneath.

ナ	マ	ヌ	ニ	ミ	モ	ヘ	ハ	ス	フ	モ	メ	ヨ	ノ

ネ	ム	ヘ	ツ	メ	ノ	ヒ	ナ	ハ	ユ	ヤ	ユ	ム	シ

ホ	ミ	マ	ク	メ	ホ	モ	ヌ	マ	ヨ	ユ	ム	ヒ	ネ

Take a 5-minute break, and then do the same for these symbols too.

ホ	コ	カ	ネ	メ	ト	ノ	モ	ユ	ハ	ク	イ	サ	フ

ヌ	ナ	ヘ	ス	ム	フ	オ	ヤ	ヨ	ツ	ヒ	ミ	ソ	シ

モ	ニ	エ	ケ	マ	ア	テ	メ	タ	キ	チ	ム	ウ	セ

Regular breaks are a vital part of the memorization process!

This time, take a 10-minute break and come back to complete these.

ミ	ユ	ツ	ア	ナ	コ	サ	ユ	カ	ヒ	オ	ハ	ネ	ヌ

ノ	モ	タ	ウ	ス	イ	ム	チ	メ	ヨ	ミ	ト	ヤ	ヘ

ク	キ	ム	ホ	ケ	ハ	ヤ	フ	セ	エ	マ	シ	テ	ニ

After a much longer break, add the romaji for each symbol below.

タ	セ	ヤ	ス	ヌ	メ	ケ	モ	ツ	ト	ム	フ	ヤ	イ

ハ	オ	ネ	ニ	ナ	テ	ウ	ハ	ヒ	ノ	コ	ク	マ	サ

シ	ム	ア	ユ	ユ	カ	ホ	ミ	キ	チ	ヨ	ミ	エ	ヘ

K5. The R & W Columns + N

This is your final group of basic katakana to learn. After these few pages, you will have learned all of the basic kana symbols. The section that follows will cover additional sounds that kana are used to represent. Fortunately, there are no new symbols to learn.

Symbols in this learning block.

ラ	リ	ル	レ	ロ
ra	**ri**	**ru**	**re**	**ro**
ワ		ヲ		ン
wa		**wo**		**n**

Pronunciation

Refer to the exercises in the hiragana section to assist with pronunciation *'r-'* sounds.

ra

ラ

Sounds a lot like the 'ra-' in rabbit.

ラ ① ②

Practice writing ラ by tracing these characters, using **two** strokes.

Try to maintain accurate shapes while writing ラ on a smaller scale.

Mnemonic.

Examples.

- Similar to hiragana, long-eared rabbit
- Umbrellas simply stop the rain.

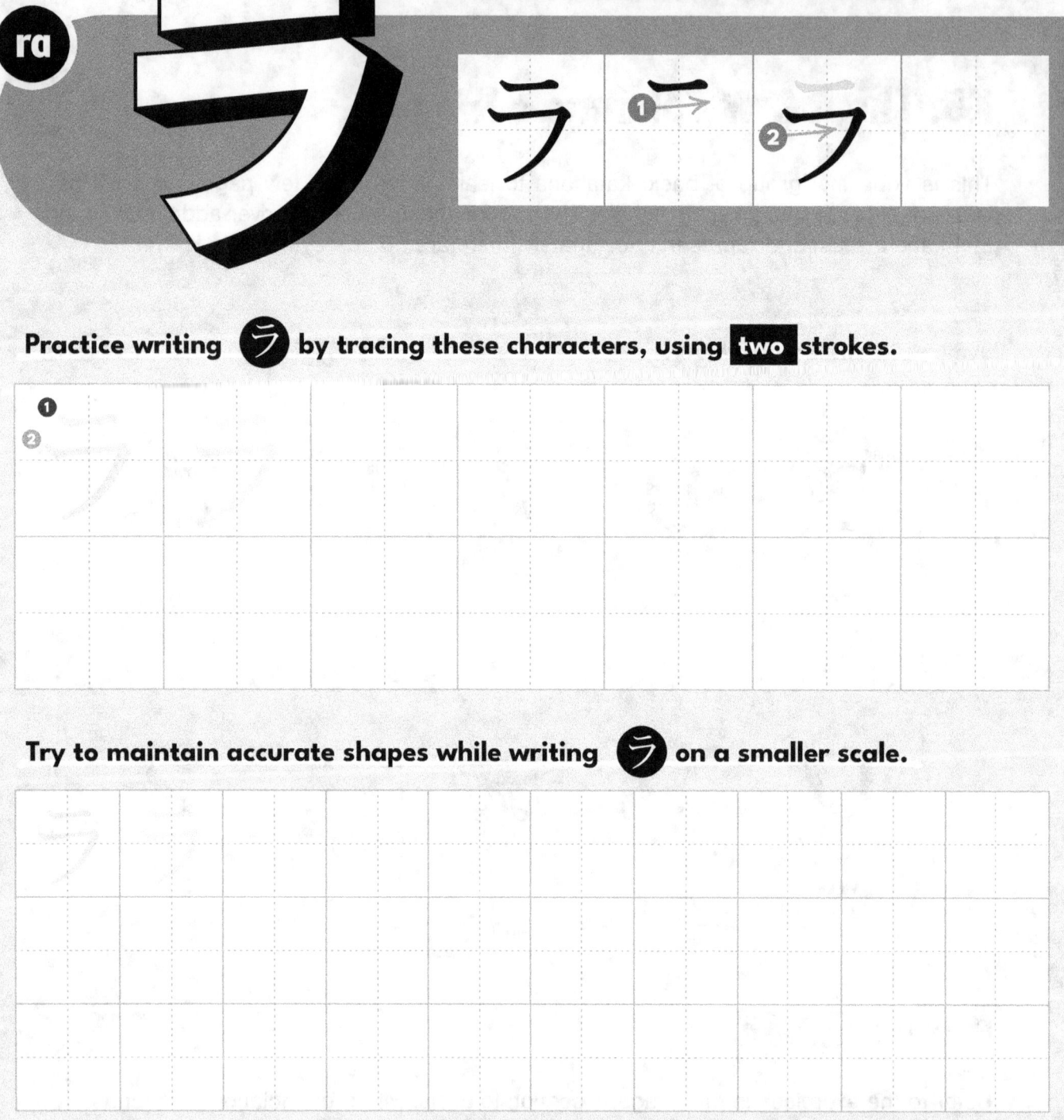

ri リ

Sounds a lot like the 'rea-' in reach.

Practice writing リ by tracing these characters, using **two** strokes.

Try to maintain accurate shapes while writing リ on a smaller scale.

Mnemonic.

Examples.

- Same as hiragana
- Two reeds
- Reaching arms

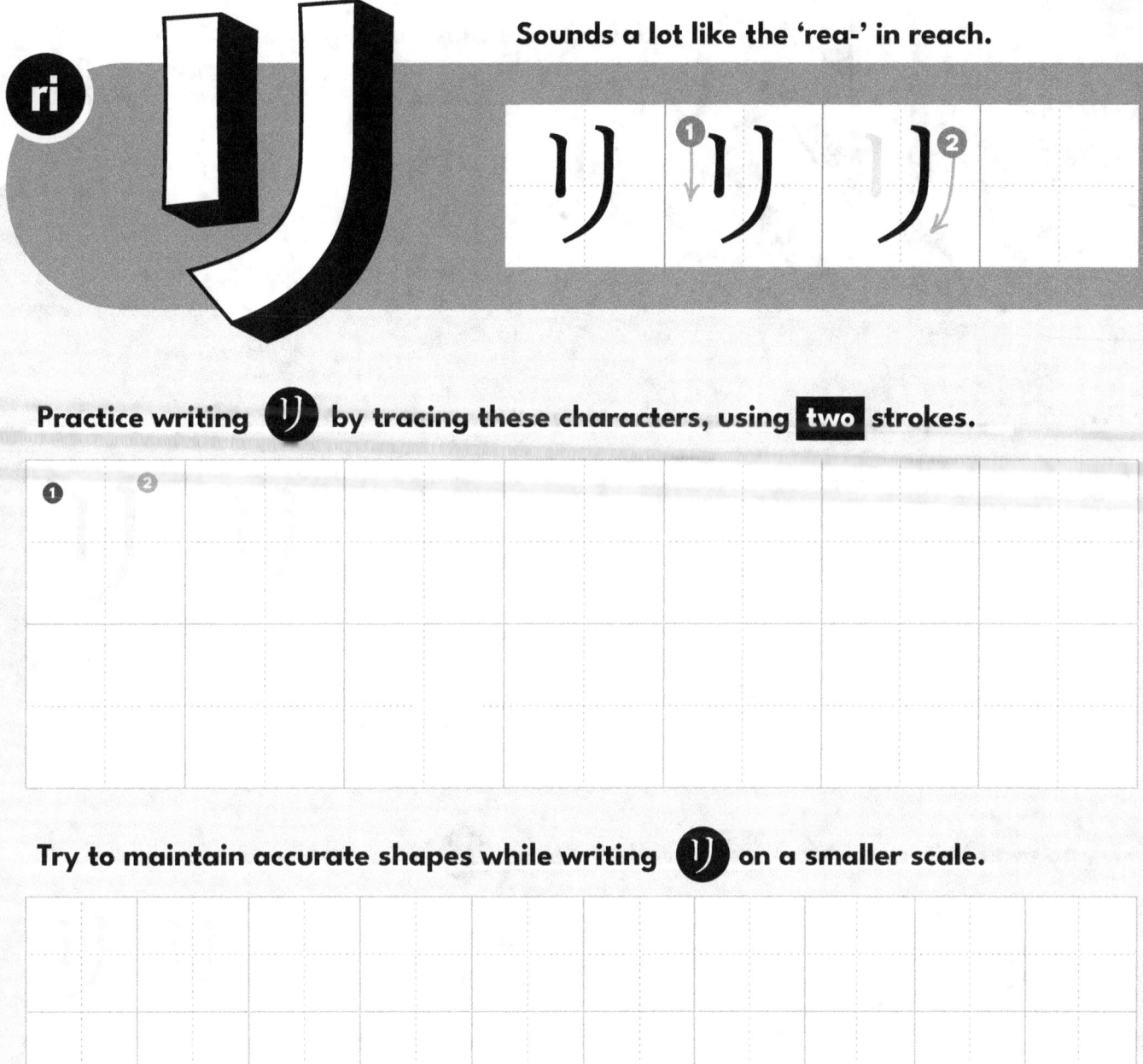

ru ル

Sounds like the '-ru' in guru.

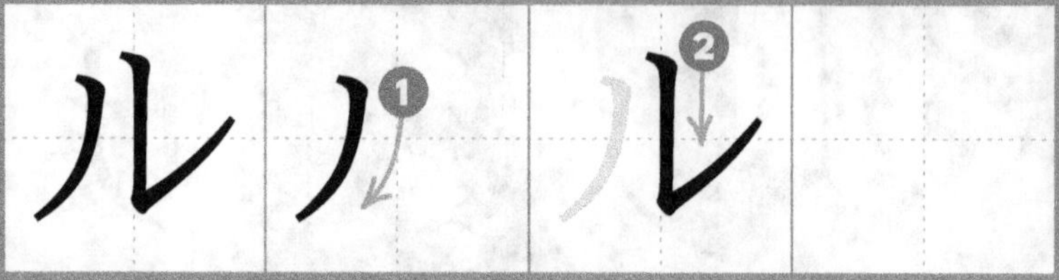

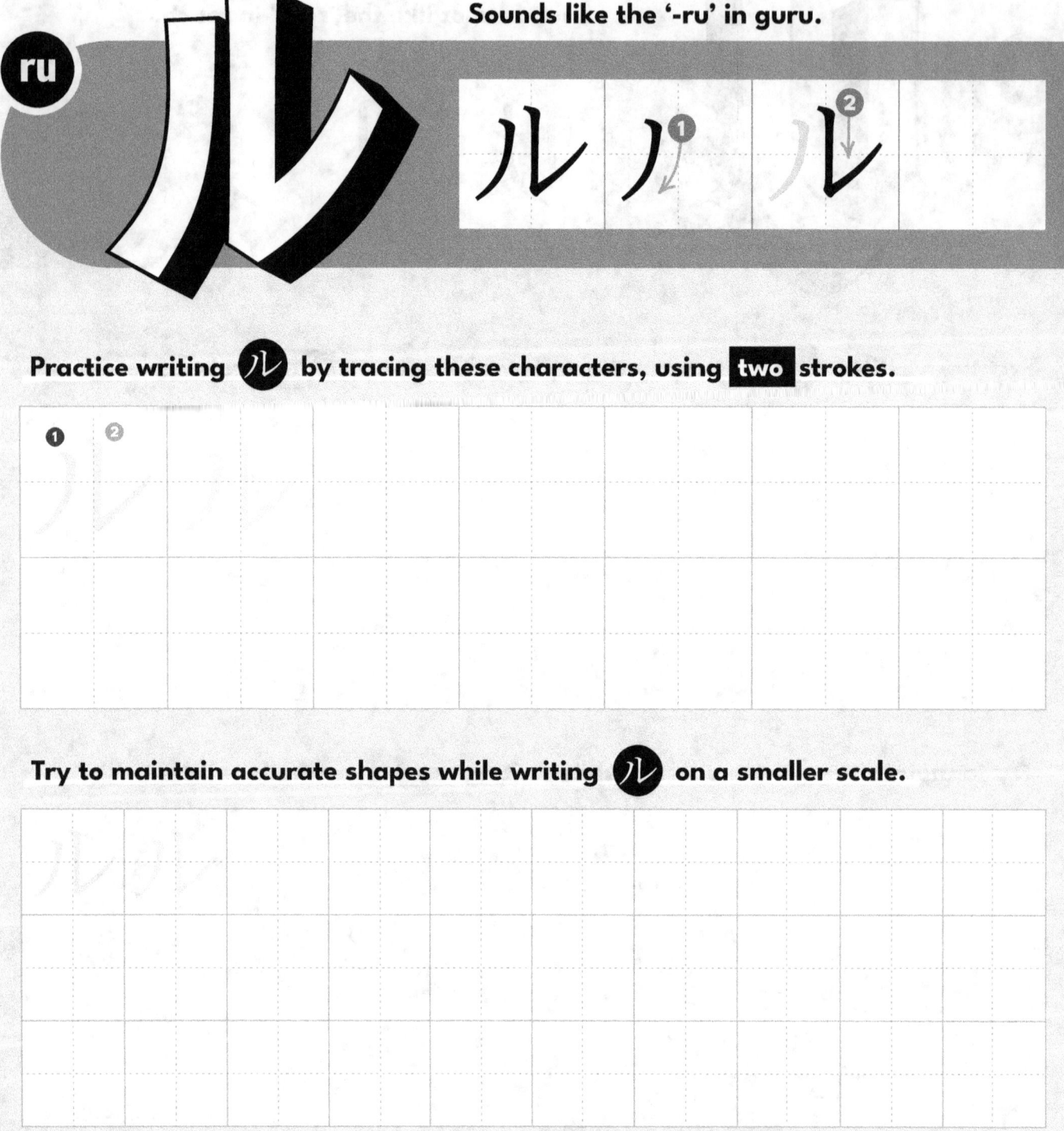

Practice writing ル by tracing these characters, using two strokes.

Try to maintain accurate shapes while writing ル on a smaller scale.

Mnemonic.

Examples.

- Routes one and two
- A tree's roots

Sounds like the 'ra-' in race, like 'ray'.

re

レ

レ レ

Practice writing レ by tracing these characters, using one stroke.

Try to maintain accurate shapes while writing レ on a smaller scale.

Mnemonic.

Examples.

- Like hiragana 'shi' but she has long red hair.
- Lemon wedge, which is 'remon' in Japanese

ro

Sounds like the '-rro' in churro.

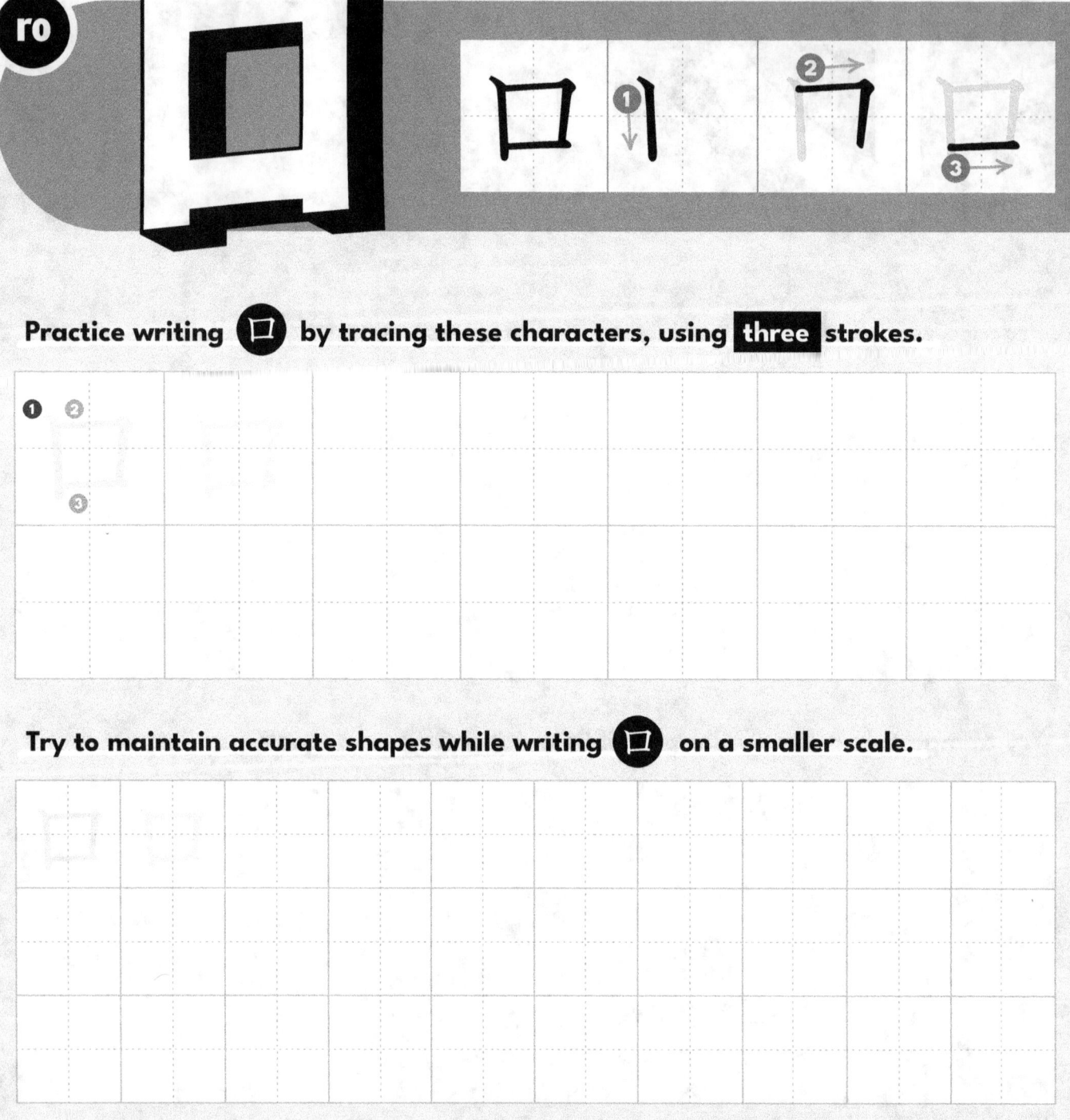

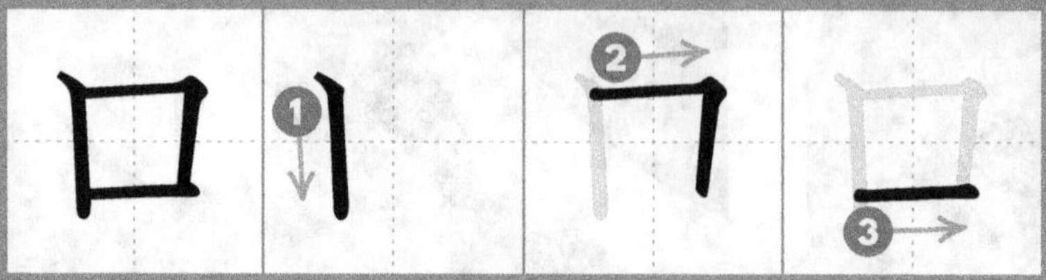

Practice writing ロ by tracing these characters, using three strokes.

Try to maintain accurate shapes while writing ロ on a smaller scale.

Mnemonic.

Examples.

- Robot head shape
- A sign that says "road tunnel ahead"

wa ワ

Sounds like the 'wa-' in wacky or wax.

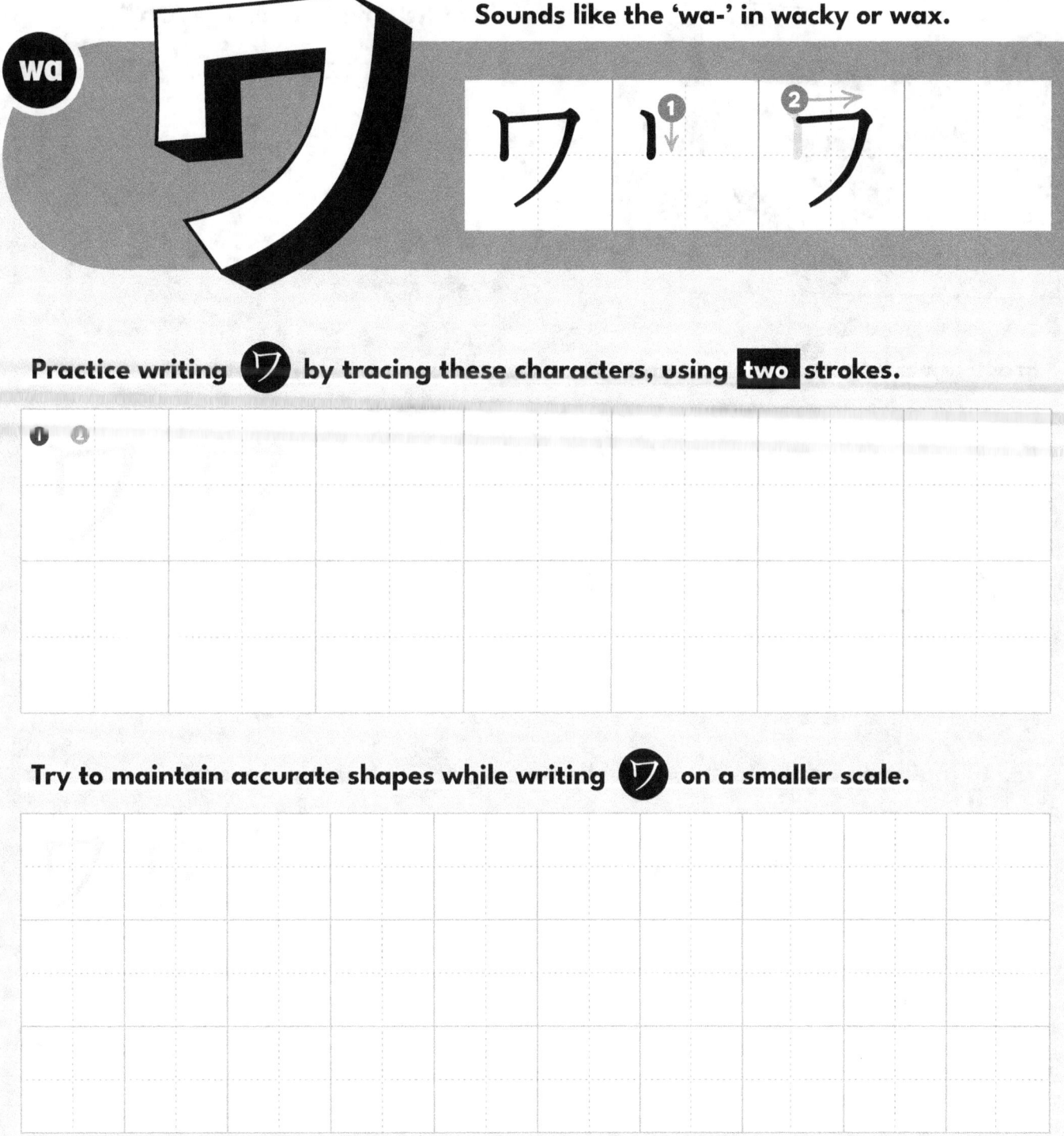

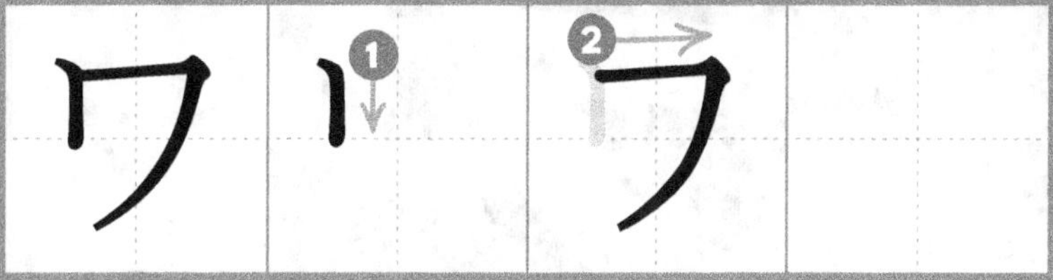

Practice writing ワ by tracing these characters, using two strokes.

Try to maintain accurate shapes while writing ワ on a smaller scale.

Mnemonic.

Examples.

- Shape of question marks... "What?"
- Picture a wine glass

wo ヲ

With a silent 'w', this sounds like 'Oh?'

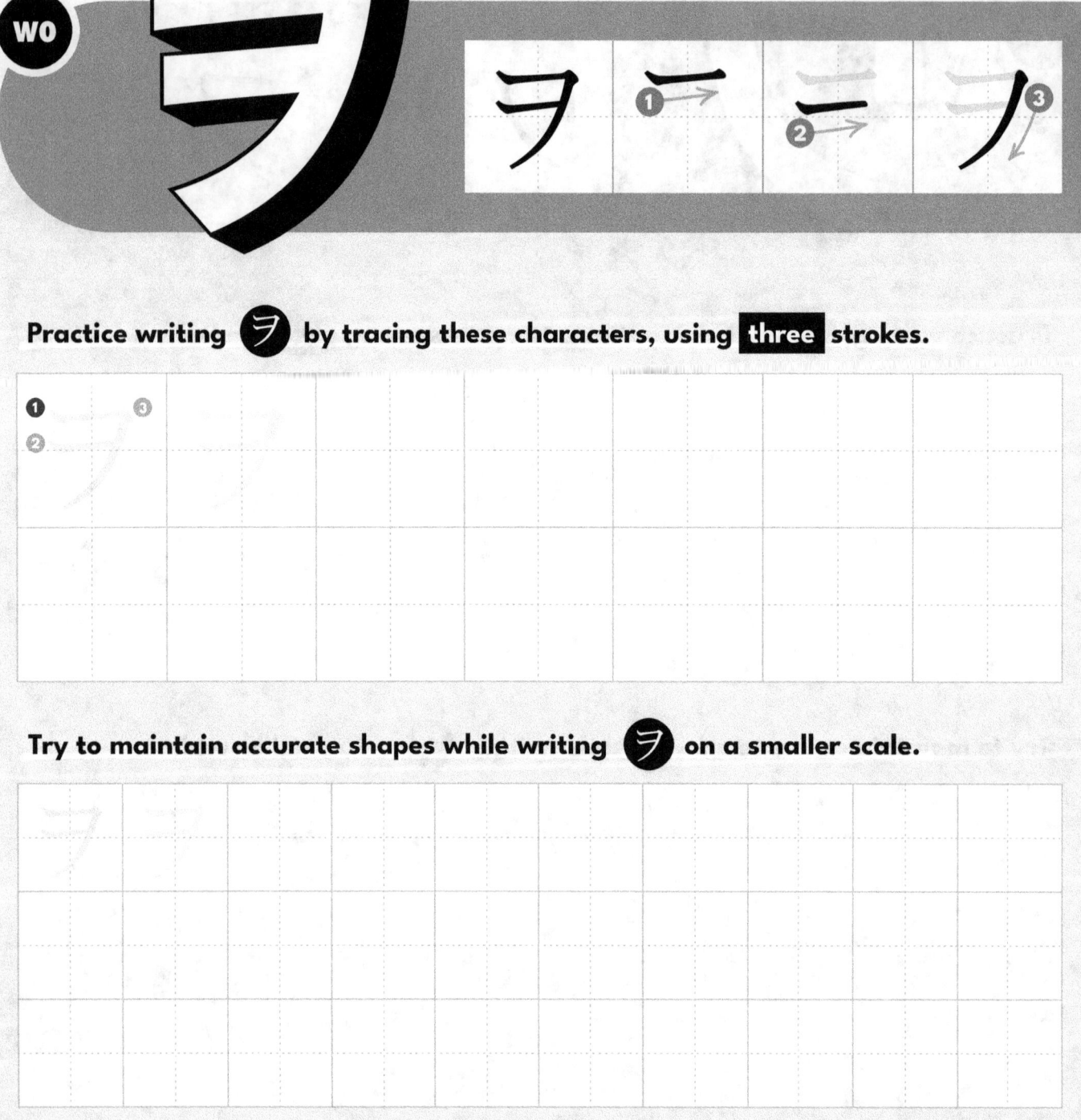

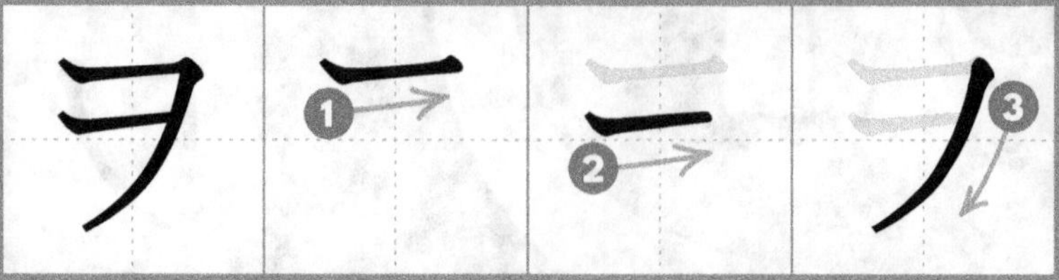

Practice writing ヲ by tracing these characters, using three strokes.

Try to maintain accurate shapes while writing ヲ on a smaller scale.

Mnemonic.

Examples.

- "Woah, a double-7!"
- 7 sticking a tongue out... "woah!"

n ン

Similar to the '-n' in plane, or 'nnn'.

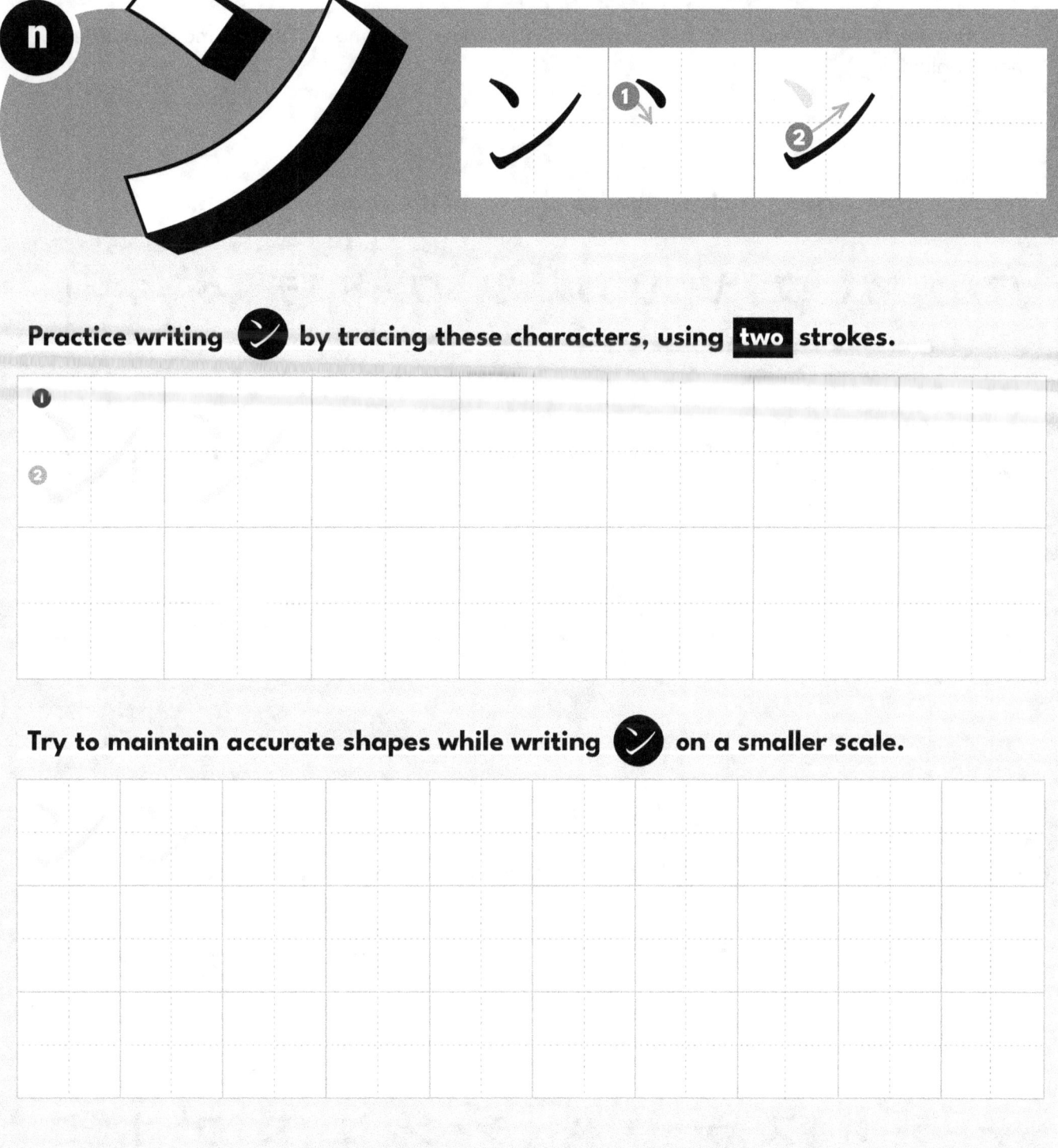

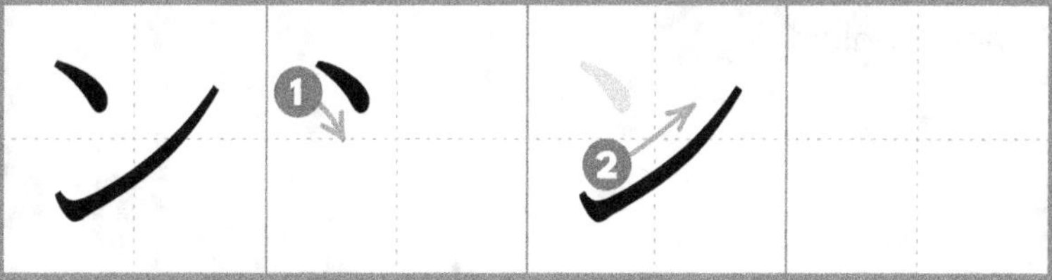

Practice writing ン by tracing these characters, using two strokes.

Try to maintain accurate shapes while writing ン on a smaller scale.

Mnemonic.

Examples.

- First, a crooked smile... now, 'shi' is wi<u>nk</u>ing (small horizontal lines compared to tsu & ni)

Now that you have learned all 46 basic katakana, the following memory exercises may be a little more challenging.

Practice pronouncing each symbol as you write the romaji beneath.

ワ	メ	ハ	フ	ヤ	リ	ル	ツ	ワ	ト	チ	ヘ	ホ	レ
ラ	ヌ	ソ	ン	ワ	リ	テ	タ	ユ	リ	ン	ム	ル	ナ
ミ	ロ	レ	ネ	マ	ヲ	ル	レ	ン	ニ	モ	ラ	ロ	ヨ

Take a 5-minute break, and then do the same for these symbols too.

ヲ	ノ	ヒ	ヲ	ロ	ノ	ヒ	ラ	エ	カ	タ	キ	ヤ	ソ
チ	ラ	オ	ス	テ	ウ	ネ	シ	ン	ニ	ヌ	フ	ホ	ミ
ワ	レ	モ	ナ	イ	リ	ヲ	セ	ヘ	コ	ケ	ワ	マ	ヨ

Take your time and try to complete each group without looking at the previous pages. Don't forget to take a break between each group.

This time, take a 10-minute break and come back to complete these.

ア	ト	ハ	ツ	ロ	ク	サ	ム	ル	メ	ユ	モ	ロ	ラ
メ	チ	ル	ム	ヨ	ヤ	ネ	モ	リ	ハ	ラ	ノ	キ	ヌ
ワ	イ	ツ	カ	ニ	ヲ	リ	コ	タ	ウ	ア	ン	レ	ロ

After a much longer break, add the romaji for each symbol below.

ヲ	マ	ン	ミ	メ	ユ	ホ	ヨ	エ	マ	シ	レ	ム	コ
イ	ワ	マ	カ	タ	ハ	ネ	マ	ツ	ヨ	チ	ニ	ヌ	ロ
ル	ウ	ノ	レ	モ	メ	ヤ	ム	ラ	ヲ	ル	キ	ア	リ

Some of the sample words in katakana may sound familiar when pronounced.

ヘリ
helicopter

メモ
memo

ヒレ
fillet

ミルク
milk

カヌー
canoe

ワニス
varnish

ローン
loan

ナイフ
knife

フレー
Hooray!

ノート
note, Notebook

タイヤ
tire

カメラ
camera

ネーム
name/reputation

ユーモア
humor

サラリー
salary

ハンマー
hammer

ヨーヨー
yo-yo

ハンカチ
handkerchief

ユニーク
unique

ネクタイ
necktie

PART 4

ひらがな
カタカナ

Additional Sounds

The basic kana characters cover a lot of the syllable sounds that we need to pronounce Japanese, but not all of them. Both sets of letters that you have just learned can be adapted with some extra annotation, to show when the sound that is normally used will need to be altered. When one of these different sounds is required the existing sets of letters are accompanied by either small marks or even extra kana. The next few pages will show you what these differences are, and how the sounds can be adapted.

Voiced Consonants

An additional set of ***'voiced'*** sounds are created by altering how we pronounce certain consonant sounds. The modified sounds are similar to their original, except that they require vibration in your vocal cords. Essentially, one of the basic consonant sounds is replaced by another, illustrated with a different *Romaji* letter.

Basic consonant sounds, such as *t-*, *s-*, and *k-*, are produced without your voice box, as the movement of air creates these sounds. You can check this by making a *'t-'* sound once or twice - *remember, it's not the letter 'T' or "tee,"* but a short 't-' sound. These are 'voiceless' consonants, and we refer to kana such as **か/カ** *(ka)* and **た/タ** *(ta)* in the same way. The modified, 'voiced' versions are made with the same mouth shapes but also by adding *your voice.* For example, the *'k-'* in **か** *(ka)* becomes a *'g-,'* and *'t-'* changes into *'d-.'*

In written Japanese, existing kana characters with different pronunciations have extra ***diacritic marks***. In this case, they are also referred to as *'voicing marks'* as the new, modified consonant sounds are *'voiced'* versions of their initial form. ***Dakuten*** are two extra lines that we draw in the upper right, similar to quotation marks, and a small circle in the same position is called ***handakuten***.

Dakuten are attached to symbols that begin with *k*, *t*, s, and *h- sounds,* while only those starting with *h- sounds* have *handakuten.* Diacritic marks are written after all other strokes have been drawn.

	k ▼	t ▼	s ▼	h ▼
+ ゛	g	d	z	b
+ ゜				p

ho	ほ ▼	ホ ▼
bo	ぼ	ボ
po	ぽ	ポ

Voicing marks have been added to the basic kana - displayed to the right.

Romaji does not accurately illustrate Japanese sounds, so some characters are marked with an asterisk to show variation from overall patterns. A 'French' 'j-' sound is better suited to 'chi' and 'shi,' while 'z-' or 'dz-' sounds are closer matches for 'tsu' and 'su.'*

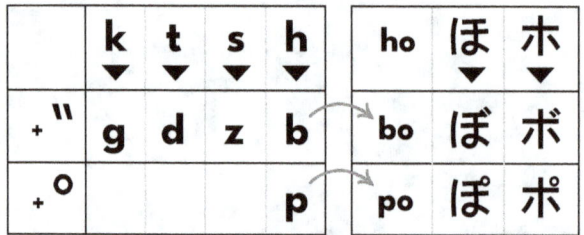

Hiragana

h/p	h/b	t/d	s/z	k/g	
ぱ pa	ば ba	だ da	ざ za	が ga	a
ぴ pi	び bi	ぢ ji (di)*	じ ji*	ぎ gi	i
ぷ pu	ぶ bu	づ zu (du)*	ず zu*	ぐ gu	u
ぺ pe	べ be	で de	ぜ ze	げ ge	e
ぽ po	ぼ bo	ど do	ぞ zo	ご go	o

Katakana

h/p	h/b	t/d	s/z	k/g	
パ pa	バ ba	ダ da	ザ za	ガ ga	a
ピ pi	ビ bi	ヂ ji (di)*	ジ ji*	ギ gi	i
プ pu	ブ bu	ヅ zu (du)*	ズ zu*	グ gu	u
ペ pe	ベ be	デ de	ゼ ze	ゲ ge	e
ポ po	ボ bo	ド do	ゾ zo	ゴ go	o

Combination Kana

Also referred to as ***compound kana***, these are the written representations of hybrid sounds made by combining two others. Essentially, an extra consonant sound is added to the front of another character. The most important thing to remember is that while we write them with two kana, they take ***one mora*** to say.

The rules for writing *compound kana* are the same for both hiragana and katakana scripts, including the new characters for *'voiced'* sounds from the previous pages.

The written form consists of one regular-sized character that usually ends with an *'-i'* sound, *such as* し/シ *(shi),* き/キ *(ki),* ち/チ *(chi), etc.,* and a second, small character, typically ゃ *(ya),* ゅ *(yu), or* ょ *(yo):*

H	き	+	よ	=	きょ
	ki		yo		kyo
K	キ	+	ヨ	=	キョ

Compound kana are used in writing completely different words to their equivalent, normal-sized counterparts. The difference in character size is more apparent when comparing words that are written using the same characters:

きよう ki-yo-u 'skillful'	ヒヨウ hi-yo-u 'cost'
きょう kyo-u 'today'	ヒョウ hyo-u 'hail'

A single mora can change the meaning of a word, but they are relatively easy to recognize with practice. A mispronounced or misheard compound sound can have a significant impact on the meaning of what is said:

Regular ゆ		
じゆう	*ji-ya-u*	"freedom"
Small ゅ		
じゅう	*jya-u*	"gun"

The chart on the next page shows the most common hybrid sounds, combining an initial character ending in an *'-i'* sound with a small symbol from the *'y-'* sounds. There is no need to memorize these characters if you can remember how to read and write a hybrid sound.

Compound kana with '-i' + 'y-' sounds tend to be associated with native Japanese words (kun'yomi). You will encounter some other, less common combination sounds, especially in words of foreign origin, but they can be considered exceptions to the rules above, and it is best to learn about those if and when you see them.

p	b	j	g	r	n	m	h	t	s	k	
ぴゃ ピャ pya	びゃ ビャ bya	じゃ ジャ ja/jya	ぎゃ ギャ gya	りゃ リャ rya	にゃ ニャ nya	みゃ ミャ mya	ひゃ ヒャ hya	ちゃ チャ cha	しゃ シャ sha	きゃ キャ kya	ya
ぴゅ ピュ pyu	びゅ ビュ byu	じゅ ジュ ju/jyu	ぎゅ ギュ gyu	りゅ リュ ryu	にゅ ニュ nyu	みゅ ミュ myu	ひゅ ヒュ hyu	ちゅ チュ chu	しゅ シュ shu	きゅ キュ kyu	yu
ぴょ ピョ pyo	びょ ビョ byo	じょ ジョ jo/jyo	ぎょ ギョ gyo	りょ リョ ryo	にょ ニョ nyo	みょ ミョ myo	ひょ ヒョ hyo	ちょ チョ cho	しょ ショ sho	きょ キョ kyo	yo

Long Vowels

Extended vowel sounds, such as *'-oo'* or *'-ee,'* are shown by adding a character or mark to the kana with the sound we need to double. They are called **長音** *(chouon)* in Japanese, and they are represented in different ways in each of the kana scripts. We can easily pronounce a long sound when talking, and the rules for writing them are not too difficult either.

When writing ***hiragana***, we add one of three vowel characters for long vowel sounds *(writing them at normal size)*:

For *'a'* sounds, it's an extra **あ** *(a)*
For *'i'* ***and*** *'e'* sounds, add **い** *(i)*
For *'u'* ***and*** *'o'* sounds, add **う** *(u)*

So, to extend the *'a'* part of **か** *(ka),* you add **あ** and write **かあ** *(ka-a)*. Similarly, to double the *'i'* in **き** *(ki),* you write **きい** *(ki-i)*. **く** becomes **くう** *(ku-u)*, and so on:

The popular examples showing the importance of correct pronunciation for long vowel sounds are to compare the Japanese spellings of 'grandfather' and 'uncle,' or 'aunt' and 'grandmother.' (*Your uncle or aunt may be offended if you refer to them as a grandparent!)*

おじさん	おじいさん
ojisan	*ojiisan*
"uncle"	"grandfather"

(the honorific title *'-san'* is added when using the respectful *Sonkeigo* speech)

Extended vowel sounds are far easier to write in ***katakana***, consisting of a simple line called the **長音符** *(chōonpu)*, or *'long sound mark,'* that follows the kana. Text in a vertical orientation has an upright line (**|**) which is located below the kana. Horizontal writing features a line that we draw horizontally, looking similar to a hyphen (**ー**):

Here, the symbols **キ** *(ku)* + **ユ** *(yu)* make combination-kana *'kyo,'* and the 'o' sound is extended with **ー** before writing the final **ト** *(to)*. For *'cake,'* you extend the *'e'* in **ケ** *(ke):*

キュート	ケーキ
kyuu to	*kee ki*
"cute"	"cake"

In Romaji, long vowel sounds can be represented by either writing the vowels out in full or using a *macron* (a diacritic mark) A macron is just a line above a vowel that shows its sound is longer when pronounced, e.g., *'Tōkyō,'* pronounced as *'Toukyou.'*

Long Consonants

Also referred to as ***double consonants***, we can write these sounds by adding a ***'small tsu'*** *(also called Sokuon)* between two kana. The consonant sound from a character that follows a small tsu should be heard twice when reading. It's the same in both hiragana and katakana, using the small **っ** and **ッ** symbols.

For example, a small **ッ** between **ロ***(ro)* and **ク** *(ku)* makes the word **ロック** pronounced as *"rokku,"* not *'ro-tsu-ku'* or *'ro-ku.'* It means 'rock (music)' as in **ロックンロール** *(rokkunrooru)*, or 'rock 'n' roll':

ロク	**ロック**
roku	ro +k ku

While words with a *small tsu* may look very similar to others, and pronunciation might not seem to vary much, they are entirely different words.

Adding a small **っ** between the characters **い** and **た** of the word **いた** makes the word **いった**. Pronunciation of this word is neither **いつた** *('i-tsu-ta')* or **いた** *('i-ta')* but, instead, **いった** is pronounced as *"i-t-ta."* The small tsu inherits a *'t-'* sound from the character **た** *(ta)*:

いた	**いった**
ita = [i][ta]	i t ta = [i][-t][ta]
"was *[there]*"	"said" *(e.g. he said yes)*
(居た)	(言った)

Small **っ** *or* **ッ** take one *mora* to pronounce, as though they were any other kana character, but they don't add an extra syllable sound. It can almost seem like you are stuttering when pronouncing words with double consonants. *The example above,* **いった** *might be spelled phonetically as "eet-ta." The extra 't' sound must be heard and squeezed into the same two morae as* **いた** *(i-ta).*

Long consonants are *'unvoiced'* in pronunciation, including those that are usually modified by *dakuten and handakuten*. In other words, *'voiced'* consonants that follow a *small tsu* are pronounced as if they do not have dakuten.

We write the word for 'bed' as **ベッド** *(beddo)*, but the **ド** *(do)* keeps its original **ト** *(to)* sound, as though written **ベット**. It's pronounced as *'be-t-to,'* not *'be-d-do.'* This word takes three *morae* to say:

ベド	**ベッド**
be-do	be d do = be-t-to
(no meaning)	"bed"

There are few words where double consonant sounds have dakuten, and they tend to be limited to foreign loanwords, so usually shown in katakana.

/////////////////////////////////// **PART 5**

Study Tools

This section provides some additional tools to aid in your studies. You could write directly in the book but feel free to cut out and copy the pages for personal use. I always try to keep the number of *empty* pages to a minimum, making room for more useful information in the earlier chapters.

The following double-sided sheets contain additional grid templates that are intended for character writing practice, with combinations of 1-inch or 0.7-inch squares, both with and without dotted center guidelines - each version should cater to a variety of purposes and preference.

Pages 185-198 contain double-sided templates that readers can cut out or copy to create a mini *flashcard* deck - helpful for revision and testing your memory. While they may not be as durable as purpose-made cards, I wanted to include them to save you from additional expense. The *cards* show individual characters and their crucial learning points. Some blank, *spare* flashcard templates in this section may be useful for creating custom cards *or replacing any that go missing!*

For those who prefer to write directly in a workbook, I have published additional companion writing practice books to use in conjunction with this publication. They each contain the different template types in this chapter. *The Kana and Kanji Companion* books are similar to writing refill pads but with Japanese writing grids. The additional *Kanji Study Companion* book is intended for the next stage of your studies and acts as a ledger, with an index area for organizing new kanji and the knowledge you collect.

My companion books are available on Amazon's global marketplaces.

(1-inch grid with guides)

Writing Practice Template

(1-inch grid with guides)

Writing Practice Template

(1-inch grid without guides)

(1-inch grid without guides)

Writing Practice Template

(1-inch grid without guides)

(1-inch grid without guides)

Writing Practice Template

(0.7-inch grid with guides)

(0.7-inch grid with guides)

Writing Practice Template

Writing Practice Template

(0.7-inch grid without guides)

(0.7-inch grid without guides)

Writing Practice Template

(0.7-inch grid without guides)

(0.7-inch grid without guides)

さ hiragana	か hiragana	あ hiragana
し hiragana	き hiragana	い hiragana
す hiragana	く hiragana	う hiragana
せ hiragana	け hiragana	え hiragana
そ hiragana	こ hiragana	お hiragana

a

Pronounce as 'ah' like the 'a' in car.

i

Sounds like 'i' in king, or 'ee' in cheek.

u

Similar to 'oo' but like the 'ue' in true.

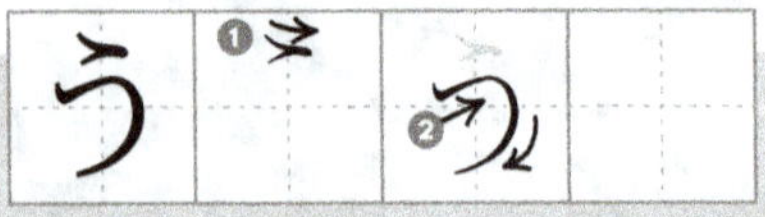

e

Pronounced as 'eh' like the 'e' in bed.

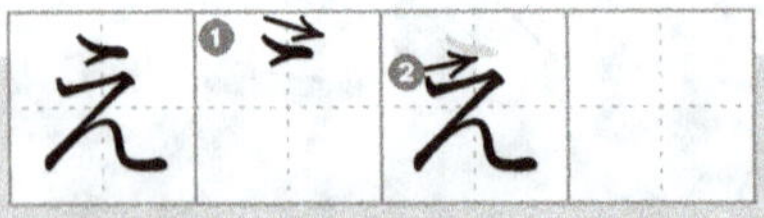

o

Sounds like the 'o' in box.

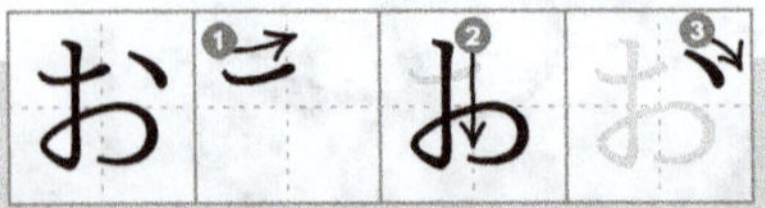

ka

Pronounce like the 'kha' in khakis.

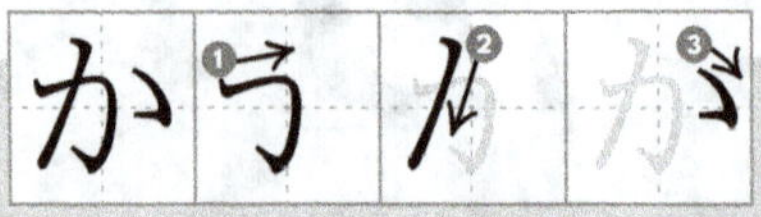

ki

This kana looks and sounds like a 'key'.

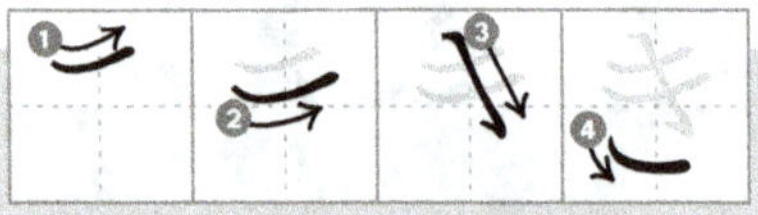

ku

Pronounced like the 'coo' in cool.

ke

Sounds like the 'ke' in kettle.

ko

Sounds like the 'co' in comb.

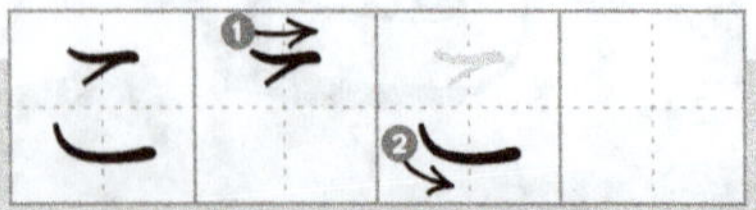

sa

Sounds like the 'sa-' in sarcasm.

shi

Sounds exactly like the 'shi' in sashimi.

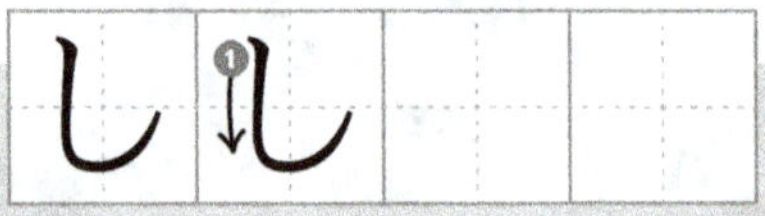

su

Sounds similar to the 'sou' in soup.

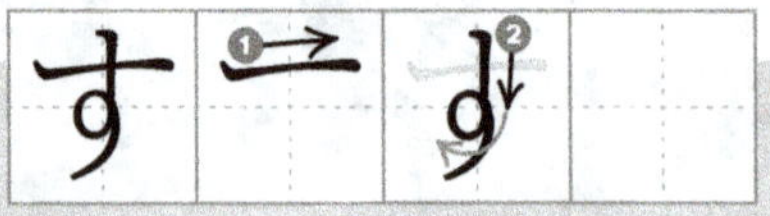

se

Pronounced 'seh' (almost like say).

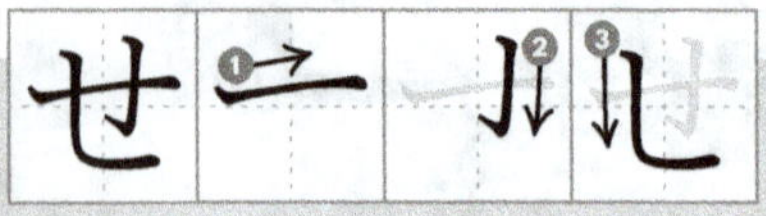

so

Sounds like the 'so-' in soccer or sorry.

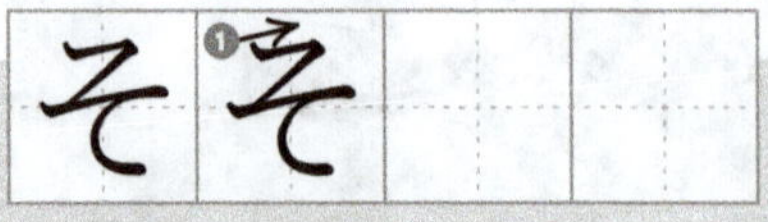

は hiragana	な hiragana	た hiragana
ひ hiragana	に hiragana	ち hiragana
ふ hiragana	ぬ hiragana	つ hiragana
へ hiragana	ね hiragana	て hiragana
ほ hiragana	の hiragana	と hiragana

ta

Sounds like the '-ta' in Santa.

た

chi

Sounds just like the 'chee' in cheeks.

ち

tsu

Sounds like 'two' and the name 'Sue'.

つ

te

Sounds like the 'te-' in teddy bear.

て

to

Sounds like the 'to-' in tonic.

と

na

Sounds just like the '-na's in banana

な

ni

Sounds similar to the word 'knee'.

に

nu

Sounds like the 'noo' in the word noon.

ぬ

ne

Sounds similar to 'nay' or 'neigh'.

ね

no

Sounds very similar to the word 'No'.

の

ha

Pronounce as 'ha' like in hand.

は

hi

Pronounced like the 'hee' in heel.

ひ

fu

Sounds like both 'fu' and 'hu' - or 'hfu'.

ふ

he

Pronounce as 'heh', almost like 'hey'.

へ

ho

Pronounce like the 'ho-' in horse.

ほ

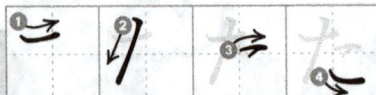

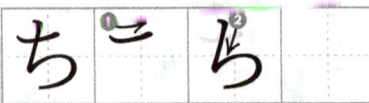

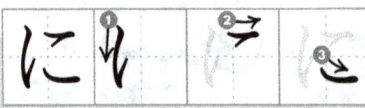

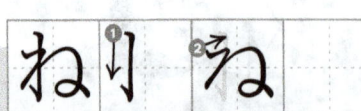

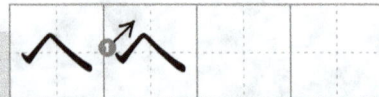

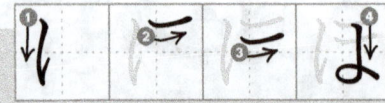

ら hiragana	や hiragana	ま hiragana
り hiragana	ゆ hiragana	み hiragana
る hiragana	よ hiragana	む hiragana
れ hiragana	わ hiragana	め hiragana
ろ hiragana	ん hiragana	も hiragana

ma

Sounds like the 'ma-' in the word man.

ま

mi

Sounds exactly like the word 'Me'.

み

mu

Similar to the 'moo' in moon.

む

me

Sounds like the 'me-' in men.

め

mo

Sounds similar to the 'mo-' in monsoon.

も

ya

Sounds much like the 'ya-' in yak.

や

yu

Sounds just like the word 'You'.

ゆ

yo

Sounds like the informal greeting 'Yo'.

よ

wa

Sounds like the 'wa-' in wacky or wax.

わ

n

Similar to the '-n' in plane, or 'nnn'.

ん

ra

Sounds a lot like the 'ra-' in rabbit.

ら

ri

Sounds a lot like the 'rea-' in reach.

り

ru

Sounds like the '-ru' in guru.

る

re

Sounds like the 'ra-' in race, like 'ray'.

れ

ro

Sounds like the '-rro' in churro.

ろ

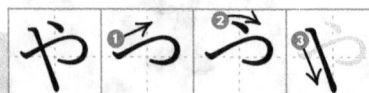

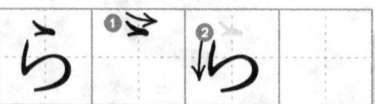

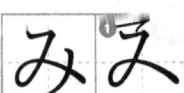

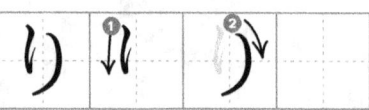

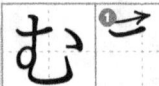

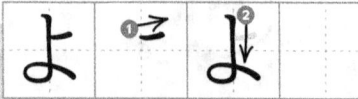

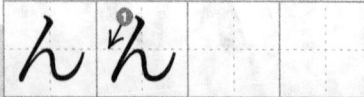

サ katakana	カ katakana	ア katakana
シ katakana	キ katakana	イ katakana
ス katakana	ク katakana	ウ katakana
セ katakana	ケ katakana	エ katakana
ソ katakana	コ katakana	オ katakana

a

Pronounce as 'ah' like the 'a' in car.

ア

i

Sounds like 'i' in king, or 'ee' in cheek.

イ

u

Similar to 'oo' but like the 'ue' in true.

ウ

e

Pronounced as 'eh' like the 'e' in bed.

エ

o

Sounds like the 'o' in box.

オ

ka

Pronounce like the 'kha' in khakis.

カ

ki

This kana looks and sounds like a 'key'.

キ

ku

Pronounced like the 'coo' in cool.

ク

ke

Sounds like the 'ke' in kettle.

ケ

ko

Sounds like the 'co' in comb.

コ

sa

Sounds like the 'sa-' in sarcasm.

サ

shi

Sounds exactly like the 'shi' in sashimi.

シ

su

Sounds similar to the 'sou' in soup.

ス

se

Pronounced 'seh' (almost like say).

セ

so

Sounds like the 'so-' in soccer or sorry.

ソ

ハ katakana	ナ katakana	タ katakana
ヒ katakana	ニ katakana	チ katakana
フ katakana	ヌ katakana	ツ katakana
ヘ katakana	ネ katakana	テ katakana
ホ katakana	ノ katakana	ト katakana

ta

Sounds like the '-ta' in Santa.

タ

chi

Sounds just like the 'chee' in cheeks.

チ

tsu

Sounds like 'two' and the name 'Sue'.

ツ

te

Sounds like the 'te-' in teddy bear.

テ

to

Sounds like the 'to-' in tonic.

ト

na

Sounds just like the '-na's in banana

ナ

ni

Sounds similar to the word 'knee'

ニ

nu

Sounds like the 'noo' in the word noon.

ヌ

ne

Sounds similar to 'nay' or 'neigh'.

ネ

no

Sounds very similar to the word 'No'.

ノ

ha

Pronounce as 'ha' like in hand.

ハ

hi

Pronounced like the 'hee' in heel.

ヒ

fu

Sounds like both 'fu' and 'hu' - or 'hfu'.

フ

he

Pronounce as 'heh', almost like 'hey'.

ヘ

ho

Pronounce like the 'ho-' in horse.

ホ

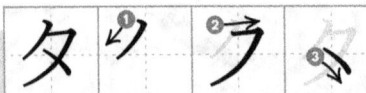

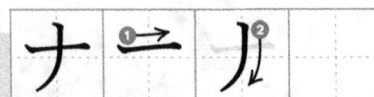

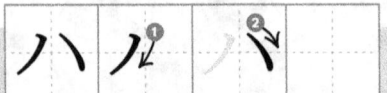

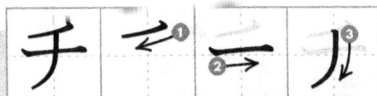

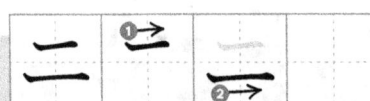

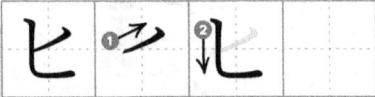

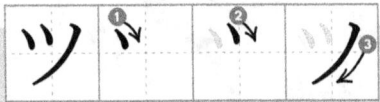

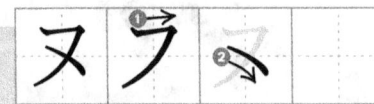

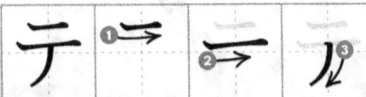

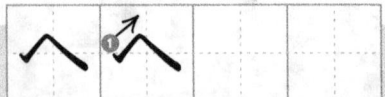

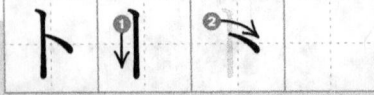

ラ katakana	ヤ katakana	マ katakana
リ katakana	ユ katakana	ミ katakana
ル katakana	ヨ katakana	ム katakana
レ katakana	ワ katakana	メ katakana
ロ katakana	ン katakana	モ katakana

ma

Sounds like the 'ma-' in the word man.

マ

mi

Sounds exactly like the word 'Me'.

ミ

mu

Similar to the 'moo' in moon.

ム

me

Sounds like the 'me-' in men.

メ

mo

Sounds similar to the 'mo-' in monsoon.

モ

ya

Sounds much like the 'ya-' in yak.

ヤ

yu

Sounds just like the word 'You'.

ユ

yo

Sounds like the informal greeting 'Yo'.

ヨ

wa

Sounds like the 'wa-' in wacky or wax.

ワ

n

Similar to the '-n' in plane, or 'nnn'.

ン

ra

Sounds a lot like the 'ra-' in rabbit.

ラ

ri

Sounds a lot like the 'rea-' in reach.

リ

ru

Sounds like the '-ru' in guru.

ル

re

Sounds like the 'ra-' in race, like 'ray'.

レ

ro

Sounds like the '-rro' in churro.

ロ

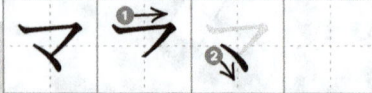

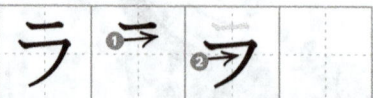

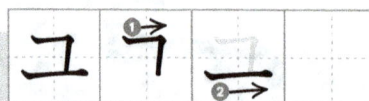

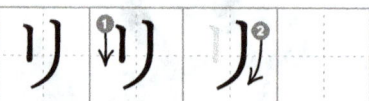

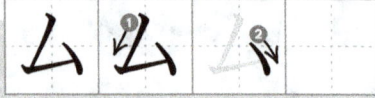

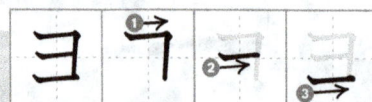

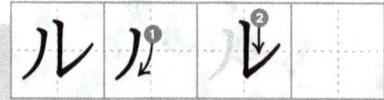

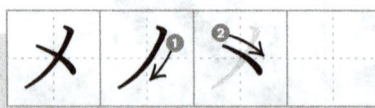

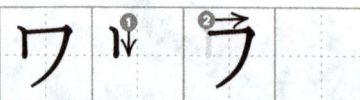

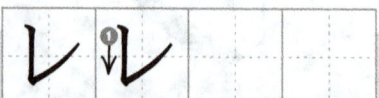

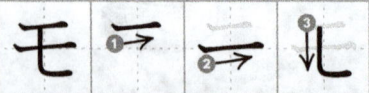

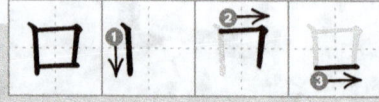

spare

つッ

small tsu

を

hiragana

spare

ああ

long vowels

ヲ

katakana

spare

ぼぽ

dakuten

しゃ

compound kana

w	r	y	m	h	n	t	s	k	H	
わ wa	ら ra	や ya	ま ma	は ha	な na	た ta	さ sa	か ka	あ a	a
	り ri		み mi	ひ hi	に ni	ち chi	し shi	き ki	い i	i
*ん n	る ru	ゆ yu	む mu	ふ fu	ぬ nu	つ tsu	す su	く ku	う u	u
	れ re		め me	へ he	ね ne	て te	せ se	け ke	え e	e
を wo	ろ ro	よ yo	も mo	ほ ho	の no	と to	そ so	こ ko	お o	o

wo

Pronounced as お
(like the O in "box")

(を is a Particle)

Small tsu っ and ッ
= double consonant sound
(adds one mora)

ロク	ロック
roku	ro +k ku

spare

wo

Pronounced as オ
(like the O in "box")

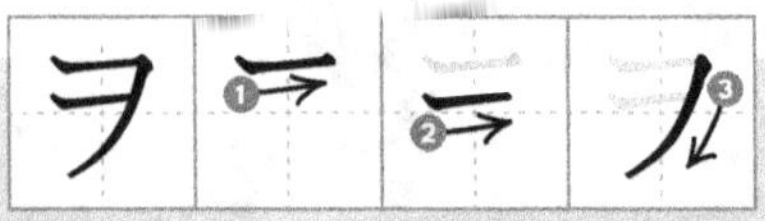

(ヲ is a Particle)

Katakana + extender

ケーキ	キュート
kee ki	kyuu to

Hiragana + extra vowel

for [a] sounds + あ (a)
for [i] / [e] sounds + い (i)
for [u] / [o] sounds + う (u)

spare

Regular kana '-i'
+ small kana 'y-'
e.g. し/き/ち + や/ゆ/よ

H	き	+	よ	=	きょ	
	ki		yo		kyo	
K	キ	+	ヨ	=	キョ	

Kana with diacritic marks
= 'voiced' consonants
dakuten ゛/ handakuten ゜

	k	t	s	h	ho	ほ	ホ
+゛	g	d	z	b	bo	ぼ	ボ
+゜				p	po	ぽ	ポ

spare

w	r	y	m	h	n	t	s	k	K	
ワ wa	ラ ra	ヤ ya	マ ma	ハ ha	ナ na	タ ta	サ sa	カ ka	ア a	a
	リ ri		ミ mi	ヒ hi	ニ ni	チ chi	シ shi	キ ki	イ i	i
*ン n	ル ru	ユ yu	ム mu	フ fu	ヌ nu	ツ tsu	ス su	ク ku	ウ u	u
	レ re		メ me	ヘ he	ネ ne	テ te	セ se	ケ ke	エ e	e
ヲ wo	ロ ro	ヨ yo	モ mo	ホ ho	ノ no	ト to	ソ so	コ ko	オ o	o

Answer Key

Check your responses to the kana revision quizzes here:

Page				
029	あう	au	あい	ai
	いえ	ie	あお	ao
	おい	oi	ああ	aa
	うえ	ue	いい	ii
	いう	iu	おう	ou

Page				
037	あい	oi	あう	au
	うえ	ue	こえ	koe
	お	o	かく	kaku
	きく	kiku	おけ	oke
	こけ	koke	かお	kao
	いけ	ike	あき	aki
	かう	kau	いう	iu
	えき	eki	あかい	akai
	いく	Iku	あおい	aoi
	ここ	koko	きおく	kioku

Page				
054	すし	sushi	とち	tochi
	つち	tsuchi	うた	uta
	そと	soto	かた	kata
	さけ	sake	しち	shichi
	こと	koto	さす	sasu
	くつ	kutsu	あした	ashita
	かこ	kako	とおい	tooi
	てつ	tetsu	きせつ	kisetsu
	せき	sato	さとい	satoi
	たつ	tatsu	ちかてつ	chikatetsu

Page				
068	なに	nani	きぬ	kinu
	ほね	hone	ほし	hoshi
	ぬの	nuno	ひと	hito
	ひふ	hifu	のき	noki
	へた	heta	にし	nishi
	はな	wana	はいく	waiku
	ふね	fune	かたな	katana
	かに	kani	せいふ	seifu
	ひな	hina	いのしし	inoshishi
	はし	washi	へいそつ	heisotsu

Page				
080	やま	yama	むね	mune
	ゆめ	yume	きもの	kimono
	よむ	yomu	さしみ	sashimi
	もも	momo	ゆかた	yukata
	みや	miya	えまき	emaki
	こめ	kome	みこし	mikoshi
	つゆ	tsuyu	うきよえ	ukiyoe
	むし	mushi	せともの	setomono
	まつ	matsu	すきやき	sukiyaki
	うめ	ume		

Page				
093	わん	wan	さくら	sakura
	てら	tera	うちわ	uchiwa
	つる	tsuru	まつり	matsuri
	これ	kore	ほたる	hotaru
	ふろ	furo	ふとん	futon
	のり	nori	れきし	rekishi
	はる	haru	わふく	wafuku
	れい	rei	りろん	riron
	しろ	shiro	ひのまる	hinomaru
	にほん	nihon	さむらい	samurai

Page				
124	カツ	katsu	コーチ	kōchi
	アイス	aisu	ソース	sōsu
	ケーキ	kēki	スキー	sukī
	アウト	auto	タクシー	takushī
	サーチ	sāchi	ステーキ	sutēki
	コート	kōto	セーター	sētā
	ツアー	tsuā	サーカス	sākasu
	テスト	tesuto	オーケー	ōkē
	シーツ	shītsu	エーカー	ēkā

Page				
160	ヘリ	heri	タイヤ	taiya
	メモ	memo	カメラ	kamera
	ヒレ	hire	ネーム	nēmu
	ミルク	miruku	ユーモア	yūmoa
	カヌー	kanū	サラリー	sararī
	ワニス	wanisu	ハンマー	hanmā
	ローン	rōn	ヨーヨー	yōyō
	ナイフ	naifu	ハンカチ	hankachi
	フレー	furē	ユニーク	yunīku
	ノート	nōto	ネクタイ	nekutai

Answer Key

Check your responses to the kana revision quizzes here:

Page 029	あう	au	あい	ai
	いえ	ie	あお	ao
	おい	oi	ああ	aa
	うえ	ue	いい	ii
	いう	iu	おう	ou

Page 037	あい	oi	あう	au
	うえ	ue	こえ	koe
	お	o	かく	kaku
	きく	kiku	おけ	oke
	こけ	koke	かお	kao
	いけ	ike	あき	aki
	かう	kau	いう	iu
	えき	eki	あかい	akai
	いく	iku	あおい	aoi
	ここ	koko	きおく	kioku

Page 054	すし	sushi	とち	tochi
	つち	tsuchi	うた	uta
	そと	soto	かた	kata
	さけ	sake	しち	shichi
	こと	koto	さす	sasu
	くつ	kutsu	あした	ashita
	かこ	kako	とおい	tooi
	てつ	tetsu	きせつ	kisetsu
	せき	sato	さとい	satoi
	たつ	tatsu	ちかてつ	chikatetsu

Page 068	なに	nani	きぬ	kinu
	ほね	hone	ほし	hoshi
	ぬの	nuno	ひと	hito
	ひふ	hifu	のき	noki
	へた	heta	にし	nishi
	はな	wana	はいく	waiku
	ふね	fune	かたな	katana
	かに	kani	せいふ	seifu
	ひな	hina	いのしし	inoshishi
	はし	washi	へいそつ	heisotsu

Page 080	やま	yama	むね	mune
	ゆめ	yume	きもの	kimono
	よむ	yomu	さしみ	sashimi
	もも	momo	ゆかた	yukata
	みや	miya	えまき	emaki
	こめ	kome	みこし	mikoshi
	つゆ	tsuyu	うきよえ	ukiyoe
	むし	mushi	せともの	setomono
	まつ	matsu	すきやき	sukiyaki
	うめ	ume		

Page 093	わん	wan	さくら	sakura
	てら	tera	うちわ	uchiwa
	つる	tsuru	まつり	matsuri
	これ	kore	ほたる	hotaru
	ふろ	furo	ふとん	futon
	のり	nori	れきし	rekishi
	はる	haru	わふく	wafuku
	れい	rei	りろん	riron
	しろ	shiro	ひのまる	hinomaru
	にほん	nihon	さむらい	samurai

Page 124	カツ	katsu	コーチ	kōchi
	アイス	aisu	ソース	sōsu
	ケーキ	kēki	スキー	sukī
	アウト	auto	タクシー	takushī
	サーチ	sāchi	ステーキ	sutēki
	コート	kōto	セーター	sētā
	ツアー	tsuā	サーカス	sākasu
	テスト	tesuto	オーケー	ōkē
	シーツ	shītsu	エーカー	ēkā

Page 160	ヘリ	heri	タイヤ	taiya
	メモ	memo	カメラ	kamera
	ヒレ	hire	ネーム	nēmu
	ミルク	miruku	ユーモア	yūmoa
	カヌー	kanū	サラリー	sararī
	ワニス	wanisu	ハンマー	hanmā
	ローン	rōn	ヨーヨー	yōyō
	ナイフ	naifu	ハンカチ	hankachi
	フレー	furē	ユニーク	yunīku
	ノート	nōto	ネクタイ	nekutai

Thank you

Congratulations on your progress with the Japanese language!

I hope that you found this *combined Hiragana and Katakana* volume from my *Japanese Made Simple* series of workbooks useful and enjoyable. Thank you for choosing it from the wide selection of other titles that are available to buy! If you enjoyed learning about the kana scripts in this way, you should consider the next book in the series, teaching all about Kanji and covering over 100+ commonly used characters and their vocabulary. I have also now combined this book with the kanji book to create an all-in-one volume and teach about grammar, Japanese culture, and more!

The process of writing, designing and independently publishing books is both challening and enjoyable. I make every effort to produce accurate language guides but it's easy to overlook little details here and there. Please let me know if you found any problems or mistakes in this book, so that I can promptly fix them for other readers.

Lastly, I wanted to ask you for a small favor...

It's incredibly satisfying to hear from people who are as keen about learning foreign languages as I am - especially when they have used one of my books. When you have a moment to spare, I would be grateful if you could consider leaving your feedback and a review on Amazon. We all rely on reviews to make our buying decisions, and your positive feedback is really helpful to *'the little guys'* and independent writers like me.

Let me know if there's anything I can do to improve my content and if there's anything else you would like to see in follow-up books. I look forward to hearing what you think!

Until next time, *arigatōgozaimasu!*

ありがとうございます!!

Dan.

Learning Hiragana and Katakana

(Japanese Made Simple)

A Beginner's Guide and Integrated Workbook

Learn how to read, write and speak Japanese, with the Kana alphabets

Dan Akiyama

www.ingramcontent.com/pod-product-compliance
Lightning Source LLC
Chambersburg PA
CBHW080019130526
44590CB00046B/3701
9781739238759